Small Firm Formation and Regional Economic Development

This edited work addresses the critical role played by small firm formation in the regeneration of urban, regional and industrial areas. It contains a wide range of in-depth and comparative research, based on several detailed case studies, that forms the basis for a universal consideration of the significant factors in determining rates of new business start-ups.

Drawing on studies and expertise from around the world, the book describes the transition from research to policy and covers the prerequisites to successful new firm formation policies. At a time when new firm formation is promoted by central and local government, business development agencies and the private sector, this book questions the economic dependence on small firms and explores the relevance of networking, information and advice.

Chapters by academics are complemented by contributions from consultants and business development agencies, making this an essential book for anyone interested in regional regeneration.

Michael Danson is Reader in Economics at the University of Paisley and is a leading researcher and analyst in economic policy.

Routledge Studies in Small Business

1. **Small Firm Formation and Regional Economic Development**
   Edited by Michael W. Danson

Small Firm Formation and Regional Economic Development

Edited by Michael W. Danson

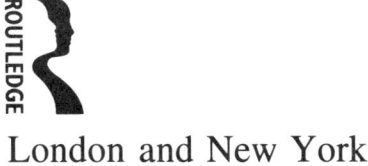

London and New York

To my parents

who were never given the chance

First published 1996
by Routledge
11 New Fetter Lane, London EC4P 4EE

Simultaneously published in the USA and Canada
by Routledge
29 West 35th Street, New York, NY 10001

Typeset in Times by
J&L Composition Ltd, Filey, North Yorkshire
Printed and bound in Great Britain by
Biddles Ltd, Guildford and King's Lynn

British Library Cataloguing in Publication Data
A catalogue record for this book is available from the British Library

Library of Congress Cataloguing in Publication Data
A catalogue record for this book has been requested

ISBN 0–415–12970–2

Contents

Figures

Tables

Contributors

Brian Ashcroft, Fraser of Allander Institute, University of Strathclyde

Martin R. Binks, Department of Economics, University of Nottingham

Tony Clarke, Department of Applied Social Studies, University of Paisley

Michael W. Danson, Department of Economics and Management, University of Paisley

David Devins, Policy Research Unit, Leeds Metropolitan University

Christine T. Ennew, School of Management and Finance, University of Nottingham

Colin Gallagher, Trends Business Research Ltd, Newcastle upon Tyne

Richard T. Harrison, Centre for Executive Development, University of Ulster

Richard Holt, Business Strategies Ltd

John Kidd, Trends Business Research Ltd, Newcastle upon Tyne

Catherine Kirk, Department of Economics, Glasgow Caledonian University

Claire M. Leitch, Centre for Executive Development, University of Ulster

James H. Love, Department of Economics, University of Strathclyde

Alasdair McNicoll, Research, Scottish Enterprise

Ronald W. McQuaid, Department of Industrial and Business Studies, Napier University

Paul Miller, Department of Economics, University of Newcastle upon Tyne

David North, Centre for Enterprise and Economic Development, Middlesex University

David Smallbone, Centre for Enterprise and Economic Development, Middlesex University

John Struthers, Department of Economics and Management, University of Paisley

Geoff Whittam, Department of Economics and Management, University of Paisley

John Wylie, External Relations, University of Paisley

Alistair Young, Department of Economics and Management, University of Paisley

Preface

This volume arises from a seminar convened in January 1994 in Ayr, Strathclyde at the Craigie Campus of the University of Paisley around the theme of 'New Firm Formation and Regional Economic Development'. Over 100 academics, policymakers, practitioners and consultants attended the meeting representing the public and private sectors from all parts of the British Isles. As anticipated, the conference was wide-ranging and influential, providing the opportunity to analyse and discuss the innovative work of academics, government and business development organisations on the regional variation in the rates of business start-ups, on the causes of differences, on policy proposals, etc. Speakers from the public and private sectors, academia and consultancies presented papers on the key elements of the new directions of this critical policy area: finance, networking, cultural influences, education. As representatives from local and national agencies participated in the meeting, interaction between higher education institutions, policymakers and practitioners was a strong dimension of the seminar. With the success of the meeting and the importance attached to incorporating the feedback on the contributions from the participants, the improved papers from the meeting are being more widely disseminated through refereed publications: the international journal *Small Business Economics*, published in early 1995 and, of course, this volume in the Routledge Studies in Small Business series.

David J. Storey
Series Editor

Acknowledgements

We wish to acknowledge the support of the Economic and Social Research Council (ESRC), grant number R45126418393, and of Scottish Enterprise in the organisation of the original conference and in the funding of the ESRC Urban and Regional Economics Seminar Group; of Dr Ron Botham, Head of Research and Industrial Strategy at Scottish Enterprise for his invaluable contributions in the realisation of the Seminar, and Professor David Storey for his encouragement to publish the papers.

Mike Danson
April 1995

1 New firm formation and regional economic development

An introduction and review of the Scottish experience

Michael W. Danson

INTRODUCTION

Over the last two decades there has been an increasing realisation of the importance of small and medium enterprises (SMEs) to the development and health of the national and regional economy, as any reader of this series or of the journals in this area will be well aware. As a corollary of this, there has been a perceived need to intervene in the market to ensure that the high proportion of SMEs which fail each year are replaced, and to promote the creation of new businesses to compensate for the decline in large plants. A measure of the potential importance of improving the rate at which new firms are formed is demonstrated by Ashcroft and Love in Chapter 2 of this volume. They show that, on average, the development of each new company will lead to four net new jobs being created after four or five years. Competitive pressures from more efficient enterprises and imports, sectoral-specific decline, industrial restructuring and other forces in the marketplace have all led to differential degrees of new firm formation across regions and nations. The different rates of success across areas in meeting the challenges of a more flexible economic world and of attempting to overcome the effects of the decline of dominant plants and industries have led to a concomitant expansion in research and analysis into these regional developments and their business environments. In recent times these Western experiences, analyses and policies have been extended to Eastern Europe and the former Soviet Union as these economies have undergone massive restructuring.

The role of governments and their agencies in addressing these changes has been well rehearsed over the years, with seemingly little left to discover and few new ways to intervene to be found. Nevertheless, the chapters in this book demonstrate that many of the debates are unresolved, while new directions for research and areas of analysis are still being identified. A major source for such developments arose from the enquiry into business birth rates, embarked on in 1993 by Scottish Enterprise, the regional development agency for Scotland, the main findings being published towards the end of that year (Scottish Enterprise 1993). The enquiry into this one area is enlightening because it demonstrates that many subtle and complex factors affect potential entrepreneurs and their ability to establish and nurture a company. The variation in the importance of access to capital, the availability and provision of appropriate property, and of academic–industry links are well documented, but this series of studies appears to have uncovered evidence of a number of other elements in the infra- and superstructure of the Scottish economy which could be recognised as having powerful effects on the rates of new firm formation. In particular, entrepreneurial potential and cultural issues, which have been raised in terms of a dependency culture in certain disadvantaged and depressed communities, were explored in some depth. Critically, this research seemed to suggest that the failure of 'enterprise' to take hold in such areas was less apparent on more careful inspection. Indeed, not only was this myth of an antienterprise culture severely undermined, but also the research programme revealed a reluctance of business development agencies and professionals to promote and encourage entrepreneurship amongst certain sections of the community: women, the working class, council house residents and the young.

   This introduction presents an overview of the research programme of Scottish Enterprise, along with other papers delivered to a conference on 'New Firm Formation and Regional Economic Development' in early 1994 in Ayr, Scotland, organised by the Economic and Social Research Council – through the Urban and Regional Economics Seminar Group – with Scottish Enterprise. Some of the contributions to that meeting are being published separately in special editions of the journals *Small Business Economics* and *Regional Studies*. Also, and as a measure of the continuing interest in this subject and in the Scottish Enterprise programme in particular, some of the chapters in this volume were not integral to the initial research programme, although they were included in the conference or directly stimulated by it. They are complementary to the Scottish Enterprise studies in that they take many of the key issues forward, but usually by introducing further issues that have significance beyond Scotland.

SCOTLAND'S BUSINESS BIRTH RATE

The objectives of the Scottish Enterprise enquiry were to provide improved understanding of the role of new firm formation in economic development and to explain why Scotland had a lower rate of business creation than other regional and national economies. The research programme was undertaken by in-house specialists, from the Research Division, by a special New Ventures Team drawn from several departments and by a number of external consultancies. Ten studies were completed, using different methodologies and perspectives. The research focused on 'genuine' business start-ups, excluding management buy-outs and privatisations. The team identified two key concepts: the 'business life-cycle' and 'segmentation'. The former gave rise to two key questions:

● Why does Scotland generate so few new ventures?
● Why does Scotland generate so few new ventures which grow into substantial companies?

The business life-cycle approach was developed from an alternative perspective by Reid (1995), who did not contribute to the Scottish Enterprise programme. More academic and technical than most of the programme, his analysis concluded that young small firms 'experience a trade-off between profitability and growth' (Reid 1995: 89), and very small firms grow faster than larger micro-firms. As will be demonstrated later, this trade-off may conflict with the needs of capital providers who seek quick returns. Both results suggest churning in the micro-level stock of firms, with induced displacement. Chapter 3 of this volume by Smallbone and North is in broad agreement, showing that younger firms tend to create more jobs than older firms and therefore to grow more. As newer firms are inclined to have higher mortality rates also, however, they argue for support for all SMEs given their potential to grow, irrespective of age.

On segmentation, the Scottish Enterprise programme addressed the varying rates of new firm formation across companies – by structure, product, process – and across entrepreneurs – by background and circumstances – to investigate the operation of the process of entrepreneurial development in different market milieux. In this volume, Smallbone and North; Gallagher, Kidd and Miller; Clarke; and Harrison and Leitch are concerned with the former, and Ennew and Binks; McNicoll; Whittam and Kirk; Struthers, Wylie and Young; and Holt with the latter.

Within this overall framework the Scottish Enterprise programme analysed a number of key issues:

- Scotland's new firm performance;
- individual and sectoral case studies;
- business environment;
- entrepreneurial potential and cultural issues.

The work of the Scottish Enterprise programme in each of these areas will be discussed in turn with arguments from comparable studies introduced where appropriate.

SCOTLAND'S NEW FIRM PERFORMANCE

This element of the study was undertaken by PIEDA using VAT trends data, and by Trends Business Research (Gallagher, Kidd and Miller, this volume), using Dun and Bradstreet records of independent companies set up in 1978 and still operating in 1990 in Scotland, South East England and the West Midlands. The Fraser of Allander Institute contributed an econometric analysis (Ashcroft and Love, this volume) of Scotland's new start-ups' performance compared with the rest of the UK and of the impact of new firms on job creation.

These studies suggested that new firm formation would continue to be of importance for the rest of the decade, stimulated by an increased SME sector. The analysis confirmed the persistent low rates of enterprise creation in Scotland, although the growth of survivors was at least as good as elsewhere, if not superior. From this, Scottish Enterprise concluded that the problem was the overall birth rate, with the policy implication being that measures to expand the pool were more appropriate than 'picking winners'.

In a separate study on cross-national comparisons of business creation, Reynolds, Storey and Westhead (1994), using data on France, Germany, Italy, Sweden, the UK and the USA, argued that the rates of business start-ups do not differ greatly across countries. However, they have identified wider variations within countries, between regions in the European Union, with the birth rate in the most dynamic areas being two or three times higher than in the least fertile zones. Further discussion of this research is available in a special edition of *Regional Studies*, edited by Storey (1994). Interestingly, there was disagreement between the authors of this study with regard to the importance of, and subsequent need to avoid, displacement in policy prescriptions.

Hart and Hanvey (1995) similarly have discussed these issues with special attention to Northern Ireland. Comparable results to the Scottish analyses are presented by them, but with greater concern expressed over the level of displacement and, therefore, the long-term sustainability of policies to promote growth through the stimulation of new enterprises.

Myant (1995) has investigated new firm developments in the Czech Republic in an important addition to the literature, not only on the country itself, but also on the realities of transformation. To a greater extent than the other papers reviewed here, his work demonstrates the critical influence of local economic factors and pre-existing structures in shaping processes of new firm formation. Rather than being seen as a positive element in economic transformation, Myant considers the new firms in the Czech Republic as perhaps representing an obstacle to change.

INDIVIDUAL AND SECTORAL CASE STUDIES

In this volume, Smallbone and North highlight the need to support new firms in general through their growth and development phases. Often a lack of attention to products and markets are major weaknesses in survival and expansion phases. Their analysis demonstrates the need to focus on the individual company. Developing this approach, Scottish Enterprise sponsored research on specific sectors which were considered to exemplify significant lessons or to have a key role in the economy. A traditional Scottish industry facing both technological and competitive pressures, clothing and textiles, was analysed by David Rigby Associates; PACEC looked at high-tech examples and academic spin-offs, both areas subject to much promotion in encouraging regional regeneration; EES consultants investigated corporate venturing; and KPMG addressed the major growth sector of the 1980s – the service sector.

The analysis of clothing and textiles showed that the popular view of company failures and declining employment was disguising the actual and potential contributions of new firms to the industry in Scotland. However, their role was restricted by a lack of innovation and dynamism. Evidence from Italy and Germany suggested that there was the potential for a more significant contribution to the economy, with development through a growth in the number of new, small firms rather than in the size of existing companies seen as the best way forward.

PACEC, on high-tech and academic spin-offs, reported minor differences in the factors explaining low levels of new firm formation in these specific sectors and in the overall economy. The research base within industry was perceived as inadequate, with few organisations acting efficiently as incubators for spin-offs and new high-tech companies. The infra- and superstructures were deemed deficient in these respects, with poorly developed and weak specialist resources, social networks and information flows within the high-tech community. The lack of demand for high-tech companies is highlighted, outwith the North Sea oil industry, constraining development of a home base, and putting firms at a cost disadvantage in export markets. In comparison with other areas, notably Massachusetts, policy support, critically, was seen as less extensive.

Problems in establishing a high-tech firm are compounded by the actual process of formation and growth, with the lack of support and ambition at home stunting development opportunities. All this seemed minor compared with the situation of academic spin-offs, the authors argued, where major restrictions were identified in Scottish higher and further education institutions and in their business, funding and cultural environments in promoting new firm formation. Entrepreneurship was perceived as alien to academic traditions, and as risky and stigmatising, so that significant barriers to entry into the marketplace had been erected.

Westhead and Cowling (1995) looked at high-tech new firm formation again and came to question the certainty of such conclusions. They believe that the debates on the major factors are still unresolved. In a US study, Muniak has argued recently (1994) that there are essential conflicts between the promotion of regeneration policies based on high-tech at the urban and at the national level. In the same vein, and as seen here, much of the policy and analysis in the UK seems to suggest that the needs of local and of national economies may not be coincidental with regard to the encouragement of high-tech and academic entrepreneurs. Policies to improve new firm formation in the country as a whole may lead to differential effects across regions, perhaps providing strong virtual and vicious cycles of uneven development.

In Chapter 11 of this volume, Clarke reports on a specific study he has undertaken of the Scottish software industry. This displays many of the characteristics of a high-tech sector requiring peculiar forms of support within a general programme of assistance. Although sector-specific programmes are viewed positively, he questions the concentration of state business development agencies on a minority of export-oriented product-based companies.

Corporate venturing covers assistance to entrepreneurs or SMEs to exploit new ideas, corporate restructuring through staff creating new independent businesses, and the development of new profit centres and subsidiaries to exploit new products, processes and markets. EES Consultants suggested that Scotland is poorly provided with such approaches to regeneration and restructuring, which is unfortunate because, by reducing risk and establishing new ventures with better prospects, they offer an effective, additional element in promoting new firm formation, especially in the high-tech area.

The service sector has provided almost all the new jobs in the UK in the last decade or so. Considered as having relatively few barriers to entry, the services should present a promising area for improving Scotland's business birth rate. In looking at particular professions, technological and personal service companies, KPMG considered that perceived problems in raising finance were the key difficulty facing such entrepreneurs. Costs of finance were an associated concern, though few entrepreneurs seemed to appreciate the risks to the lender in supporting such activity. As demonstrated in the other studies, there was less dynamism in these companies than was apparent in their counterparts in the South East or the USA, with relatively little extra-regional or export marketing. Complementing this, Gallagher et al. conclude that support should be focused on wealth-creating sectors of the economy, especially in manufacturing and the higher skilled areas of professional and business services. This would go some way to providing the extra-company functions identified by KPMG in the wider business environment.

BUSINESS ENVIRONMENT

Studies for Scottish Enterprise expanded on this to consider property (PIEDA), 'business angels' (KPMG), and finance generally (Stoy Hayward). Continuing market failure seemed to be identified, even in the recession, with the market for small units being relatively tight. Shortages of serviced office accommodation and facilities for 'bad neighbour' new enterprises were highlighted, along with other problems not being addressed fully by the private sector, thus indicating more severe constraints in the upturn. Despite lower land values than in comparable areas, rents were high in private sector developments. The critical role of the public sector in providing accommodation was clear, although faith that the market would respond to further demand was held by the consultants and developers.

Mason and Harrison (1995) and Cowling and Clay (1995) extended the work of the Scottish Enterprise programme into the central factor of finance. In Chapter 5 of this volume, Ennew and Binks probe the nature of differences between Scottish and English banks in respect of their treatment of small businesses. Perhaps contradicting the findings in the Scottish Enterprise and other research programmes, they disclose a better relationship in Scotland between bank and customer with fewer perceived problems in service. However, they are unable to discern whether this is a real difference or simply a reflection of institutionalised lower expectations in Scotland. Venture capital is not only a relatively insignificant source of external funding for new ventures in Scotland but also, the agency claims, the outlook is 'anything but optimistic'. Current and seemingly endemic problems with access to seed-corn and start-up finance are threatening to become more severe in the near future. Together these findings suggest an attempt to close this widening gap with a move to the provision of risk finance by the public sector and by the private investor, the so-called 'Business Angel'. Some of the chapters on finance in *Scotland's Business Birth Rate* (Scottish Enterprise 1993) are titled 'Finance – The Big Issue?', 'Informal Investment – A Neglected Source?', and 'Finance – The Ongoing Debate', each suggesting that little has been resolved. In the report the equity gap is contrasted with the availability of money; the question of access is a major and persistent feature in the Scottish business environment, and to a greater extent than elsewhere. Given the significant power and size of the Scottish financial sector, the invention and introduction to the world of investment and unit trusts and the strong history of (savings) banking, there is an argument that 'improvements in the behaviour and performance of both lenders/investors and actual/ potential business founders' can and must be encouraged (Scottish Enterprise 1993: 50).

Drawing on search cost ideas, Mason and Harrison (1995) suggest that the public sector should underwrite the costs of bringing together business angels and entrepreneurs seeking finance, so overcoming inefficiencies, indivisibilities and risks in the market. Cowling and Clay (1995), in considering the UK government's Loan Guarantee Scheme, have argued that this relatively cost-effective job-generation and enterprise support package could be extended to aid more new firms.

While differences in experiences of dealing with the problems of new and small companies, especially in difficult trading conditions, underlie many of the perceived differences in this area, there may be a counter to these positive elements of support in Scotland. In particular, there is evidence of an in-built discrimination against certain groups by the financial and business development establishment. The Scottish Enterprise programme uncovered enlightening dimensions to these social and cultural issues.

ENTREPRENEURIAL POTENTIAL AND CULTURAL ISSUES

While many of the factors influencing enterprise creation and regional economic development raised in the Scottish Enterprise enquiry and covered in this volume are common to most communities, with the arguments well rehearsed elsewhere, the identification of entrepreneurial potential and cultural issues as significant does add an extra dimension to our understanding of the processes involved in new firm formation. The research directly challenges the business development community in Scotland to address its own behaviour and attitudes to potential entrepreneurs. Extensive interviewing across several countries and substantial reviews of the literature were used to establish the comparative levels of interest in entrepreneurship, of perceptions and experience of entrepreneurship and of social attitudes towards enterprise. Perhaps because of a particular reaction to Thatcherism, but undoubtedly related to a specific economic and social history, the perception of entrepreneurs by the community in Scotland was less positive than elsewhere. Even though there was recognition of their contribution to the economy, this was not sufficient to undermine the key role reserved for government intervention. Persistent unemployment, poverty and deprivation, against a relative economic decline of 80 years' duration (Danson 1991), have thralled Scots to the philosophy of collective intervention to generate jobs. Entrepreneurs were seen in these surveys as being less caring and community-oriented than the respondents.

Although further analysis showed a lower pool of self-confessed, potential entrepreneurs, there was still a substantial proportion of the adult population who believed they had the ability and desire to run their own business. These statistics suggest that there was no anti-enterprise or dependency culture; rather, with much unexploited potential, a barrier to converting desire into reality seemed to be abroad.

To identify if the problems could be isolated elsewhere in Scottish society, interviews with the business development industry and amongst opinion formers were undertaken. These demonstrated that such professionals exhibited complacency, a less than positive attitude towards policies promoting new, small and medium enterprises, and their own dependency culture. They tended to believe that native Scots entrepreneurs could not be dynamic animals in the regeneration process. A misperception of the characteristics of indigenous people, and therefore of potential entrepreneurs, was not uncommon, with some agencies suggesting *higher* barriers were required to limit entry by local businesses into the market. Failure was seen in a very negative way, in contrast to the USA, where it is far more acceptable to fail and try again.

Most of these business development executives are also involved in the other strands of regional economic development strategies as practised by Scottish Enterprise, local enterprise companies, public–private sector partnerships, etc. Many of the concepts at the heart of their organisations, such as the encouragement of inward investment, the avoidance and fear of displacement, the provision of business advice, suggest that they may, in their implementation, corrupt the promotion of new firm formation in ways not identified before. So, while dominant and branch plants have been considered as destroyers of entrepreneurship (Fothergill and Gudgin 1982; Storey 1982), the reality may be more complex, with a dependency on external investment and expertise and a positive neglect of native entrepreneurs compounding bureaucratic insensitivities, contradictory performance indicators and alien corporate cultures. Further, as Ashcroft and Love argue here, the traditional old industrial areas have poor employment and new firm creation records, suggesting the ongoing importance of past-dominated and narrow economic structures. With over half of all exports, value added and investment in manufacturing being derived from electronics and whisky, neither of which has a significant indigenous presence, Scotland is a prime example of such a past-dominated, narrow economy. External control and ownership have been promoted to the direct and indirect detriment of Scottish enterprise and entrepreneurs.

In some regions problems of job loss and poor employment performance encompass the existing stock of firms as well as new firm formation rates. There is evidence that regional development agencies and government departments have been opposing management spin-offs, effectively scuppering the opportunities for technology-based developments in sanctioning the closure of R&D laboratories in nationalised industries, and dampening enthusiasm and support for management/worker rescues of branch plant closures (Strathclyde Regional Council 1988; Danson 1991). The rationale behind this is that, with the views of overseas owners and future investors paramount, the position of inward investment agencies cannot be compromised in the international market for mobile capital.

As mentioned above, concerns over displacement dominate much thinking, while there is scant recognition given to the longer term processes of innovation, dynamism and efficiency. Protecting the *status quo* is preferred to encouraging indigenous start-ups (Scottish Enterprise 1993: 23).

This research is indicative of a wider, growing interest in the concept and importance of social networks in the entrepreneurial creation process. Again, these particular studies revealed Scotland as having a more extreme set of rules and social mores in determining support and advice. Those who would have most difficulty establishing a business elsewhere – the young, women and the working class – appear to face higher hurdles in Scotland than in the South East of England and beyond. Lack of security and also of alternative employment in the event of failure, and the effects on family life of creating a new firm are the major concerns of potential entrepreneurs, according to the Scottish Enterprise report (1993: 24). The authors believe these problems could be overcome in some instances by means of wider discussion with informed contacts and existing entrepreneurs. This seems all the more important given the less than positive attitude of business development organisations. Unfortunately, the low level of entrepreneurship identified in the programme above becomes self-perpetuating in these circumstances, compounding the earlier barriers to enterprise.

Knowing an entrepreneur is an important 'rocket' in the process of converting potential into actual business creators; those who are most easily dissuaded from making the transition are those least likely to have a set of relevant contacts. With reference to the details on financial support, the greater severity of funding problems in Scotland is associated with the lower penetration of the ideology of the property-owning democracy. With the UK funding bodies' preference for mortgages on the borrower's home to be used as collateral, there is an additional barrier to establishing the company where owner occupation of housing has tended to be low traditionally.

McNicoll in Chapter 6 of this volume discusses this set of elements in more detail, concluding that positive encouragement to progress the idea of becoming an entrepreneur would often be sufficient, within the environment of all the other hurdles and obstacles, to prevent most potential new ventures from failing to reach the starting line. The need to encourage networking, he suggests, is important if new firm formation rates are to be improved. McQuaid in Chapter 7 and

Whittam and Kirk in Chapter 8 develop these arguments further, analysing the role of both formal and informal networks in Scotland and Italy. While they support such moves as have been made by the Scottish Enterprise Network, they again raise the issue of the failure to include small entrepreneurs in the process and discussion of decision-making. Achieving economies of scale in business services, a prerequisite for overall improvement, would require a comprehensive and effective system of networking which the proposals do not encourage.

Struthers, Wylie and Young in Chapter 9 here add an interesting discussion of recent developments in Russia, where the restructuring of the last few years has highlighted a number of key issues. Not least among these are the importance of market-defining characteristics (indeed prerequisites) of property rights, contract laws, information and degrees of risk and uncertainty. The influence of organisations and individuals within current and former networks is shown to be significant in the processes of new firm formation and business development. In many ways the significance of this chapter is in its reflection of what may be underdeveloped or weak in the case of other areas. Placing Scotland, for instance, in the continuum between Russia and Massachusetts should be illuminating with regard to the need for policy intervention in the market.

This discussion on the role of information and networks is extended by Devins, in Chapter 10, when he considers measures taken to overcome market failure in business advice and knowledge. The dual need to monitor and evaluate advice programmes and services, and to know the companies supported, are seen as essential to the long-term health of the new firm sector.

The final two chapters in this volume, by Holt and Harrison and Leitch, discuss in some detail the stages of identifying local economic development strategies, and within that context the forming and implementing of the role of new firm programmes. The contribution by Holt provides a stimulating discussion on the methodology of this process, with the suggestion that prioritisation of new firms should not necessarily be the preferred route for a particular area. The lessons proposed by Holt – that local business development strategies must be constructed, analysed, debated and reviewed, with liaison between agency staff, consultants and others, are paralleled by Harrison and Leitch. In considering the Northern Ireland experience, they argue for the establishment of entrepreneurial teams to progress business ideas and opportunities, positively assembling collections of talent and expertise, rather than an approach which passively supports the market.

The consensus, here as earlier, is for intervention to overcome market failure in the labour, capital, land and knowledge sectors.

CONCLUSION

In the Scottish Enterprise enquiry extensive research on one particular national economy suggests that complex interrelationships between a number of factors can restrict the flow of potential entrepreneurs to the marketplace. In the case of Scotland these are often seen in more extreme forms than elsewhere in the UK or the developed world. Of greater concern, given the lack of state intervention to expand production or to manage aggregate demand, the greater competition for foreign direct investment and the increased competitive pressures within the single European market, are the revealed preferences of the business development agencies and professionals established to promote new firm formation.

Successful launches of new enterprises are delivered in many instances *despite* the business culture and industry, rather than because of its efforts. This argument by the Scottish Enterprise report is supported by frequent references to the very different conditions in Massachusetts, Germany and South East England. However, the experiences of Scotland are repeated in more or less similar ways across deprived and depressed regions of the UK and the EU, as the work of Hart and Hanvey (1995) amongst others, has shown. The specific problems of Scotland and the interest generated by the research programme relate to the discussions on social networks and their exclusivity in a small nation, and to the difficulties in controlling and influencing financial systems in a global investment centre.

Historical analysis of new firm formation, regional economic development and owner occupation: patterns and policies of stability?

It has been shown here that, underpinning the promotion of new firm formation and enterprise by Scottish Enterprise and others is a set of observations, presented as theory, which link regional economic performance to the rate of business start-ups. Thus, Scotland and other laggard regions are compared (by, *inter alia*, Ashcroft and Love, Gallagher et al., and Smallbone and North, all in this volume; and by Hart and Hanvey 1995) unfavourably with the South East of England with its high numbers of small and medium enterprises, its growth in new businesses and its virtuous cycles of economic development in the last two decades. The implication advanced in the literature is that there is a causal relationship between improved small company performance and enhanced levels of regional growth, and only by emulating these rates of new firm formation could Scotland close the gap in overall economic performance.

Well-founded research findings in the last few years have also drawn a connection between the degree of prosperity in a region and the level and growth in owner occupation. Further, the overspill effects created by a property-owning culture are believed to be self-reinforcing. Again, these conclusions have been based on cross-sectional and time-series analyses of data of the 1970s and 1980s.

Adopting these two theses, Scottish Enterprise have extended the application of the methodology, identifying interrelationships between all three variables: owner occupation, new firm formation and economic performance, arguing that important feedback mechanisms sustain these processes of cumulative causation. Now, while much of the evidence to support these policy prescriptions focuses on the recent history of the appropriate regional and industrial economies, as if they are timeless truths certain in their predictability, the data and their analyses do not extend beyond 1990. The recession of the early 1990s has begun to stimulate work on the consequences of the fall in house prices and of negative equity in the South East, and lead researchers to consider whether new sets of structural relations now exist between (private residential) capital and wider economic prosperity. However, little attention has been paid to the possibility that parallel changes in the new firm formation/economic development interaction may have been underway since 1990. Yet such considerations obviously should raise questions over whether the Scottish Enterprise policies may be introducing instabilities into the Scottish economy, albeit unexpectedly. Rather than relying on the traditional, established causal relationships which seem to operate favourably in the South East and in Massachusetts, these policies in reality may be based on spurious and short-term phenomena.

As important, recent reworking and updating of the US data (by Fieser 1994, for example) suggests rather less certainty over the benefits of a reliance on new firm formation; medium sized companies appear to return the best performance in the long run, with small firms showing no better than average and tending on the basis of many indicators to be unstable.

This discussion seems to warrant an extended re-examination of the short-term movements in economic variables, with an opportunity to analyse the long-term stability of their relationships with each other. The policy relevance of a study on the stability of these functions is self-evident, not least because of the possibility that a breakdown or even reversal in the structural relationships would appear to under-mine the rationale of following the South East model of economic development. If such a prosperous and cohesive economy suffers adversely in a downturn because of inherent destabilising linkages, then the implications for a disadvantaged area could be even more severe.

In the early 1980s, local government in Britain joined the debate on the future economic development of towns, conurbations and regions. One particular aspect of this concerned the balance of support to be given to new firms, inward investors and established indigenous medium and large employers. In the case of several local authori-ties, including Sheffield and the Greater London Council (1985), it was argued that the last of these was the critical sector for regenera-tion, and strategies were initiated accordingly. The debate on the development of these areas for the rest of this century and the beginning of the next seems to have lost touch with some of the analysis that underpinned these strategies. It would seem that, in the rush to support new firms, the benefits of a more coherent and integrated approach has been forsaken. History suggests that the Chapters in this volume are part of the story of economic develop-ment at the regional level; other dimensions are also worthy of attention and in time will undoubtedly receive it.

This volume, along with the special editions of *Small Business Economics* (Danson 1995) and *Regional Studies* (Storey 1994), has progressed many of the themes and issues raised in this area. Never-theless, as Westhead and Cowling (1995) argue, the jury is still debating many of these. Further research and action is required, undoubtedly, before entrepreneurship can play a full role in the regeneration of the regional economies of Europe, East and West.

BIBLIOGRAPHY

Cowling, M. and Clay, C. (1995) 'A preliminary analysis of factors influen-cing take-up rates on the loan guarantee scheme', *Small Business Econom-ics*, 7: 141–52.

Danson, M. W. (1991) 'The Scottish economy: the development of under-development?', *Planning Outlook*, 34, 2: 89–95.

Danson, M. W. (ed.) (1995) 'New firm formation and regional economic development', *Small Business Economics*, 7: 81–97.

Fieser, J. B. (1994) 'Job creation and firm size: the debate reconsidered', mimeo., US Department of Commerce: Washington.

Fothergill, S. and Gudgin, G. (1982) *Unequal Growth: Urban and Regional Employment Change in the UK*, London: Heinemann.

Greater London Council (1985) *The London Industrial Strategy*, London: GLC.

Hart, M. and Hanvey, E. (1995) 'Job generation and new and small firms: some evidence from the late 1980s', *Small Business Economics*, 7: 97–109.

Mason, C. M. and Harrison, R. T. (1995) 'Closing the regional equity gap: the role of informal venture capital', *Small Business Economics*, 7: 153–72.

Muniak, D. C. (1994) 'Economic development, national high-technology policy and America's cities', *Regional Studies*, 28, 8: 803–10.

Myant, M. (1995) 'Transforming the Czech and Slovak economies: evidence at the district level', *Regional Studies*, 29, 8 (forthcoming).

Reid, G. C. (1995) 'Early life-cycle behaviour of micro-firms in Scotland', *Small Business Economics*, 7: 89–95.

Reynolds, P. D., Storey, D. J. and Westhead, P. (1994) 'Cross-national comparisons of the variations in new firm formation rates', *Regional Studies*, 28, 4: 443–56.

Scottish Enterprise (1993) *Scotland's Business Birth Rate*, Glasgow: Scottish Enterprise.

Storey, D. J. (1982) *Entrepreneurship and the New Firm*, London: Croom Helm.

Storey, D. J. (ed.) (1994) *Regional Studies*, 28, 4.

Strathclyde Regional Council (1988) 'Caterpillar working party report to EIDC', mimeo., Glasgow: Strathclyde Regional Council.

Westhead, P. and Cowling, M. (1995) 'Employment change in independent owner-managed high-technology firms in Great Britain', *Small Business Economics*, 7: 111–40.

2 Employment change and new firm formation in UK counties, 1981–9

Brian Ashcroft and James H. Love

INTRODUCTION

In this chapter we explore the relationship between employment change and new firm formation at the UK county level during the 1980s. The research reported here was stimulated and sponsored by Scottish Enterprise (SEN). Previous research had shown that Scotland's regions generally exhibited a low rate of new firm formation compared with their UK counterparts. Our earlier work offered some pointers to the reasons for Scotland's underperformance, but as SEN moved towards the development of an initiative aimed at raising the rate of new firm formation in Scotland the agency felt that it was important to understand the role and significance of new firm formation in net job creation. Clearly, to the extent that firm formation is found to be of limited significance to net employment change, then the justification for a policy supporting firm formation is reduced.[1]

Part 1 of the chapter discusses the role of new firm formation in effecting net employment change at the local level. In Part 2 a model of net employment change at the UK county level is specified and particular attention is given to the variables which might be expected to influence county employment change in addition to firm formation. Part 3 discusses the data on new firm formation and net employment change as well as the measures used to proxy the other influences on net job change. The estimation procedures are then discussed and the results presented and analysed. Finally, the chapter concludes by highlighting the principal findings of the research.

THE ROLE OF NEW FIRM FORMATION IN NET EMPLOYMENT CHANGE

Figure 2.1 provides a schematic view of the job-generation process. The level of jobs provided in an economy may change as new or existing firms respond to variations in product demand or general factor supply conditions. Job creation may occur through expansions of capacity and/or output in existing local firms, or via new firm formation or incoming, inward investment. Job losses, on the other hand, must by definition occur only in existing firms through contractions or closure. However, the extent to which these well-known components of change are associated with specific job change will depend on conditions in the local labour market, such as how wages are determined, and the available supply of labour by occupation and skill. In any one period, the balance of new jobs and lost jobs will be reflected in a net change in employment in the local area.

The principal interest of this chapter is the role of new firm formation in the regional job-generation process. Figure 2.1 indicates that the effect of new firm formation on new jobs and net job creation will amount to more than the direct jobs provided by the new firm. Indirect effects on the demand for local products will have

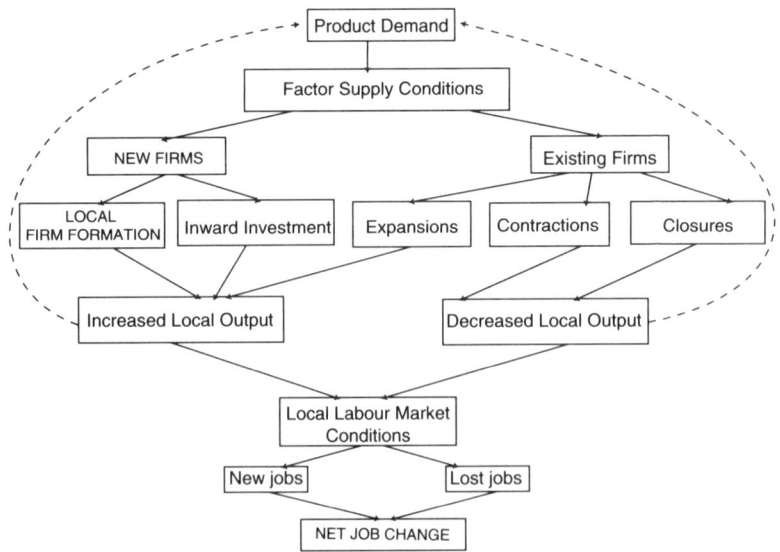

Figure 2.1 New firm formation and the job-generation process

further repercussions for the components of job change – the dotted 'feedback loop' in the figure. As favourable linkage, income multiplier effects and an increase in product prices occur in other sectors, activity in existing firms, further new firm formation and inward investment may be stimulated.

New firm formation may, however, generate displacement effects in the local economy. To the extent that local labour market conditions result in a general increase in both nominal and real wages following the increased labour demand associated with new firm formation, the impact on output and jobs will be correspondingly lower in the regional economy as a whole. Moreover, while the addition to capacity provided by firm formation will tend to lower the prices of competing products, providing some stimulus to demand, output and employment in the short run, in the longer run reduced product prices will lower the return to investment producing an eventual contraction of capacity and jobs.

McGregor et al. (1993) have shown that following an exogenous investment injection into the local economy, the ultimate impact on output and jobs depends on the assumptions made with regard to the regional labour market and the extent to which the investment brings new demand to the region. If firm formation is treated as analogous to an exogenous investment injection, then the analysis of McGregor et al. (1993) suggests that ultimately there will be no net increase in equilibrium employment if the new firms simply compete with existing ones. However, in the short to medium run, the extent of the favourable impact on net output and job creation will depend on conditions in the local labour market, with fixed nominal and fixed real wage closures tending to be associated with a greater impact. Similarly, where firm formation brings in new demand to the region, thus tending to raise equilibrium output and employment, the extent of the impact will be governed by the particular state of the local labour market.

Further favourable impacts on regional output and employment may occur in at least two ways. First, firm formation may *indirectly* induce a switch in demand in favour of the region as existing firms substitute the local products of the new firm for imports. Second, by serving as a vehicle for product and process innovations new firms may raise, directly and indirectly,[2] the productive efficiency of the local economy.

A MODEL OF NET EMPLOYMENT CHANGE AND FIRM FORMATION AT THE UK COUNTY LEVEL

We hypothesise that, on average, new firm formation will be associated with a given positive effect on net employment change at the county level. Of course, new firm formation will not be the only influence on county net employment change. Figure 2.1 makes clear that net job creation will be the consequence of employment change in existing firms and inward investment, as well as of new firm formation. We therefore need to select variables that favour institutional forms other than new firm formation in effecting employment change across counties, i. e., the expansion, contraction and closure of existing firms and the inward entry of firms and branches.

Against this background, and in the light of the discussion of the determinants of net employment change as illustrated by Figure 2.1, we have chosen the following variables to be included within the estimating equation, in addition to a measure of the rate of new firm formation (NFF):

- EPPC: proxy for the economic potential of each county. The variable proxies access to wealthy markets and therefore the potential demand for a county's goods and services. We would expect EPPC to display a positive sign.

- PD: the density of population in each county and proxy for the congestion costs and space limitations faced by firms in densely populated urban areas. We would expect this variable to have a negative sign if congestion costs of population density militate against employment change in high density areas.

- LAF: proxy for the presence of large, existing firms in the county. The argument here is that in counties where the proportion of large firms is relatively high – and small firms and new firm formation are relatively low – the significance of large and existing firms to employment change within the county will be relatively greater than firm births. Accordingly, we would expect that this variable should display a positive sign.

- EARN: proxy for the average nominal wage of employees in each county. Counties with higher values of EARN might be expected to substitute other co-operating factors for labour and so employment change per existing firm should be lower, all other things being equal. We would, therefore, expect this variable to display a negative sign.

- PRATE: participation rate in each county. This variable is used to partly proxy the supply of labour at the county level. Higher participation rates should be associated with a greater labour supply. To the extent that the effect of a higher labour supply on employment change is not mediated, other things being equal, through the proxy for wages, i. e., EARN, then one would expect PRATE to have an independent effect on employment change. A higher PRATE might be expected to be associated positively with county net employment change.

- PCPOP: the percentage change in county population over the study period. County population will change principally through net migration. It might be expected that migration, as another component of labour supply, would affect employment change for much the same reasons as offered to justify the inclusion of PRATE. In addition, since migrants bring spending from wealth with them, demand should also be higher the greater the percentage change in population. For both these reasons we would expect the coefficient on this variable to display a positive sign.

- RP: proxy for the availability of regional policy incentives in each county during the study period and would be expected to be positively related to net employment change.

We therefore have the following equation to be estimated:

$$\text{DEMP} = \alpha_1 + \beta_1\text{NFF} + \beta_2\text{EPPC} + \beta_3\text{LAF} + \beta_4\text{EARN} + \beta_5\text{PRATE} + \beta_6\text{PD} + \beta_7\text{PCPOP} + \beta_8\text{RP} + \mu_1 \tag{1}$$

where:
DEMP is the change in county employment per head of the working population; NFF is county new firm formation per head of the working population; μ_1 is an error term; and all the remaining variables are as defined above.

County working population is employed as a scale variable to allow for the varying size of counties on new firm formation and net employment change, see Ashcroft and Love (1994).

Finally, in view of the potential feedback effects from firm formation to employment change to firm formation which were noted in Figure 2.1, the estimation must allow for the possibility of a simultaneous relationship between the two.

ESTIMATION AND RESULTS

(a) Data

The dependent variable in the estimation below is employment change 1981–9 expressed per head of working population. Firm formation is measured by VAT registrations per head of working population; this is lagged by one year, i.e., for the period 1980–8. While VAT registrations are not perfect indicators of firm formation (Ganguly 1982), they have the advantage of being collected on a nationally consistent basis and are available at a suitably disaggregated spatial level.

Figure 2.2 plots these two variables for the 64 British counties (local authority regions in the case of Scotland). There is clearly a strong positive correlation between them (correlation coefficient = 0.67), and the simple 'line of best fit' is also shown. Table 2.1 shows the proxies adopted for the remaining independent variables in the estimated equation. The derivations of EARN, PRATE, PD and PCPOP are fairly obvious; all four relate principally to local factor supply conditions (EARN, PRATE and PCPOP specifically to labour supply), while PCPOP may also act as an indicator of demand.

The economic potential variable (EPPC) attempts to go beyond merely the wealth of the local market, and allow for 'spillover' demand effects from access to other proximate local markets which will vary in their level of demand. Note that the two variables which proxy to a greater or lesser product demand conditions EPPC and PCPOP are not highly correlated (r = 0.135). The variable LAF proxies the employment generation effects of large and existing firms. All of these independent variables are expressed as appropriate rates.

The final variable (RP) proxies the strength of regional policy in the county concerned. A dummy variable was constructed which took the value of 3 if the county had been scheduled as a Special Development Area; a value of 2 was assigned where the county had been a Development Area, 1 where the county had been an Intermediate Area, and 0 if the county had not been in receipt of regional assistance. The values assigned to each county were then weighted to allow for the years during the study period when the county had been designated as one of the three types of policy-assisted area. Counties which continued to be Special or Development Areas therefore received greater weight than those moving to a lower assisted status

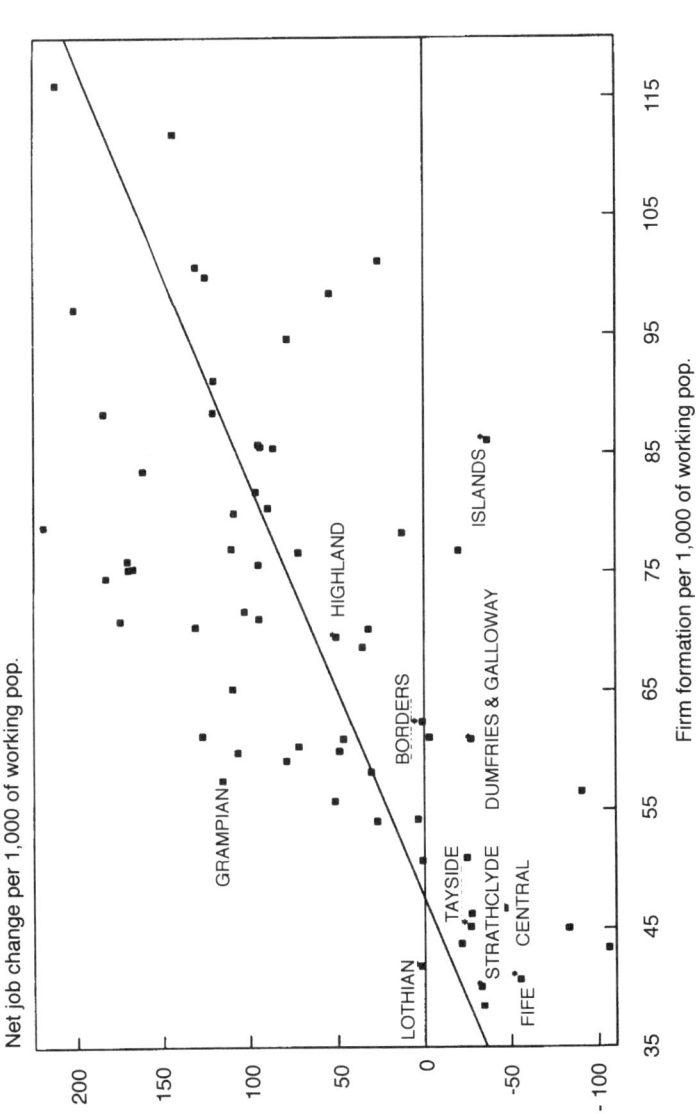

Figure 2.2. Firm formation and net job change (UK counties), 1980–9

Table 2.1 Variables used in estimation

Variable	Proxy for	Definition	Source
DEMP	Employment change	Employment change 1981–9/ working population	Regional Trends
NFF	Firm formation	VAT registrations 1980–8 per head of working population	Employment Department
EPPC	Economic potential	Σ(GDP/distance from each county) divided by working population	Various
LAF	Effect of large firms	% of manufacturing employment in plants with >10 employees	Business Monitor PA1003
EARN	Average earnings	Average annual wage	Regional Trends
PRATE	Participation rate	(Employees in employment + unemployed + self employed)/population aged 16–60	Various (1987 data)
PD	Population density	Population per hectare	Regional Trends
PCPOP	Change in population	Percentage change in population 1979–87	Census of Population
RP	Regional policy effect	Dummy variable (see text)	Various

Note: All data are at the county level and refer to 1984 unless otherwise stated.

or those completely de-scheduled at some time during the study period.

(b) Estimation and results

We are primarily interested in the relationship between firm formation and employment change, allowing for other influences which occur contemporaneously. The most obvious method of estimating equation 1 is by ordinary least squares. However, because there is a strong univariate relationship between these two key variables and because of the potential feedback effects illustrated in Figure 2.1, we must acknowledge the possibility of reverse causation between firm formation and employment change. Precisely such a relationship is postulated for Germany by Audretsch and Fritsch (1992), where employment growth is used as a proxy for regional economic growth.

We therefore test for the existence of a simultaneous system of the following type:

$$DEMP = \alpha_1 + \beta_1 NFF + \beta_2 X_1 + \mu_1$$

$$NFF = \alpha_2 + \beta_3 DEMP + \beta_4 X_2 + \mu_2$$

Where: X_1 is a vector of exogenous determinants of DEMP;
X_2 is a vector of exogenous determinants of NFF.

Estimation of such a system requires first that the determinants of firm formation be established in order to form the vector X_2. From our previous work (Ashcroft et al., 1991) we have developed a sound parsimonious model of firm formation at the county level, allowing this to be done. When a two-stage least squares version of the above system was estimated, the parameter β_3 was found to be consistently positive and statistically significant – the hypothesis of simultaneity cannot be rejected. The endogenous variables cannot therefore be assumed to be distributed independently of the stochastic disturbance terms μ_1 and μ_2, and so OLS estimation will result in inconsistent estimates. The results described below are therefore estimated using a 2SLS version of equation 1.

The results of estimating equation 1 are shown in Table 2.2. In model 1, all the independent variables are entered into the estimated equation. The coefficient on NFF is positive and highly statistically significant, suggesting that firm formation is indeed an important determinant of employment change. The coefficients on LAF, PRATE, PD and PCPOP are also statistically significant, and have the hypothesised signs. The significant coefficient on LAF suggests that where the proportion of 'large' firms is high – and small firms and earlier firm formation relatively low – existing firms have a greater effect on employment change within the county. The results for PRATE and PCPOP suggest that a higher participation rate and change in county population both have a positive effect on county employment change. The negative sign on the coefficient for PD indicates that employment growth is lower in more densely populated areas *ceteris paribus*, suggesting that congestion costs may be having real effects in such areas.

Table 2.2 Results of 2SLS estimation

Model	NFF	EPPC	LAF	EARN	PRATE	PD	PCPOP	RP	Constant	R^2	F	DW
1	4.877** (1.004)	-0.638 (0.685)	18.619** (5.037)	0.017 (0.017)	357.842** (113.323)	-0.028* (0.010)	1.809* (0.735)	4.901 (10.143)	-2390.58** (616.654)	0.702	19.482	1.685
2	4.515** (0.945)	—	17.281** (4.923)	0.014 (0.016)	358.985** (113.073)	-0.027* (0.010)	1.855* (0.730)	2.694 (9.927)	-2229.50** (604.958)	0.705	22.518	1.637
3	4.403** (0.886)	-0.472 (0.661)	16.283** (4.464)	—	377.659** (111.012)	-0.027* (0.010)	1.903* (0.724)	0.385 (9.079)	-2035.13** (506.486)	0.705	22.473	1.692
4	4.174** (0.851)	—	15.511** (4.435)	—	374.465** (111.120)	-0.026* (0.010)	1.925** (0.722)	-0.761 (9.005)	-1953.71** (506.861)	0.707	26.396	1.660
5	4.214** (0.683)	—	15.656** (3.998)	—	378.691** (98.024)	-0.026* (0.010)	1.937** (0.709)	—	-1974.02** (434.785)	0.713	32.227	1.657

Notes: (a) Dependent variable is DEMP as defined in Table 2.1.
(b) Standard errors are shown in brackets.
(c) Significant at ** 1%, * 5% on a two-tailed t-test.
(d) Number of observations = 64.

However, EPPC, EARN and RP all have insignificant coefficients. Models 2 and 3 therefore drop EPPC and EARN respectively from the estimation; these omissions result in virtually no change to the significant variables, and result in a slight improvement in the overall fit of the model. In model 4, both EPPC and EARN are removed. Once again there is very little change to the estimated coefficients, and the coefficient on RP remains insignificant.

Model 5 represents the preferred, parsimonious version. This estimation explains a high proportion of the variance in the dependent variable (adjusted R^2 = 0.713). The Durbin–Watson statistic for all five estimations falls within the inconclusive range, suggesting that the possibility of positive first-order serial correlation cannot be excluded.

CONCLUSIONS

In this chapter we have explored the relationship between firm formation and net employment change focusing on the UK counties during the 1980s. As far as we are aware there have been no previous attempts – at least for the UK – to estimate the relation formally. The research reported in this paper is preliminary so our findings must be viewed with caution. Nevertheless, it does appear that firm formation is strongly associated with net employment change at the UK county level. If the point estimate of our preferred equation is taken, then one new firm was on average associated with the creation of just over four net new jobs during the study period. This is not to say that one new firm directly creates four jobs, but rather that for each new firm four additional jobs will be added to the stock of county employment after four to five years,[3] given the indirect effects, including displacement, on existing firms and the subsequent closure of some of the new starts.

Tables 2.3 and 2.4 provide, respectively, a county ranking of actual employment change per 1,000 of the working population (Table 2.3) and a ranking of the predicted employment change that would have occurred if each county had displayed the mean county firm formation rate during the study period, other things remaining equal (Table 2.4). The obvious implication of this procedure is that counties with firm formation rates below the mean county rate register a predicted employment performance above the actual, while the opposite applies for those counties displaying above average firm formation rates. The value of this procedure is that it allows us to identify groups of

Table 2.3 Employment change in British counties (per 1,000 of working population), 1981–9

1	Northamptonshire	219.098	33	Isle of Wight	71.868
2	Powys	211.814	34	Staffordshire	71.849
3	Buckinghamshire	201.101	35	East Sussex	54.005
4	West Sussex	184.342	36	South Glamorgan	51.441
5	Cambridgeshire	183.095	37	Leicestershire	50.396
6	Clwyd	174.688	38	Derbyshire	48.791
7	Shropshire	170.545	39	West Yorkshire	46.407
8	Suffolk	170.063	40	Highland	35.434
9	Oxfordshire	167.179	41	Lancashire	32.049
10	Berkshire	161.408	42	Gwent	30.566
11	Cornwall	146.737	43	Mid Glamorgan	27.320
12	Wiltshire	130.986	44	Dyfed	26.170
13	Surrey	130.768	45	Hertfordshire	12.762
14	Cumbria	127.158	46	Northumberland	3.673
15	Dorset	125.095	47	Lothian	1.731
16	Somerset	120.747	48	Nottinghamshire	1.153

17	Devon	120.276	49	Borders	0.837
18	Grampian	115.112	50	Greater Manchester	−3.156
19	North Yorkshire	109.874	51	Greater London	−19.974
20	Avon	109.335	52	Cleveland	−21.508
21	Norfolk	108.410	53	West Midlands	−24.649
22	Humberside	106.377	54	Tayside	−26.675
23	Warwickshire	102.399	55	Dumfries & Galloway	−27.010
24	Gloucestershire	96.016	56	Durham	−27.256
25	Bedfordshire	94.593	57	Strathclyde	−32.712
26	Gwynedd	94.478	58	Tyne & Wear	−34.083
27	Hampshire	94.024	59	Islands	−36.712
28	Hereford & Worcs	93.505	60	Central	−46.322
29	Lincolnshire	88.985	61	Fife	−55.218
30	Kent	85.908	62	South Yorkshire	−83.332
31	Cheshire	78.710	63	West Glamorgan	−90.809
32	Essex	77.935	64	Merseyside	−105.875

Table 2.4 Predicted employment change in British counties (per 1,000 of working population) with the mean county firm formation rate, 1981–9

1	Northamptonshire	182.64	33	Northumberland	71.11
2	Clwyd	171.54	34	Fife	69.18
3	Grampian	169.32	35	Norfolk	67.69
4	Cumbria	165.038	36	West Midlands	56.43
5	Cambridgeshire	164.83	37	Leicestershire	53.14
6	Humberside	150.20	38	Central	52.93
7	Suffolk	148.78	39	Gloucestershire	47.33
8	Shropshire	146.10	40	Lincolnshire	45.99
9	Oxfordshire	145.48	41	Isle of Wight	44.61
10	Avon	130.37	42	Somerset	43.81
11	Wiltshire	130.10	43	Highland	41.73
12	Cheshire	125.46	44	Greater Manchester	35.36
13	Lothian	121.19	45	Borders	33.71
14	Staffordshire	113.51	46	Lancashire	32.07
15	South Glamorgan	112.31	47	Devon	31.88
16	West Sussex	107.59	48	Gwynedd	29.01

17	Berkshire	105.29
18	Tyne & Wear	99.69
19	Warwickshire	96.06
20	Mid Glamorgan	95.39
21	Strathclyde	94.22
22	Derbyshire	92.16
23	Hampshire	90.25
24	Cleveland	90.05
25	Buckinghamshire	87.51
26	West Yorkshire	85.42
27	Nottinghamshire	83.17
28	North Yorkshire	81.33
29	Gwent	81.30
30	Tayside	78.94
31	Durham	73.80
32	Bedfordshire	71.58
49	Hereford & Worcs	28.88
50	South Yorkshire	22.76
51	Kent	21.68
52	Powys	18.69
53	Dumfries & Galloway	12.19
54	Merseyside	7.32
55	Surrey	2.19
56	Dorset	0.07
57	Hertfordshire	−21.31
58	Essex	−25.06
59	Cornwall	−28.99
60	West Glamorgan	−33.04
61	Greater London	−47.73
62	East Sussex	−65.10
63	Islands	−103.53
64	Dyfed	−104.38

Table 2.5 Groups of British counties by contribution of firm formation to employment change, 1981–9

IMPSTNG	ABOVE	IMPWEAK	DETSTNG	BELOW	DETWEAK
Grampian	Tyne & Wear	Merseyside	Buckinghamshire	Powys	Dyfed
Cheshire	Strathclyde	South Yorkshire	West Sussex	Cornwall	East Sussex
Humberside	Fife	Central	Berkshire	Surrey	Islands
Staffordshire	Lothian	West Midlands	Norfolk	Dorset	Hertfordshire
Cumbria	Cleveland	West Glamorgan	Northamptonshire	Essex	Greater London
Avon	Tayside	Dumfries & Galloway	North Yorkshire	Devon	
		Greater Manchester			
	Durham	Borders	Shropshire	Somerset	
	Nottingham	Highland	Bedfordshire	Gwynedd	
	Mid Glamorgan	Leicestershire	Oxfordshire	Hereford & Worcs	
	Northumberland	Lancashire	Suffolk	Kent	
	South Glamorgan		Cambridgeshire	Gloucestershire	
	Gwent		Warwickshire	Lincolnshire	
	Derbyshire		Hampshire	Isle of Wight	
	West Yorkshire		Clwyd		
			Wiltshire		

Note: See text for definition of column headings

counties defined by the relative contribution of firm formation to their actual employment performance. This is done in Table 2.5.

In Table 2.5, the British counties are placed in six groups. The first three groups (IMPSTNG, ABOVE and IMPWEAK) are the counties which exhibited a firm formation rate below the average for the British counties, while the latter three groups (DETSTNG, BELOW and DETWEAK) contain the counties with above average firm formation rates. The two groups, ABOVE and BELOW, contain those counties where firm formation is estimated to have had a major relative contribution to county employment change. So, the ABOVE group contains counties which displayed below average (and usually low) firm formation rates, below average employment performance, and where the application of the mean county firm formation rate has an estimated effect on county employment sufficient to raise predicted employment performance above the mean county rate. The counties in each group are ranked by the size of the effect. So, Tyne and Wear exhibited an actual employment change of −34.083 and after the application of the mean county firm formation rate, the county's predicted employment performance rises to 99.69, considerably above the mean county employment change of 64.6. This has the effect of moving Tyne and Wear from 58 in the actual employment performance rankings to 18 in the rankings of predicted employment.

The IMPSTNG group contains six counties which exhibited below average firm formation rates but above average actual employment performance, clearly for reasons other than firm formation. Movement of these counties to the mean firm formation rate simply serves to improve an already strong employment performance. Conversely, the IMPWEAK group contains counties displaying both below average employment performance and firm formation rates and where the application of the mean county firm formation rate is not sufficient to raise the county above the mean county employment performance. So, Merseyside had the worst employment performance over the period (−105.875) ranking 64, and the imposition of the mean county firm formation rate raises predicted employment to 7.32 (rank 54), suggesting that Merseyside's employment problems embrace much more than a weak firm formation rate.

The counties experiencing above average firm formation rates are also placed into three groups. The BELOW group contains those counties where application of the mean county firm formation rate is sufficient to move the county from above average to below average employment performance, with each county ranked by size of effect.

So, Powys ranked 2 on actual employment performance (211.814) but after the application of the mean county firm formation rate its ranking slips dramatically to 52 on predicted employment performance (18.69), suggesting the importance of new firm formation to the county's strong jobs performance. In the other two groups, the imposition of the mean county firm formation rate is not sufficient in DETSTNG to move the counties from above to below average employment change, while in DETWEAK the procedure simply serves to reinforce an already weak, below average, employment performance. In both these latter two groups we can conclude that a superior firm formation performance was relatively marginal to their overall employment prospects.

Overall, these findings suggest that in about two-fifths (27) of British counties above or below average firm formation rates have had crucial significance to employment outturns, while in the remainder, above or below average job change reflects differences in the performance of the stock of existing firms as well as rates of new firm formation.

ACKNOWLEDGEMENTS

We are grateful to Scottish Enterprise for sponsoring the research contained in this chapter and in particular to Ron Botham and Jonathan Slow for their helpful advice and comments. All errors and omissions remain our own.

NOTES

1 While such a finding might reduce the justification for a policy initiative in support of firm formation it does not necessarily *remove* it. Firm formation may be the vehicle for the introduction of product and process innovations into the regional economy and for new technology generally. New firms may also serve to diversify the regional economy and by increasing local supply to larger externally controlled plants present in the economy may serve to integrate the external sector much more into the local economy. For these reasons, new firm formation may be very important to the long-run development of the regional economy, even if its contribution to net job creation in the short to medium run is slight.
2 New firms may serve to raise regional productive efficiency indirectly by supplying superior intermediate products to local companies and/or via demonstration effects of best practice operation to other local firms.
3 Four to five years is the average period for employment to build up in each new firm with a study period of nine years.

BIBLIOGRAPHY

Ashcroft, B., Love, J. H. and Malloy, E. (1991) 'New firm formation in the British counties with special reference to Scotland', *Regional Studies*, 25: 395–409.

Ashcroft, B. and Love, J. H. (1994) 'Firm births and employment change: the British counties, 1981–89', mimeo., Fraser of Allander Institute and Department of Economics, University of Strathclyde.

Audretsch, D. B. and Fritsch, M. (1992) 'Market dynamics and regional development in the Federal Republic of Germany', Discussion Paper FS IV 92–6, Wissenschaftszentrum, Berlin.

Ganguly, A. (1982) 'Births and deaths of firms in the UK in 1980', *British Business*, 29 January: 204–7.

McGregor, P. G., Swales, J. K., Ying, Y. P. and Le Tissier, S. (1993) 'The impact of foreign direct investment: a simulation approach', report to Scottish Enterprise National, Fraser of Allander Institute, University of Strathclyde.

3 Survival, growth and age of SMEs
Some implications for regional economic development

David Smallbone and David North

INTRODUCTION

Aims of this chapter

This chapter aims to contribute to a discussion of the role of small and medium size enterprises (SMEs) in regional economic development and to identify some of the policy issues that need to be considered if this contribution is to be maximised. Any assessment of the role of SMEs in economic development must consider their ability to survive and grow and, in particular, their ability to create employment. It also needs to include the extent to which they are able to contribute to the development of competitive regional economies. In both cases, it is necessary to take a long-term view which recognises that the needs, problems and economic impacts of SMEs may change as firms which survive the critical early years evolve into more established concerns. Such a view is taken in this chapter through an examination of the evolution of a panel of manufacturing SMEs over a 10-year period.

This chapter is concerned with established firms rather than new firms; in fact, all firms in the study which survived the 1980s were at least 10 years old at the time they were interviewed in 1990. However, the composition of the panel includes firms of different ages and includes 'young firms' (founded in the 1970s) as well as more mature firms (defined here as those founded before 1970). Since it is often argued that the contribution of SMEs to employment growth diminishes with the age of the firm (Dunne and Hughes 1990: 12; University of Cambridge 1992: 14), one aim of this chapter is to compare the contribution of the younger firms to employment generation with that of their older counterparts.

By comparing the contribution of established SMEs of different ages to economic development, the chapter aims to enter the targeting debate about the types of SMEs which justify prioritised support. Within the context of a strategy of focusing policy support on firms which can contribute to regional economic development in the longer term, the aim is to see if there is a case for targeting firms in particular age groups, such as young firms, and also to identify the constraints and problems which young firms face in evolving into more mature businesses. In this case the objective is to contribute to the policy debate about the support needs of young businesses that have successfully navigated the difficult early years after start-up.

There is evidence of a growing interest in the UK in the contribution of *established SMEs* to the economy which is reflected in policy initiatives such as the DTI's *Business Link* (DTI 1993: 7). The 1980s saw a substantial growth in the number of small businesses as well as in the number and variety of policy initiatives designed to encourage and support them. In the early 1980s, the emphasis in public policy was on increasing the rate of new business formation, but more recently there has been a growing recognition of the importance of helping expanding firms overcome growth constraints and of encouraging established small firms to maintain and improve competitiveness (Advisory Council on Science and Technology 1990: 67; Hughes 1991: 478). It has also been argued that putting more money into start-ups is less cost effective than helping established SMEs grow faster (Storey 1993: 15). It is the growing recognition of the contribution of established SMEs to economic development which provides the policy context for this chapter.

The data-base and its use in the chapter

The empirical evidence presented here is drawn from a study entitled 'A Longitudinal Study of Adjustment Processes in Mature Manufacturing SMEs during the 1980s' (part of the ESRC's Small Business Research Initiative).[1] To be included in the study, firms had to be independently owned and with a work-force of less than 100 employees in the base year (1979); they also had to be in one of eight manufacturing sectors (see Table 3.2). The starting point for the study was a data-base consisting of firms in London which had been interviewed in 1979 and 1981 as part of a previous study covering the period 1976–81 (Leigh et al. 1983). Of the 293 firms from this previous study which met the above criteria, 124 were found no longer to be in existence in 1990. Of the 169 which had survived, 126 were interviewed again in 1990/1 as part of the present study. In addition to this London panel, firms which met the above criteria were also selected from other locations, since one of the underlying aims of the present study has been to compare the development of similar SMEs during the 1980s in contrasting types of location. Thus, 100 firms were selected from the outer metropolitan area (OMA) (mainly Hertfordshire and Essex), and a further 80 firms from 'remote' rural locations in northern England. A specific aim was to try to match the sectoral mix of firms drawn from the OMA and remote rural locations with that for Greater London as far as possible. Taken together, therefore, the three geographical panels comprised 306 SMEs which were in existence in 1979 and had survived to at least 1990/1. In-depth interviews with the owners/managers of these firms were carried out in 1990/1 and wherever possible the interview data were supplemented with data drawn from company accounts.

Most of the analysis reported in this chapter will be based on the combined panel of 306 firms and will be concerned with comparing the development of surviving firms of different ages during the 1980s. For the purpose of this chapter , the 'young firms' will be defined as those which were less than 10 years old in the base year of the study, i.e., 1979. In other words, they were firms which were established during the 1970s and their performance during the subsequent decade will be compared with that of firms which were already at least 10 years old in 1979. Thus, there are 119 firms (39 per cent of the total panel) which will be regarded as the 'young firms' in the subsequent analysis. The main part of the chapter will focus on comparing the development during the 1980s of these 119 'young firms' with that of their 187 older surviving counterparts, in terms of their performance, problems and contribution to employment generation during the period. However, since one of the factors which affects a firm's long-term contribution to employment change is its ability to survive, the first part of the chapter uses the longitudinal data-base for London-based companies to make some analysis of survivability in terms of the age of firms. The rest of the chapter is focused on three main questions:

• How does the contribution of 'young firms' to employment growth compare with that of older SMEs during the period 1979–90?
• To what extent were firms founded in the 1970s able to evolve into mature, established SMEs by the end of the 1980s?
• What problems did young firms face in making the transition into established SMEs?

The approach used throughout the chapter is first to present our main empirical findings with respect to each of the questions under consideration. This is followed by an attempt to draw out the implications for policy both in terms of the contribution of these 'young' firms to economic development and also the extent to which this might be increased with greater policy support. The concluding section of the chapter summarises our interpretation of the policy implications which arise from the analysis, focusing on the extent to which the contribution of SMEs to economic development appears to vary with the age of firm, and also on the policy support needs of growing young firms.

HOW DOES THE CONTRIBUTION OF 'YOUNG FIRMS' TO EMPLOYMENT GROWTH COMPARE WITH THAT OF OLDER SMEs DURING THE PERIOD 1979–90?

In making an assessment of the contribution of firms of different ages to employment generation over a period of time, it is necessary to consider the effect of any difference in the survival rates of firms as well as in the propensity of those firms which survive, to create jobs. Our longitudinal data-base enables us to assess the impact of any difference in the survival rates between SMEs of different ages on employment; an assessment of the contribution to employment generation by surviving firms of different ages includes those in the OMA and remote rural areas also (i.e., n = 306).

The survivability of young and mature SMEs

(i) *Barely half of the firms under 10 years old at any one time are likely to be able to survive over the next decade to create additional jobs.*

It is well known that there is a high risk of failure in the first few years of establishing a business. For example, it has been shown that 36 per cent of all VAT registered businesses fail within three years of registration (Stanworth and Gray 1991: 11). While our own study has not been concerned with the prospects of new business start-ups, it is possible to compare the survival rates of firms of different ages. Because our longitudinal data-base for London firms includes data on their development during the period 1976–9, a comparison can be made between those firms which did manage to survive the subsequent decade and those that did not (for a full discussion see North, Leigh and Smallbone 1991, 1992). In this particular chapter, the focus is on a comparison of the survival rates of those London firms which were set up during the 1970s (i.e., firms which would have been less than 10 years old in 1979, the base year for our study), with those firms which were set up earlier.

As shown in Table 3.1, the ability of the firms established in the 1970s to survive the 1980s was significantly lower than that of the older firms; just under half of the 1970s firms were still in existence in 1990, compared with nearly two-thirds of those set up before 1970. Put differently, the 1970s firms comprised 25 per cent of all the firms in the London panel which survived the 1980s, but 38 per cent of those which did not survive. Therefore, these findings not only confirm that there is likely to be a high turnover in the stock of young firms within any regional economy, but also that it can take a new firm up to 20 years to become firmly established and reasonably secure.

Since the impact of non-survival on employment depends on the size of the non-surviving firms as well as their number, it is also necessary to compare the younger and older firms in terms of the jobs lost as a result of non-survival. The 47 firms in our London panel which were set up in the 1970s but did not survive the 1980s, accounted for 730 jobs in 1979 (a mean loss of 15.5 jobs per firm). This compares with the loss of 1901 jobs in the 76 older firms which did not survive (a mean loss of 25 jobs per firm). Thus, although the survival chances of older firms are better than those of young firms, the employment impact of this is partly offset by the generally larger employment size of the older firms which went out of business. One way of assessing the combined impact of these two effects is to average the jobs lost through non-survival over all the firms in each age group in 1979 (i.e., the survivors and non-survivors combined). This shows that non-survival accounted for the loss of slightly more jobs in the case of the older firms; for the 89 young firms in the London panel, a mean of 8.2 jobs per firm were lost during the 1980s as a result of the non-survival of 53 per cent of them, whereas for the 202 older firms a mean of 9.4 jobs were lost through the non-survival of 38 per cent of them.

From a regional economic development standpoint, the above findings would appear to have two main policy implications. First, given the less than 50 per cent chance of survival amongst firms which are less than 10 years old, one challenge for policy-makers is to identify those young firms which are most likely to survive over a 10-year period and create additional jobs. This is where an understanding of those factors most likely to influence survival is crucial. Second, while it might be tempting to argue that measures should be

Table 3.1 The survivability of firms by age group (London panel)

Year of formation	Number of firms in 1979 panel	Non-survivors	Survivors
Pre-1950	90 (100%)	36 (40%)	54 (60%)
1950–69	112 (100%)	40 (36%)	72 (64%)
1970–79	89 (100%)	47 (53%)	42 (47%)
All firms	291 (100%)	123*(42%)	168*(58%)

Notes: (a) * the year of formation is unknown for 1 non-surviving and 1 surviving firm
(b) chi-square value of 6.21 (df = 2) shows that there is a significant difference at the 0.05 level

taken to try to increase survival rates amongst young firms, our evidence suggests that there is little justification for separating out the youngest firms for special attention compared with older firms, at least on the basis of the jobs which would be lost. If policies to increase survival rates are desirable for employment retention, they should apply to both young and old firms alike.

(ii) *The propensity of a young firm to survive clearly depends upon the sector which it is in.*

A sectoral strategy is one approach to targeting SMEs for prioritised policy support. In this respect, our study has shown marked sectoral variations in the survival rates of firms within the London panel, with the printing and electronics sectors having very high survival rates at one extreme, compared with clothing and the toys and games sectors at the other (Table 3.2). The extent of the sectoral variation in survival rates is greater than that reported in some other studies (Storey 1994: 94) which is almost certainly associated with the level of sectoral disaggregation used. In this particular study, we defined 'sector' in terms of specific four-digit codes of the Standard Industrial Classification (SIC) which means that we are more likely to pick up variations in market conditions than in studies where broad Divisions of the SIC are used.

While the survival chances of the young firms accords to this sectoral pattern, within most sectors there was a contrast between the survival rates of young and older firms. For example in furniture, only 35 per cent of the firms set up in the 1970s survived until 1990 compared with 55 per cent of those established earlier; in industrial plant, the equivalent survival rates were 47 per cent for younger firms

Table 3.2 Sectoral variations in survival rates for London firms (London panel)

Sector	Firms in 1979 No.	Survival rate 79–90 %
Clothing	67	24
Electronics	34	79
Furniture	55	49
Industrial plant	36	67
Instruments	17	65
Pharmaceuticals	11	82
Printing	56	88
Toys and games	17	35
Total	293	58

and 80 per cent for older firms. The sole exception to this pattern was the clothing sector, where the survival rate was lowest amongst the oldest firms: only 16 per cent of those which had been established for at least 20 years in 1979 survived until 1990, compared with 32 per cent of those less than 10 years old. From a policy perspective, the marked variations between sectors in small business survival rates supports the case for including a sectoral dimension within a targeting strategy. The sectoral dimension is important if policy support is to avoid simply adding to the number of firms in what are already overcrowded and/or declining subsectors.

(iii) *Young firms are particularly vulnerable when they operate in highly competitive product/market areas, are heavily dependent on a few customers and have not evolved sufficiently to spread their risks over a number of (related) products and markets.*

Whether or not a firm survives over a particular period will depend upon the interrelationship between a number of factors and processes, many of which will be affected by the forces operating within the sector that the firm is competing in. Our comparison of surviving and non-surviving firms in the London panel suggests that the most satisfactory interpretations of survivability involve a consideration of the interplay between various aspects of management behaviour (including their product and market strategies) on the one hand and sectoral conditions on the other (for a discussion of the key influences on survivability in different sectors see North, Leigh and Smallbone

1991: 24–31, 1992: 22–5). Space only permits a brief summary of the various factors influencing survivability here.

The strength of market demand combined with the intensity of competition are clearly two of the most important external factors influencing survivability, and this helps to explain the different survival chances of firms in the different sectors. Thus, young firms in the commercial printing industry in London faced a generally buoyant market during the 1980s associated with the growth of the business services and finance sectors. Young clothing firms on the other hand faced a fiercely competitive situation characterised by the import of cheaper garments from low labour cost countries, particularly in the Far East and Southern Europe.

Within sectors, our comparison of surviving and non-surviving firms showed that the non-survival of a business was usually involuntary and could be explained in terms of the failure of the owners/ managers to overcome particular weaknesses in their firms' products and markets. When we focus on those firms set up in the 1970s which did not survive, these weaknesses are particularly evident. A firm's chances of survival can depend upon its ability to develop a degree of product differentiation and a clear market focus, yet many young firms (most notably in the clothing, electronics, furniture, and industrial plant sectors) had been unable to achieve this, being overdependent upon non-specialist subcontracting work and relying on achieving competitiveness on the basis of price rather than the use of more customer-focused, non-price tactics.

Young firms were also particularly vulnerable because, unlike their older counterparts, they had not evolved sufficiently to be able to spread their risks over a number of (related) products and markets. They also invariably suffered from having a narrow customer base. Young firms in the clothing and industrial plant sectors (and also in the furniture sector to some extent), were commonly dependent upon just one or two customers; this meant they were left without a market when their customers decided to source from elsewhere or, in some cases, went out of business themselves.

In several respects, therefore, the non-surviving firms in our London panel which were set up during the 1970s had not been able to develop by the beginning of the 1980s the characteristics normally associated with established businesses. Although many of the founders of these firms had experience of working in the sector previously, it was taking them several years to build up a supporting network of suppliers and customers, a reputation for quality work and a reliable work-force. Even though they had been in existence for up to 10 years, many of them were still marginal businesses operating in crowded subsectors of the industry in 1979. While they had been largely carried along by market trends during the 1970s, many of them could no longer survive in competition with more established firms once demand dropped back in the recession of the early 1980s.

On the basis of this analysis, therefore, it can be argued that any policy initiatives concerned with trying to improve the survival chances of young firms as part of a wider strategy of strengthening a regional economy need to focus on assisting these firms to develop and implement product and market strategies. Clearly such strategies will need to be tailored to particular sectoral conditions, but they are likely to include helping young firms to achieve greater product differentiation and a more distinctive market focus, progress towards producing higher value added products, diversification of products and/or markets, and a broadening of their customer base.

Employment growth in surviving firms: the age dimension

Having considered the evidence on non-surviving SMEs from our London panel, the rest of the chapter will be concerned with a discussion of those SMEs which survived during the 1980s. This will be based on a comparison of young and mature SMEs in the entire panel (i.e., the London, OMA and rural panels combined – n = 306), although differences between the younger firms in the different types of location are highlighted where appropriate.

(i) *Job generation is closely tied to output growth in all age groups; most new jobs are created by firms which at least double their real turnover over 10 years.*

One of the key findings of the study as a whole is that job creation during the period 1979–90 was closely related to the growth of the firm in output terms (measured in terms of deflated sales turnover 1979–90) (see North, Smallbone and Leigh 1993: 221–4). However, because of productivity improvements, a firm typically had to increase its real sales turnover by two and a half times in order to double its employment. In fact, the best performing firms in growth terms accounted for nearly three-quarters of all new jobs which were created; the 70 firms which attained 'high growth' status (23 per cent of all firms) accounted for 71 per cent of all new jobs, creating 25 new jobs each on average. Thus, from a policy perspective, it would appear that the best way of generating employment in the longer term is to focus support on firms with the greatest growth potential. When we focus on the younger firms, it is clear that this strong relationship between employment generation and growth in output still holds. Thus, the majority of new jobs in the younger firms were created by those which managed to at least double their real sales turnover over the period 1979–90. In fact, a higher proportion of younger firms compared to older firms more than doubled their size (in terms of the value of output) during this period: 56 per cent of the firms founded in the 1970s compared with just 25 per cent of the firms founded before 1970. The nature of this growth performance will be discussed below, but it does lead us to expect a much better employment performance by the surviving younger firms during the 1980s compared to their older counterparts.

(ii) *At an aggregate level, firms founded in the 1970s contribute most of the net increase in employment between 1979 and 1990.*

At first sight, the employment contribution of the younger SMEs dwarfs that of older firms during the 1980s; for example, 1,126 out of the 1,159 net increase in jobs in the total panel (i.e., 97 per cent) was attributable to these young firms (Table 3.3). The firms set up in the 1970s almost doubled their employment between 1979 and 1990, this being a median increase per firm of five jobs (the mean increase of 10 jobs showing the effect of some extreme cases). The importance of the 55 per cent of young firms which more than doubled their turnover is underlined by the fact that they accounted for 1096 (i.e., 97 per cent) of the net employment increase of the younger firms, and 94.5 per cent of that of all firms. From the point of view of *net* employment creation, therefore, the contribution of these young, fast-growing firms is predominant.

However, the contribution of more mature firms to net employment creation is not insignificant. While it was admittedly much smaller than the net increase of the young firms, there was a 8.7 per cent increase in the employment of the surviving firms which had been in existence for between 10 and 30 years in 1979. However, firms in the oldest age category (i.e., those founded before 1950) did show a net decrease in their employment between 1979 and 1990 of 7.8 per cent. Nevertheless, because they were larger on average than those in the younger age categories, these older SMEs still represented a substantial proportion of the total employment in the panel in 1990: 30 per cent of employment in 23 per cent of the number of firms. In terms of

Table 3.3 Total employment and employment change by age of firm (combined panel)

	Pre-1950	1950–69	1970–9	All firms
1979 Employment				
Total	2,406	2,554	1,240	6,200
Mean firm size	34.4	22.4	10.6	20.7
Median size	24.5	20.0	5.5	12.0
1990 Employment				
Total	2,218	2,775	2,366	7,359
Mean firm size	31.7	24.3	20.4	24.5
Median size	16.0	17.5	12.0	15.0
Net absolute change	−188	+221	+1,126	+1,159
% change	−7.8%	+8.7%	+90.8%	+18.7%
Change per firm				
Mean	−2.7	+1.9	+9.7	+3.9
Median	−1.0	0	+5.0	+1.0
No. of firms	70	114	116	300*

Note: * it was not possible to classify six firms because of inadequate data

a region's future employment prospects, therefore, a concern for new job creation in young firms should not be at the expense of a concern for facilitating employment creation in some more mature firms.

(iii) *A more disaggregated analysis of employment change shows that older firms had a higher propensity to reduce employment during the 1980s than younger firms.*

While the net employment change measure is important in showing the overall employment potential of surviving firms of different ages, it does tend to undervalue the part that the more mature firms play in employment generation. Tables 3.4 and 3.5 help to give a fuller picture of the employment changes that occurred at the individual firm level.

As might be expected, the main reason why the contribution of older firms to net employment change was inferior to that of younger firms was that they had a much higher propensity to reduce their employment during the 1980s. Overall, just over a third of the surviving firms in the total panel are responsible for the 1,345 jobs which were shed between 1979 and 1990, and 88 per cent of these jobs were lost from firms which were in existence prior to 1970

Table 3.4 Jobs gained and lost, 1979–90, by age of firm (combined panel)

	Pre-1950	1950–69	1970–9	All firms
Jobs gained	437	778	1,289	2,504
	(17.5%)	(31%)	(51.5%)	(100%)
Jobs lost	625	557	163	1,345
	(46.5%)	(41.4%)	(12.1%)	(100%)
Net change	−188	+221	+1,126	+1,159
No. of firms	70	114	116	300*

Note: * it was not possible to classify six firms because of inadequate data

(Table 3.4). Whereas just 19 per cent of firms established in the 1970s reduced employment between 1979 and 1990, 41 per cent of those founded between 1950 and 1969 and 56 per cent of those founded prior to 1950 did so. Many of these older SMEs also tended to be amongst the largest in the panel and, as we have shown elsewhere, firms employing more than 50 are more likely to reduce than increase their employment (North, Smallbone and Leigh 1993: 220).

As well as showing the effect of those older firms which reduced their employment, the disaggregated picture also shows that a substantial number of more mature firms expanded their employment during the 1980s. In terms of the additional jobs created, firms set up

Table 3.5 Absolute change in employment, 1979–90, and age of firm (combined panel)

No. of jobs gained/lost	Pre-1950	1950–69	1970–9	All firms
>30 gain	6	8	12	26
+20–29	1	4	7	12
+10–19	6	12	19	37
+1–9	15	24	43	82
0	3	19	13	35
-1–9	26	26	16	68
-10–19	5	11	4	20
-20–29	0	6	1	7
>30 loss	8	4	1	12
Total	70	114	116	300*

Note: (a) * it was not possible to classify six firms because of inadequate data
(b) the units in this table refer to the number of firms

before 1970 actually accounted for almost half of new jobs; moreover, 41 per cent of these firms actually increased their employment in the 1980s compared with 70 per cent of the younger firms. Since firms founded in the 1970s were typically still smaller in 1990 than the majority of their older counterparts, it is not surprising that their contribution to absolute employment change tended to decrease as the number of jobs being considered increased (Table 3.5). Thus, focusing on firms increasing employment by 20 or more between 1979 and 1990, 10 per cent of firms founded pre-1950, 11 per cent of those founded between 1950 and 1969 and 16 per cent of those founded in the 1970s achieved such increases. For firms increasing employment by 30 or more in the 1980s, the corresponding proportions are 9 per cent, 7 per cent and 10 per cent respectively.

This more disaggregated evidence provides further support for the argument that older SMEs, as well as younger ones, have an important role to play in job creation. With respect to targeting, our survey evidence suggests that an exclusive emphasis on younger firms would be misplaced, because a minority of mature firms at any one time are also increasing employment. Essentially, this is because job generation in small firms over an extended period of time results from business growth, and growth in small firms can be a very discontinuous process. As a consequence, even some very mature firms can demonstrate fast growth during certain periods. Thus, from a targeting perspective, some mature firms can be well worth supporting.

(iv) *The ability of surviving SMEs to generate employment varies spatially, being highest in rural areas and lowest in urban areas. Young firms make the largest contribution to net job creation in all types of location.*

Although surviving SMEs increased employment over the decade in all three types of location, there are clear differences in the magnitude of the increases. As other recent studies have also found (e.g., Coombes et al. 1991; Keeble et al. 1992; University of Cambridge 1992), the employment creation potential of small firms in urban areas is typically less than that of comparable firms in non-urban areas. Our own findings are broadly consistent with these other studies, demonstrating that it was firms in remote rural areas which achieved the best employment performance, and London firms the worst: rural firms achieved a 51 per cent net increase in employment between 1979 and 1990 compared with 23 per cent for the OMA firms and 7 per cent for the London firms. Our previous analysis has shown that these differences are not the result of the remote rural areas having a significantly higher proportion of growth firms than urban areas, but rather because of differences in the ways in which SMEs achieved growth in urban and rural environments (North and Smallbone 1995). Growth was less likely to be translated into direct employment creation in an urban context because it was found that increased externalisation and the more intensive use of labour by urban firms reduced the need to expand the work-force to achieve growth, whereas in rural contexts the growth of the firm was more likely to lead directly to employment increases.

The SMEs which were set up during the 1970s proved to be the main contributors to net job creation in all three types of location. However, whereas the young SMEs in both the remote rural and outer metropolitan locations more than doubled their employment over the decade (increases of 137 per cent and 129 per cent respectively), the young London firms only achieved an increase of 43 per cent, which is in line with the poorer overall employment performance of the London firms as a whole. In terms of the average number of jobs created, it was the 1970s outer metropolitan firms which performed best, achieving a median increase of six jobs per firm against five and 2.5 for their London and rural counterparts respectively. There was also a more marked contrast between the net employment increases of the young firms and the net employment decreases of the more mature firms in the case of the OMA panel than in either the London or rural panels. In fact, in the case of the rural panel, some of the older SMEs performed particularly well. Rural firms founded between 1950 and 1969 outperformed their counterparts in London and the OMA in terms of employment change during the 1980s, largely because of the much lower levels of job losses among surviving companies; the rural firms in this age group increased their employment by 58 per cent compared with decreases of 1 per cent and 6 per cent for their London and OMA counterparts. Thus, the better employment growth performance of the rural firms was not simply the result of them tending to be younger and smaller than urban firms but was also due to the important employment-generation role played by some of the more mature firms. Policy-makers need to be aware of the different relationship between output growth and employment growth in SMEs in different types of location.

TO WHAT EXTENT WERE FIRMS FOUNDED IN THE 1970s ABLE TO EVOLVE INTO MATURE, ESTABLISHED SMEs BY THE END OF THE 1980s?

In this section, the aim is to see to what extent the growth performance of the younger firms compared with older firms justifies targeted support and if so, what forms of support should be prioritised. To achieve this, a comparison is made between the growth performance (1979–90) of firms founded in the 1970s with that of older firms. This is followed by an attempt to highlight those aspects of business development in which young firms appeared particularly active in evolving into established businesses during the 1980s. This leads to the final section of the chapter where the distinctive problems and challenges faced by young businesses in making the transition into more established firms are identified.

(i) *Overall, firms founded in the 1970s grew more strongly in the 1980s than older firms and a significant minority had evolved into sound growing businesses by the end of the 1980s.*

In order to compare the growth performance of the firms within our study over the period 1979–90, each firm was assigned to one of five performance groups, based on the change that occurred in real sales turnover in the period studied. Additional criteria were used to distinguish between two types of rapidly growing firms. The aim was to separate those where rapid growth was combined with consistent profitability and a size which increases their chances of being able to cope with major external shocks such as the loss of a major customer, from firms where rapid growth had been achieved but at the expense of other weaknesses. The groups are defined in Figure 3.1.

Table 3.6 shows that 70 per cent of firms founded in the 1970s were able to increase real turnover between 1979 and 1990 and 56 per cent more than doubled it; this compares with 44 per cent and 25 per cent respectively of firms founded before 1970. It can be argued that the ability of younger firms to achieve growth is affected by their typically lower absolute turnover in 1979.[2] Nevertheless, the fact that there is little difference between the different age groups in the propensity of firms to achieve 'high growth' performance in the 1980s is a particular achievement for the younger firms: a quarter of firms founded in the 1970s were able to meet the same growth, size and profitability criteria as their more established counterparts. Indeed, as we have argued elsewhere, high growth performance is

Group 1 ('high growth'): these are firms that more than doubled their sales turnover in real terms 1979–90, that reached a sufficient size by 1990 to give them the capacity for continued viability and that were consistently profitable.

Group 2 ('strong growth'): these are firms which at least doubled real turnover 1979–90 but failed to reach £0.5m turnover and/or to maintain consistent profitability.

Group 3 ('moderate growth'): these are firms which increased real turnover by between 1.5 and 2 times 1979–90.

Group 4 ('stable'): these are firms which stayed about the same size in terms of output value, having increased real turnover by between 1.0 and 1.5 times 1979–90.

Group 5 ('declining'): these are firms which actually declined in terms of real turnover 1979–90.

Figure 3.1 Performance groups

more associated with a firm's commitment to growth and the types of strategy followed, than with objective characteristics such as age, size or sector (Smallbone, North and Leigh 1993a: 86–7).

One of the factors influencing the stronger growth performance of younger firms during the 1980s is that they were more likely to be growth-oriented than older firms: 92 per cent of firms founded in the 1970s were aiming to grow during the 1980s compared with 66 per cent of older businesses; 47 per cent had a strong growth objective compared with 36 per cent of older firms. One reason why ageing businesses may grow less rapidly than young firms is because an individual's motivation to continue to expand the business may

Table 3.6 Age of firm and growth performance, 1979–90 (combined panel)

Age of firm	Group 1 firms		Group 2 firms		Group 3 firms		Group 4 firms		Group 5 firms		All firms
	No.	%	No.	%	No.	%	No.	%	No.	%	No.
Pre-1950	13	19	3	4	13	19	22	31	19	27	70
1950–69	26	23	4	3	23	20	21	18	41	36	115
1970–9	30	25	36	31	17	14	22	18	14	12	119
Total	69	23	43	14	53	17	55	18	74	24	304[*]

Note: * there are two firms for which we do not have accurate age data

decline once they have achieved a 'satisfactory' level of income from their enterprise. It is such cases that lead some writers to point to an association between the age and experience of the leader of the firm and the stage of development of the business (Chell and Haworth 1992). Such an association may be found in some first-generation businesses but, more generally, the age and life-cycle characteristics of the leader of the firm may be a more important influence on the firm's growth orientation than the age of the business *per se*.

Clearly, the combination of their higher degree of growth orientation and stronger overall growth performance makes these younger firms a potentially interesting group from a policy perspective, particularly when their employment growth performance is also taken into account. At the same time, it is a mistake to think that rapid growth is only found in very young firms. Since very few of the firms in this study were within one or two years of start-up in 1979, even our 'young firms' are not new firms. Moreover, the growth performance of the older firms in the study indicates the potential contribution of even very mature SMEs to regional economic development. Age is one factor influencing both the importance of the growth objective and a firm's ability to achieve growth, but it is not a determining factor. Thus, policy-makers need to be sensitive to the growth potential and support needs of firms of different ages.

(ii) *Almost a third of businesses founded in the 1970s demonstrated an ability to achieve fast sales growth in the 1980s but had other weaknesses.*

One potential weakness of the growth performance of younger firms in the 1980s is demonstrated by the fact that 31 per cent of firms founded in the 1970s are in our Group 2 performance category. These are firms which at least doubled their real turnover over the decade but which had failed to reach a sufficient size after 10 years (£0.5m sales turnover) and/or consistent profitability to be considered sound established businesses. Either way, they would seem to be an important target for policy support if their development over a long period of time is to be secured.

In fact, 16 of the 36 (44 per cent) Group 2 firms founded in the 1970s showed a profit in only one of the three years preceding the interview (i.e., 1987/8–1989/90); in half these cases, sales turnover in 1990 had reached the £0.5m threshold needed to justify inclusion in the high-growth category. The experience of these young Group 2 firms in the 1980s supports the view, expressed by other writers, that many fast growth firms do need external support if their growth performance is to be sustained and their potential for job generation in the longer term to be fulfilled (Storey and Johnson 1987: 225–6).

(iii) *To survive and grow over 10 years, young firms need to pay particular attention to developing their markets and to diversifying their customer base.*

Our previous analysis of the factors influencing survival and non-survival emphasised the failure of managers in non-surviving companies in overcoming particular weaknesses in the firm's approach to products and markets. The evidence presented below shows that younger firms which survived the 1980s had typically been able to rectify these deficiencies, since by 1990 firms founded in the 1970s were largely indistinguishable from older firms in these respects.

One of the challenges facing young businesses is the need to broaden their customer base in order to reduce dependence on a small number of major customers. Firms founded in the 1970s which survived the 1980s had been successful in achieving this so that by 1990 they appeared similar to older companies in this respect (see Table 3.7). While a broadening of the customer base over the decade was a characteristic of growing firms of all ages, this was particularly the case for *young* growth companies: 80 per cent of those which increased real turnover between 1979 and 1990 had been able to increase the number of customers.

Table 3.7 Proportion of sales to the three largest customers, 1990 (combined panel)

Per cent of turnover	Founded pre-1970		Founded 1970–9		All firms	
	No.	*%*	*No.*	*%*	*No.*	*%*
1–20	59	33	45	39	104	35
21–40	48	27	24	21	72	24
41–60	32	18	21	18	53	18
61–80	24	13	14	12	38	13
81–100	17	9	12	10	29	10
All firms	180	100	116	100	296[*]	100

Notes: (a) *there are 10 firms excluded from this table because of inadequate data
(b) a chi-square value of 1.91 (df = 4) indicates no significant difference at the 0.05 level

Table 3.8 Geographic market orientation[a] and age of firm (combined panel)

Market orientation 1990[b]	Founded pre-1970		Founded 1970–9		All firms	
	No.	%	No.	%	No.	%
National/ International	87	47	52	44	139	46
Regional	98	53	67	56	165	54
All firms	185	100	119	100	304[c]	100

Notes: (a) geographic market orientation is based on at least 50% of sales turnover
(b) international market orientation = more than 50% of total sales revenue from exports; national market orientation = more than 50% of sales outside the local/regional market; local/regional market orientation = more than 50% of sales in local or regional markets
(c) there are two firms excluded from this table because of inadequate data

Another weakness identified in firms which did not survive the 1980s was their tendency to rely on achieving competitiveness through price rather than non-price factors. Firms founded in the 1970s which survived the 1980s were particularly active in using non-price competitive tactics so that by 1990 they were less likely to rely solely on price than their older counterparts: 28 per cent of younger firms; 37 per cent of older firms. While price competitiveness is a necessary part of the tactics of most firms, it is not a sufficient condition for either survival or growth. SME managers must be encouraged to pay close attention to non-price factors such as product distinctiveness, sales and marketing, the quality of service to customers, whether or not they see growth as an important objective for the firm.

One of the factors which influences the contribution of SMEs to regional economic development is their ability to develop sales outside their local and regional economies, since this is a mechanism for generating additional aggregate income and minimising displacement effects within the region. Our evidence is that younger firms which survived the 1980s had been able to broaden their geographic market base successfully, so that by 1990 they were largely indistinguishable from older firms in this respect also (see Table 3.8).

Similarly, if we focus specifically on firms involvement in export activity, we also find that by 1990 young firms were largely indistinguishable from their older counterparts (Table 3.9). By 1990,

Table 3.9 Export activity by age of firm (combined panel)

% of sales turnover exported	Founded pre-1970		Founded 1970–9		All firms	
	1979	1990	1979	1990	1979	1990
None	62	59	75	57	67	58
1–24	24	26	11	23	19	25
25–49	7	8	4	6	6	7
More than 50	6	7	11	14	8	10
All firms	100	100	100	100	100	100

Note: a chi-square value for 1990 data of 4.56 (df = 3) indicates no significant difference at the 0.05 level

therefore, firms founded in the 1970s were able successfully to develop similar geographic market coverage to the more established firms although the extent to which they needed to do this varied between the sectors.

The overall conclusion is that by 1990, firms founded in the 1970s which survived had very similar profiles to their more mature counterparts in terms of a number of product and market characteristics. Indeed, their survival may be said to have been influenced by their ability to successfully address the key aspects of product and market development which our previous survivor/non-survivor analysis highlighted.

WHAT PROBLEMS DID YOUNG FIRMS FACE IN MAKING THE TRANSITION INTO ESTABLISHED SMEs?

Although by 1990, firms founded in the 1970s appear largely indistinguishable from older firms in many respects, this does not mean the transition was easy nor that it is complete. To investigate this, managers were also asked about the factors that had constrained the development of their firms during the 1980s. In fact, there was little overall difference in the pattern of responses between firms of different ages; in general, the relative importance of different types of constraint on the development of surviving firms over the period varied more between sectors and between locations than with age of firm. Nevertheless, there are some young firms which did appear to face particular difficulties.

In the early part of the chapter, it was demonstrated that once a firm has survived the difficult early years after start-up and become 'established', its ability to generate jobs is closely linked to its ability to achieve business growth, and this applies to firms of all ages. However, for *some* young firms, achieving growth can present particular demands on the company's resource base which need to be met if the firm is to continue to grow and create jobs in the longer term. Policy-makers need to recognise and address these challenges and problems if the contribution of this type of firm to economic development is to be maximised. Our analysis of the problems faced by young firms in evolving into established SMEs during the 1980s, aims to draw attention to those aspects of business development where there appears to be a need for some external assistance to extend the firm's internal resource base, and to those types of young firm where the need appears to be greatest.

(i) *Young firms (especially growing businesses) are more constrained by a shortage of development finance than older firms.*

Among surviving companies overall, there was little evidence that problems in financing development were an important issue for the majority of firms, and in this respect our findings support the results of other recent studies (e.g., DTI 1991: 13). Managers were asked specifically if a shortage of development finance had held back the development of the company in the late 1980s: 68 per cent of firms overall stated that it was not a problem and only 21 per cent described it as a major problem (see Table 3.10). However, firms founded in the 1970s showed a higher propensity to refer to a development finance gap than older firms: 43 per cent compared with 25 per cent of firms founded before 1970 and a higher proportion also saw this as a major constraint on the development of the firm during this late 1980s period.

Clearly, development finance is most likely to be required by businesses that are aiming to grow and it is the younger firms which have the highest commitment to growth. Thus, a more detailed investigation of the firms in which a 'finance gap' is most seriously constraining business development reveals that they are particularly concentrated in our Group 2 performance category. In fact, 39 per cent of the younger firms in this performance group stated that a shortage of development finance had been a *major* constraint on the development of the firm in the late 1980s compared with 22 per cent of other young firms. These Group 2 firms are those which have

Table 3.10 Shortage of development finance and age of firm (combined panel)

Shortage of development finance	Founded 1970–9		Founded pre-1970		All firms	
	No.	%	No.	%	No.	%
No problem	68	57	139	75	207	68
Problem identified	51	43	47	25	98	32
(major problem)	(32	27)	(32	17)	(64	21)
Total	119	100	186	100	305	100

Notes: (a) managers were asked if a shortage of development finance had held back the development of the firm during the period 1987–90.
(b) a chi-square value for problem identified/not identified of 9.43 (df = 1) shows that there is a significant difference at the 0.01 level
(c) a chi-square value for no problem/major/minor problem of 9.65 (df = 2) shows that there is a significant difference at the 0.01 level

demonstrated an ability to achieve fast turnover growth over a 10-year period but have other potential weaknesses (specifically inconsistent profitability and/or a failure to achieve a sufficient size after 10 years to suggest that they would be resilient to external 'shocks'). The majority (84 per cent) of firms in this performance group were founded in the 1970s.

Rapid growth can stretch the limited resource base of many small firms and it is a mistake to think that fast growth firms do not need external assistance. The Group 2 firms in this study are a potentially important target group for policy support, first, because their performance indicates their potential for longer term growth, but second, because their weaknesses threaten their ability to maintain growth, or perhaps even to survive. For example, only one of the 14 young Group 2 firms which reported a major development finance gap was consistently profitable in the late 1980s and half were profitable in only one of the three years 1987–9. It could be argued that the problems these firms faced in raising development finance are as much a result of their inability to manage growth successfully as a supply-side failure in the market for finance. However, either way these firms would seem to be potentially important targets for policy support. Other studies have also pointed to the financial constraints on growing businesses (University of Cambridge 1992: 26–9) and in view of the considerable body of evidence which shows that a major part of the contribution of SMEs to employment growth

Table 3.11 Percentage reporting cash flow problems and age of firm (combined panel)

	Founded pre-1970	Founded 1970-9
Cash flow problems		
% all firms	46	57
% high-growth firms	36	60
% growing firms	39	57
Major cash flow problems		
% all firms	18	29
% high-growth firms	10	33
% growing firms	12	34

comes from a minority of high growth businesses, it is important that the constraints on the development of such firms are addressed.

(ii) *Cash flow problems are another feature of young growing businesses.*

Managers were also asked if the firm experienced problems in managing its cash flow. While there was some tendency for younger firms to be more prone to cash flow problems than older firms, once again it was the young growing business where the problem was most commonly reported (see Table 3.11). Major cash flow problems were reported in a third of firms founded in the 1970s which achieved growth in the 1980s. Among older businesses, on the other hand, major cash flow problems were much less common.

Although our financial data are insufficiently detailed to enable a systematic analysis of the reasons for these cash flow problems, the interviews with managers revealed that common causes of problems in controlling working capital in these businesses included overstocking, extending over-lengthy credit, buying costly assets and over-trading caused by expanding more rapidly than the resource base of the business is able to cope with.

(iii) *Relocation is frequently part of the evolution of relatively young, growing businesses.*

Table 3.12 shows that 38 per cent of all firms in the study relocated in the 1980s. Although there was a predictable tendency for relocation to be more common in the case of growing firms (52 per cent of firms

Table 3.12 Relocation, 1979–90, and age of firm (combined panel)

Date of establishment	Relocated 1970–9		No relocation 1979–90		All firms	
	No.	%	No.	%	No.	%
Pre-1970	50	27	135	73	185	100
1970–9	65	55	54	45	119	100
All firms	115	38	189	62	304	100

which increased real turnover 1979–90 relocated during the same period), the fact that one-fifth of the firms in which real turnover remained stable or declined over the period (Groups 4 and 5) also relocated, shows that relocation is not solely associated with growth. The most common reasons given by managers for relocating were related to site characteristics in general, and to property in particular. 'Space constraints' was by far the most common single reason for relocating overall, and particularly in the case of the younger firms: 72 per cent compared with 42 per cent of older movers.

Table 3.12 also shows that relocation was a particular feature of the development of the younger firms in the panel; in fact, 55 per cent of firms founded in the 1970s relocated in the 1980s. It is the combination of age and growth characteristics which explains why it is Group 2 firms which show the greatest propensity to relocate: 72 per cent compared with 45 per cent of the other growth firms and 21 per cent of stable and declining firms. It is this Group 2 performance category which contains a subset of relatively young firms whose growth over the decade meant that they outgrew their premises and relocation was an integral part of their evolution into more sizeable and successful businesses. Young firms are more likely to outgrow their premises than older firms partly because a given increase in capacity will have a greater proportional effect on the extra space required and partly because their more limited resources makes them less able to invest in their long term space needs.

From a policy perspective, relocation may be associated with a period in the development of the business when external assistance may be particularly useful. For a small manufacturing company, relocation can be a difficult experience, not least because of the disruption to production and the associated difficulty of maintaining continuity of supplies to customers. This in turn can have implications for cash flow, placing considerable demands on the financial and management resource base of the company. From a policy perspective, it is also important to note that the majority of relocating firms moved a relatively short distance; this tendency being particularly pronounced in the remote rural firms. In London, 48 per cent of relocating firms moved to another part of the same borough and a further 26 per cent to elsewhere in London. In the remote rural panel, 90 per cent of relocations were 'local' in that they were to another part of the same village, or to a neighbouring village. Thus, SMEs in these remote rural locations are particularly tied to their local areas. One implication for policy is that if the growth potential of SMEs is to be realised, it is important that an adequate supply of suitable premises is available in *all* types of location. However, this can present a particular challenge to policy-makers in some of the rural areas, since there may be planning implications involved in responding to the need for larger premises for growing firms in some localities.

(iv) *Extending the geographic extent of market coverage can present a particular challenge for younger firms.*

Although it has already been demonstrated that by 1990 there was little difference overall in the geographic market orientation of firms in the different age groups, this is one aspect of market development which can represent a particular challenge for the young growing business. In order to investigate this aspect, we classified the geographic market orientation of each firm in 1979 and 1990 on the basis of where the majority of their sales revenue was generated.

Younger firms showed the highest propensity to make this form of market adjustment over the decade: 19 per cent of firms founded in the 1970s changed their geographic market orientation in the 1980s compared with just 8 per cent of older firms. However, a firm's location was also one of the factors which influenced its propensity to adjust in this way. Whereas in London, the scale and diversity of the market meant that in most sectors there was good scope for firms to grow without changing their regional market orientation, this was less evident in the remote rural areas. For remote rural firms, the need to sell outside the regional market in order to achieve growth, was a challenge which typically faced firms at a much earlier stage in their development than was the case for similar firms based in a large urban area such as London (for a more detailed discussion, see Smallbone, North and Leigh 1993b: 102–5).

This is a particular challenge for those engaged in offering policy support, because for a young firm to successfully extend its markets in this way requires more than the development of a marketing strategy. Geographic market extension can place particular demands on the financial and management resource base of a young company. Additional costs may result directly from the extension of sales and marketing over a wider area, and there may also be indirect costs which arise from the increasing problems of management control. It is important that a firm's marketing needs are set in the context of the development of all aspects of the business if successful marketing is to lead to sustained business growth in the longer term.

SUMMARISING THE IMPLICATIONS FOR POLICY

Our study of the growth and survival of manufacturing SMEs in different locations during the 1980s suggests that established SMEs have an important contribution to make to regional economic development. They have been shown to be an important source of new jobs, especially in rural and outer metropolitan locations. Younger SMEs in the study (i.e., those that have been in existence for less than 10 years) have a higher propensity to generate jobs than older SMEs, but this is partly offset by their lower chances of survival. Moreover, although younger established firms make a disproportionate contribution to net employment change, our evidence suggests that a substantial proportion of more mature SMEs also have the potential to generate additional jobs. For these reasons a strategy which targets policy support exclusively on young firms would *not* seem justified. Our evidence shows that employment creation clearly depends upon being able to realise the growth potential of *all* SMEs. It is therefore more important for policy-makers to assist SMEs of all ages to achieve this potential by overcoming possible barriers to it rather than to target firms on the basis of age characteristics. It is the growth potential of the firm and not age *per se* that matters from the point of view of its potential to generate employment.

At the same time, it is clear from the evidence presented that *some* young firms may need assistance if they are to evolve into more established businesses. One challenge for policy-makers is to help firms to develop those attributes and business practices which increase their survivability and their ability to grow. Our evidence suggests that close attention to product and market development is essential both in increasing a young firm's survival chances and in enabling it to evolve into a more established business. In this chapter we have emphasised both the failure of many young firms to overcome weaknesses in their products and markets as a cause of their non-survival and also the increasing convergence between young firms and older firms with respect to market characteristics as firms increase in age. The results of our more detailed analysis of the strategies and types of business behaviour used by surviving firms through the 1980s reinforces the importance of this aspect of business development. To survive over 10 years, all firms in the panel needed to pay some attention to products and markets while the best per-forming companies were those which were the most active in mana-ging their products and markets, i.e., in developing their customer base, taking steps to make their products competitive and in mana-ging their product portfolio (Smallbone, North and Leigh 1993a: 90–1).

However, there is a particular subset of young firms that would seem to justify targeting for policy support; these are those young firms which are growing strongly but which have other weaknesses that threaten their long-term development. The growth performance of this type of firm over 10 years indicates their potential contribution to economic development, but their size and other characteristics suggest they may need help if their development over a long period is to be secured. The particular problems highlighted in the chapter are with respect to development finance (which may be partly a result of an unwillingness of financial institutions to lend/invest in compa-nies with a record of inconsistent profitability); problems in managing cash flow; problems for rural firms which result from the need to extend geographic markets at a relatively early stage in their devel-opment; and premises-related constraints which mean that relocation is a common experience among young growing companies. Young growing firms are likely to need particular kinds of support therefore, but this should be done within the context of policies which are designed to encourage and support growing firms at different stages of development.

NOTES

1 The Economic and Social Research Council's Small Business Research Initiative includes financial contributions from Barclays Bank, Commis-sion for the European Communities (DG XXIII), Department of Employ-ment and the Rural Development Commission. The views expressed in this paper do not necessarily reflect those of the sponsoring organisations.
2 The median turnover in 1979 of firms founded in the 1970s was £60,000 compared with £256,000 for firms founded 1950–69 and £300,000 for those founded pre-1950. For firms which achieved real turnover growth in the period 1979–90 the median turnover in 1979 was £60,000 for young

firms, £300,000 for firms founded 1950–69 and £305,000 for firms founded pre-1950.

BIBLIOGRAPHY

Advisory Council on Science and Technology (1990) *The Enterprise Challenge: Overcoming the Barriers to Growth in Small Firms*, London: HMSO.

Chell, E. and Haworth, J. (1992) 'A typology of business owners and their orientation towards growth', in K. Caley, E. Chell, F. Chittenden and C. Mason (eds) *Small Enterprise Development: Policy and Practice in Action*, London: Paul Chapman.

Coombes, M., Storey, D., Watson, R., and Wynarczyk, P. (1991) 'The influence of location upon profitability and employment change in small companies', *Urban Studies*, 28, 5: 723–34.

Department of Trade and Industry (1991) *Constraints on the Growth of Small Firms*, London: HMSO.

Department of Trade and Industry (1993) *Business Links: a Prospectus for One Stop Shops for Business*, London: HMSO.

Dunne, P. and Hughes, A. (1990) 'Age, size, growth and survival: UK companies in the 1980s', Working Paper No. 4, Small Business Research Centre, University of Cambridge.

Hughes, A. (1991) 'UK small businesses in the 1980s: continuity and change', *Regional Studies*, 25, 5: 471–9.

Keeble, D., Tyler, P., Broom, G. and Lewis, J. (1992) *Business Success in the Countryside: the Performance of Rural Enterprise*, London: HMSO.

Leigh, R., North, D., Gough, J., and Escott, K. (1983) 'Monitoring manufacturing employment change in London 1976–81', London: Middlesex Polytechnic.

North, D., Leigh, R. and Smallbone D. (1991) 'A comparison of surviving and non-surviving small and medium sized manufacturing firms in London during the 1980s', Working Paper No. 1, Middlesex University, ESRC Small Business Research Initiative.

North, D., Leigh, R. and Smallbone, D. (1992) 'A comparison of surviving and non-surviving small and medium sized manufacturing firms in London during the 1980s', in K. Caley, E. Chell, F. Chittenden, and C. Mason (eds) *Small Enterprise Development: Policy and Practice in Action*, London: Paul Chapman.

North, D. and Smallbone, D. (1995) 'Employment generation and small business growth in different geographical environments', in F. Chittenden, M. Robertson and I. Marshall (eds) *Small Firms: Partnerships for Growth*, London: Paul Chapman.

North, D., Smallbone, D. and Leigh, R. (1993) 'Employment and labour process changes in small & medium sized manufacturing enterprises during the 1980s', in J. Atkinson and D. Storey (eds) *Employment, the Small Firm and the Labour Market*, London: Routledge.

Smallbone, D., North, D. and Leigh, R. (1993a) 'Strategies of high growth SMEs in the 1980s', in M. Virtanen (ed.) *Proceedings of the Conference on the Development and the Strategies of SMEs in the 1990s: Volume 2,*

Mikkeli, Finland: Small Business Centre, Helsinki School of Economics and Business Administration.

Smallbone, D., North, D. and Leigh, R. (1993b) 'The growth and survival of mature manufacturing SMEs in the 1980s: an urban-rural comparison', in D. Storey and J. Curran (eds) *Small Firms in Urban and Rural Locations*, London: Routledge.

Stanworth, J. and Gray, C. (eds) (1991) *Bolton 20 Years On: The Small Firm in the 1990s*, London: Paul Chapman.

Storey, D. (1993) 'Should we abandon support for start-up businesses?', in F. Chittenden, M. Robertson and D. Watkins (eds) *Small Firms Recession and Recovery*, London: Paul Chapman.

Storey, D. (1994) *Understanding the Small Business Sector*, London: Routledge.

Storey, D. and Johnson, S. (1987) *Job Generation and Labour Market Change*, London: Macmillan.

University of Cambridge (1992) 'The state of British enterprise: growth, innovation and competitive advantage in small and medium sized firms', Cambridge: Small Business Research Centre, University of Cambridge.

4 Empirical research on the role of new firms in Scotland

Colin Gallagher, John Kidd and Paul Miller

INTRODUCTION

There has been considerable discussion in recent years about whether it is fruitful or appropriate in the UK to encourage higher new firm birth rates. Storey (1994a), for example, after an international review of start-up performance concluded that it was not an area which deserved serious effort in the UK.

This chapter largely focuses on the start-up performance of those firms which make up our corporate base. These are small businesses which in general will trade outside of their locality and often will have more than just one employee. It is these businesses which are the true wealth-creators of the economy.

The findings of three empirical studies are presented which have examined differing aspects of the extent and impact of new firm formation in Scotland. The first is a study of the regional variation in SME firm stocks and birth rates with particular reference to Scotland. This data on regional variation complements the theoretical discussion by Storey of this topic (Storey 1994b: 67). The second compares the performance of firms born in the period 1980–2 in Scotland and the South East over the period 1980–7. Finally, the third examines the contribution of new firms to economic development in Scotland over the period 1987–91. This is the most recent study and is described in greatest detail here. All of the studies have been based upon the analysis of the large Dun and Bradstreet private sector business data-base. Significant data validation was carried out prior to all of the studies which, in general, followed the procedures described in Brace, Robson and Gallagher (1992).

VARIATIONS IN THE STOCK OF SME FIRMS ACROSS REGIONS

This study examined regional SME firm and job creation and loss over the period 1987–9, where SMEs were defined as firms with between 1 and 499 employees. The work has been described in detail in Gallagher and Robson (1992), and in Gallagher, Robson and Kerr (1994). An examination of change in the 1987 total stock of firms found significant differences in firm densities (number of firms per million of population) across regions (see Figure 4.1 and Table 4.1). The regions of the North and Scotland had the lowest firm densities, which were less than 40 per cent of that of the South East (with the highest density). In spite of this variation they very closely mirrored both the South East and the national average in terms of the proportions of their firms which had expanded, contracted died and remained stable. Thus, at first glance, the region in which a firm is based does not seem to affect the relative extent of such change. This was a surprising finding, given the traditional view that the sectoral structure of a region has a strong influence upon its economic performance. It may be that the proportion of firms with growth aspirations is regionally independent.

Each region was examined in terms of its make-up of small and large SMEs. If small SMEs are defined as those with less than 20 employees, then in the UK overall, more than 50 per cent were small. There was, again, significant variation at the regional level, and three

Table 4.1 The regional distribution of SME firms in 1987 (per million of population)

Region	Population (millions)	Firm cohort size	
		1–4	1–499
South East	17.5	11,300	22,200
West Midlands	5.2	7,800	16,200
North West	6.4	7,900	16,000
East Anglia	2.1	7,400	15,600
East Midlands	4.0	7,100	15,100
Yorks & Humberside	5.0	6,400	13,900
South West	4.7	6,700	13,500
Wales	2.9	5,300	11,000
Scotland	5.1	3,900	8,600
North	3.1	3,800	8,500
UK	55.8	7,900	16,100

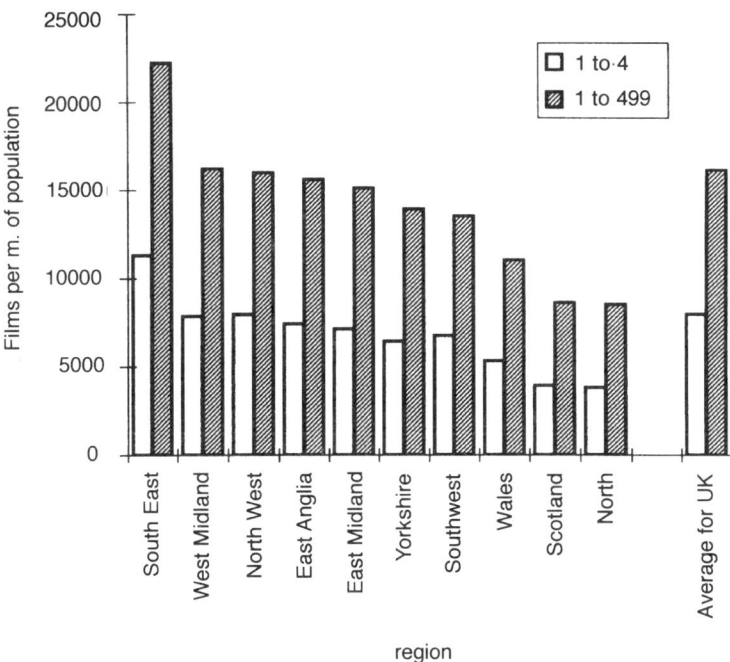

Figure 4.1. The regional distribution of SMEs in 1987

broad regional groups emerged (see Table 4.1). Wales, the East Midlands and the South East had 55 per cent of their SME employment in the small category. Yorkshire, East Anglia and the West Midlands had an average distribution of SME employment. The North and Scotland were below average with only 45 per cent of their firms with less than 20 employees. In that it is the smallest firms which make the largest contribution to job creation, these variations in employment distribution must affect the relative job creation potential of the regions.

Birth rates expressed as a percentage of initial firm stock varied to a greater extent by region than any of the other change measures (Table 4.2). Scotland in these terms had a high birth rate, but because of its exceptionally low density of firms per million of population, the absolute number of births was very low, a continuing important economic development problem. Indeed, when percentage births were arranged in descending order, the highest firm birth rate had occurred in those regions with the lowest firm densities. This variation may be due to:

Table 4.2 Regional firm births, 1987–9, as a percentage of 1987 firm stock

Region	Births*
Scotland	27
South West	24
North	22
Wales	22
South East	20
East Anglia	19
North West	19
East Midlands	18
Yorks & Humberside	18
West Midlands	17
UK	20

Note: * 1–499 cohort size

- variations in the sectoral make-up of regions;
- differing regional attitudes to new firm formation;
- the result of 'natural concentration' which leaves room for new firm births;
- the differing regional effects of government new firm formation policy.

Firm deaths, relative to the initial stock, in a given size cohort did not vary significantly across the regions. The implication is that it may be national, rather than regional, factors which principally influence SME firm death rates.

NEW FIRMS IN SCOTLAND AND THE SOUTH EAST 1980–7

This study compared the performance of 2,600 new firms that had started up between 1980 and 1982 in Scotland with 20,000 that had started in the South East over the same period. The work is described in detail in Gallagher and Miller (1993). In each region, two cohorts were identified on the basis of their high or poor subsequent performance up to 1987, and these were called, for the sake of brevity, 'flyers' and 'sinkers'. The flyers were those which, by 1987, had a turnover of at least £3.5million, or employed at least 50 people; in Scotland there were 215, or 42 per million of population and in the South East there were 1,687, or 97 per million of population. The sinkers were those which, by 1987, had a turnover of £0.25 million or less, and employed 10 or less. In Scotland there were 525 of these, or

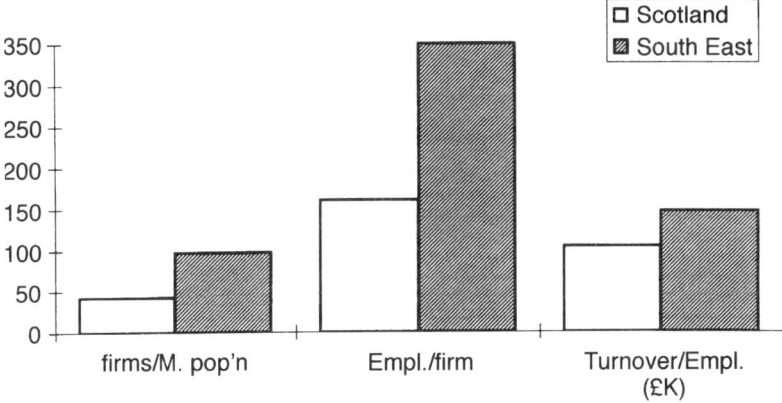

Figure 4.2 New firms, 1980–7: the 'flyers' in Scotland and the South East

103 per million of population, and in the South East there were 4,337, or 251 per million of population (see Figure 4.2 and Table 4.3).

The Scottish flyer firms had performed relatively very poorly; the South East's flyers had 40 per cent more employees. Both success and survival had been easier to achieve in the South East. Scotland had produced fewer new firms and had also produced fewer high-flying firms per head of population than had the South East. Her business service companies, such as consultants and computer services, in particular had found it difficult to achieve success. Possible reasons were that too many businesses may have been chasing too small a market, that Scottish industry did not source its services from within

Table 4.3 New firm performance in Scotland and the South East

| | The 'flyer' firms | | The 'sinker' firms | |
	Scotland	South East	Scotland	South East
Firms per million of popn.	42	97	77	251
Employees per firm	160	348	4	4
Turnover per empl. (£1,000)	103	146	27	31
Turnover per firm (£m)	16.4	50.6	0.1	0.1
Numbers of firms	215	1,687	525	4,337

the region and that the decision to use external business services is taken by headquarters located outwith Scotland.

The performance of high-tech manufacturing businesses was compared: 707 such firms in the South East and the exceptionally low number of 50 in Scotland. The most striking feature was the low proportion of high-performing flyer firms in both regions. It is apparent that new high-tech manufacturing firms grow slowly in their early years.

NEW FIRMS IN SCOTLAND 1987–91

Just how important are new firms in the Scottish economy? This study looked at all facets of the components of change from 1987 to 1991 inclusive. We concentrated here on the results of firm births. Any analysis of the components of employment and corporate change are heavily influenced by how a new firm is defined by time period, and whether the analysis looks forward, or backward. Looking forward from a point in time, the longer the time period used the more the employment generated by a set of births from say, one year, will be concentrated in fewer firms, as the numbers of firms declines by a process of economic attrition. By looking backward from the present, we can put the contribution of births over a set number of years into the context of employment and the corporate base as a whole. Births also need to be set into their context in terms of the enormous churning of firms and employment which is constantly taking place in the economy. This approach was adopted by Gallagher in studies which have looked at the whole of the UK over a series of time periods from 1971 (Daly et al. 1991, and Anon 1993a), and was the approach used in the study described here.

Table 4.4 shows the contribution of new firms in the overall context of employment and the firm population for those firms in Scotland which were born between 1987 and 1991 and which were still in existence at the end of 1991. There were 24,000 jobs involved in management buy-outs (MBOs), identified separately, between 1987 and 1991. Births created more jobs than expanding firms, but if the analysis is restricted to companies only, the reverse is true. Turbulence in terms of births and deaths was found to be inversely related to size, thus, sole proprietors and partnerships, which tend to be relatively small, were very turbulent. It cannot be concluded from this data that births are more (or less) important than expanding firms, because of the time period used. The data were further split into independent Scottish companies, Scottish-controlled subsidiaries,

Table 4.4 New firms in Scotland, 1987–91, by type of entity

Type of company	Firms No.	Employees No.
Independent Scottish companies	11,710	67,400
Scottish-controlled subsidiaries	1,000	8,000
Other UK-controlled subsidiaries	550	5,100
Foreign-controlled companies	80	8,100
Sole proprietors	24,200	40,300
Partnerships	12,700	33,700
Management buy outs (MBOs)	210	24,200
Total	50,440	186,700

other UK-controlled subsidiaries and foreign-controlled companies, and also by different size bands and sectors.

Figure 4.3 shows the size distribution of the employment in company births in the four types of company by size. The overwhelming importance of independent Scottish company births was apparent, with over 67,000 employed at the end of 1991 compared, for example, to just over 8,000 in new foreign-controlled companies. Small independent Scottish companies dominated the numbers of births, such that 85 per cent had less than 10 employees at the end of 1991. Foreign company births (the majority in manufacturing) were quite clearly different in that 76 per cent of their employment is in companies of at least 100 employees, compared to only 2 per cent amongst the independent Scottish company births. Figure 4.4 shows the sectoral distribution of the employment in the different types of company births and Figure 4.5 shows the sectoral distribution of the number of company births. The sector with the largest numbers of new companies and jobs in births amongst the independent Scottish companies is other services, with manufacturing second.

Table 4.5 shows the percentages that births between 1987 and 1991 made up of employment in the four types of company in 1991. It is amongst the independent Scottish companies that births contributed the largest proportion of total employment in 1991. Table 4.6 shows the percentage share of employment in births of the total employment split by sector and size band, for all companies. Overall, 10 per cent of employment in companies in Scotland in 1991 was in companies which had been formed between 1987 and 1991 inclusive, but this varied across the different sectors. Births made up the largest proportion of employment in the other services sector.

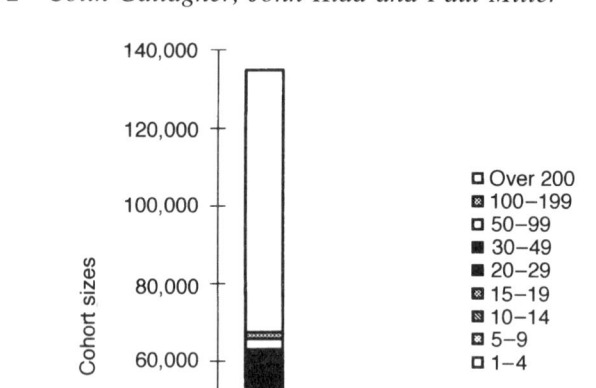

Figure 4.3 The firm size distribution of employment in Scottish births, 1980–7

Table 4.5 Employment in company births in Scotland, 1987–91

		Employment	
Type of company	*Births*	*Total*	*%*
Independent Scottish companies	67,400	426,600	15.8
Scottish-controlled subsidiaries	8,000	159,100	5.0
Other UK-controlled subsidiaries	5,100	133,500	3.8
Foreign-controlled companies	8,100	121,800	6.7
Total	88,600	841,000	10.5

Table 4.6 Percentage employment in births, 1987–91, by sector

Size band	Manu.	Constr.	Transp. & Comm.	W'sale	Retail	F I P*	Other servs	Ag., f&f	Mining	Total
1–4	84.4	71.0	72.5	72.1	53.4	73.1	80.0	14.3	33.3	69.8
5–9	62.3	46.6	55.9	37.9	26.7	41.6	48.8	8.7	40.4	40.9
10–19	40.1	32.0	29.7	20.9	20.2	35.8	32.6	8.1	25.5	28.6
20–49	17.2	11.9	18.7	11.2	13.8	15.8	22.9	4.1	19.6	15.1
50–99	5.6	3.8	10.7	2.0	4.1	19.0	7.6	13.3	17.7	5.5
100–199	5.1	0.0	0.0	0.0	3.3	0.0	12.8	0.0	0.0	3.7
200–499	2.7	0.0	5.1	0.0	2.7	0.0	0.0	0.0	0.0	1.8
over 500	2.1	0.0	0.0	0.0	0.0	0.0	2.3	0.0	0.0	1.1
Total	7.7	10.9	8.8	12.2	10.3	11.5	20.2	4.4	5.7	10.5

Note: * Finance, insurance and property

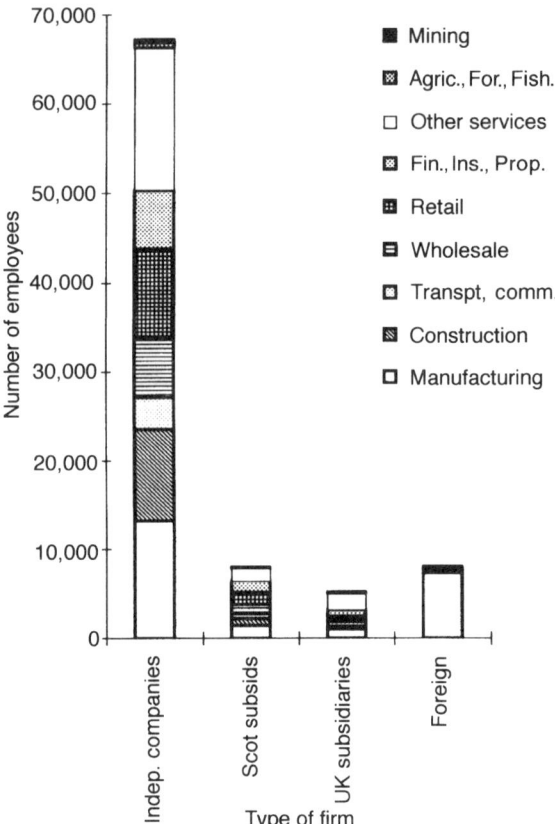

Figure 4.4 The sectoral distribution of employment in Scottish births, 1980–7

Twenty per cent of employment was in companies which had been formed in and after 1987. As we would expect, the manufacturing sector had only 7.7 per cent of its employment in companies formed since 1987, with a size distribution which was more weighted towards large firms.

Most births are of course located in the three smallest size bands and within these births make their greatest contributions in manufacturing and in other services. Apart from agriculture, forestry and fishing and mining, retail is the sector where births make their smallest impact in the smallest size bands (even though as a proportion of all employment, births in the retail sector as a whole make a greater impact upon employment than those in manufacturing and construction).

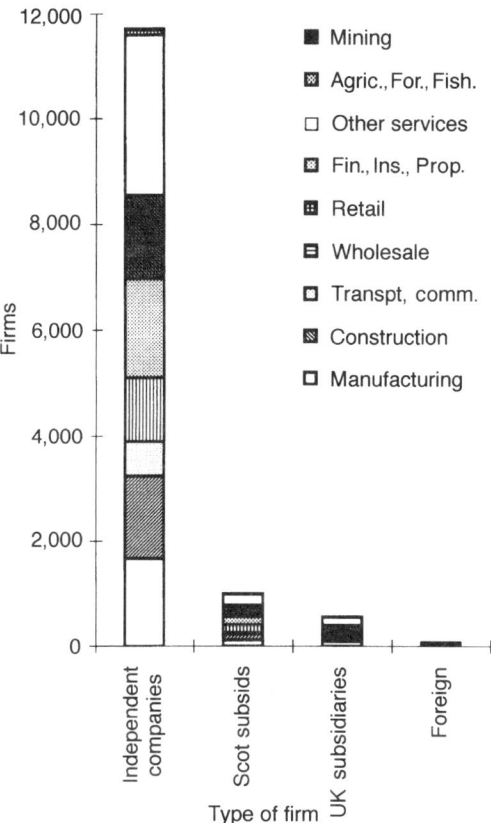

Figure 4.5 The sectoral distribution of firms in Scottish births, 1980–7

Table 4.7 shows the percentage share of the number of births between 1987 and 1991 of the number of companies in 1991 in each sector and size band. Finance, insurance and property and other services stand out from the other sectors with 60 per cent of all companies existing in 1991 having been born between 1987 and 1991 inclusive.

Table 4.7 Percentage firm births, 1987–91, by sector

Size band	Manu.	Constr.	Transp. & Comm.	W'sale	Retail	F I P*	Other servs	Ag., f&f	Mining	Total
1–4	84.7	71.5	71.5	72.2	56.5	73.5	80.8	13.8	34.3	70.6
5–9	63.6	47.9	56.5	38.1	27.7	41.7	49.3	10.3	44.5	41.9
10–19	41.8	32.8	29.9	20.4	19.9	36.2	32.8	7.7	28.2	28.9
20–49	18.7	13.4	20.0	12.2	14.9	15.2	22.4	3.8	16.7	16.0
50–99	5.9	3.8	11.7	2.0	4.3	17.8	7.7	16.2	11.9	5.7
100–199	5.1	0.0	0.0	0.0	3.8	0.0	13.6	0.0	0.0	3.8
200–499	2.0	0.0	7.3	0.0	3.2	0.0	0.0	0.0	0.0	1.7
over 500	3.2	0.0	0.0	0.0	0.0	0.0	4.3	0.0	0.0	2.1
Total	41.9	42.2	49.8	40.4	36.5	59.3	59.1	10.0	25.4	45.2

Note: * Finance, insurance and property

THE SURPLUS OF BIRTHS OVER DEATHS 1987–91

A key feature of the corporate scene in Scotland between 1987 and 1991 was the surplus of births over deaths. This is not quite as positive as it may initially sound; on average, firm deaths involved more jobs than births and thus a gain in employment was not so apparent. VAT registrations exceeded de-registrations in Scotland in each year between 1987 and 1991 and by 11,400 in total. This represents an increase in the stock of VAT registered businesses of 12.7 per cent over the five years. Although this may sound impressive, the percentage increase for the UK as a whole was 16.8 per cent and for the South East of England 22.4 per cent. There were around 5,000 more company births than deaths in Scotland between 1987 and 1991, concentrated amongst independent Scottish companies and in the smallest 1–4 size band. The situation was different by 1993, with a 10 per cent drop across the whole of the UK.

The other services sector covers such high value added activities as management consultancy, computer programming and research and development, and also the less economically important activities of hairdressers, laundry services and car repair shops, and the importance of births in this sector is apparent. Amongst independent companies, births accounted for 23 per cent of the employment while its share of total employment in 1987 was only 12 per cent. However, this high level of birth activity was matched by high company deaths, where 44 per cent of all of the other services companies in existence in Scotland at the start of 1987 had ceased to exist by the end of 1991, compared to 35 per cent overall. We cannot say how far this high level of births is a natural economic trend and how far it has been assisted by additional factors, such as the Enterprise Allowance Scheme (Meager 1992).

FOREIGN-CONTROLLED BIRTHS IN MANUFACTURING

There were a number of large inward investments in manufacturing (e.g., Compaq Computer Manufacturing, Avex Electronics, OKI and JVC). These start-ups obviously involve very different issues compared to the small independent start-ups. Foreign-controlled companies created 32 per cent of the jobs in company births in manufacturing compared to 9 per cent overall in Scotland. Hood (1991) has suggested that Scotland is now facing much greater competition from other locations in Europe such as Spain and Cen-

Table 4.8 Firm stock, birth rates and death rates in Scotland

Type	Firms	Net increase 1987–91		
	1987	*No.*	*%*	*% annual*
Companies	25,500	4,600	19.0	3.5
Sole props and partnerships	80,000	6,400	8.0	1.6
Total	105,000	11,000	11.0	2.0

tral and Eastern Europe for new inward investment. Foreign companies made a positive impact upon manufacturing employment in Scotland between 1987 and 1991, but whether they can continue to do so will depend largely on the future strategies of multinationals with sites both in Scotland and elsewhere in Europe.

Is the relationship between firm stock, birth rate, and death rate important? Any increase in the total stock of firms will result only if the birth rate is greater than the death rate in the longer run. Increasing the stock of businesses is not simply about achieving more start-ups; it is also about improving the survival chances of both the existing stock and the new births. The net increase in the stock of firms is the small difference between the two large change rates of birth and death. In 1987 there were 105,000 firms in Scotland (see Table 4.8), and the net increase over the five-year period was an additional 2 per cent per annum. In contrast, firm density in Scotland (firms per million of population) has traditionally been only about half of that in the South East, and it is essential to try to narrow this gap. The Scottish Enterprise target of a 50 per cent increase in the birth rate (Anon 1993b) by the year 2000 implies a gross increase of the order of 3 per cent per year, which looks achievable.

CONCLUSIONS

Does Scotland need a higher new firm birth rate? New firms born between 1987 and 1991 made a large contribution to employment in Scotland at the end of 1991. The Scottish birth rate was high in terms of the existing stock of businesses, but low in terms of new firms per head of population. Scotland's rate of increase in the stock of businesses in terms of new firms per head of population (12.7 per cent) was well below the national average (16.8 per cent), and far below that of the South East (22.4 per cent). Thus, while the UK as a whole may not need to stimulate births, Scotland does. A very low density of the smallest SMEs with less than 20 employees was found in Scotland. It is these firms which make the largest contribution to job creation, and this must hamper the regions relative job creation potential severely.

Traditionally, changes in the death rate have unfortunately been observed to tend to follow birth rates. Thus, in addition to trying to increase the birth rate, ways need to be explored to restrain this increase in the death rate. The new firms' issue is one of quality as well as quantity, and more careful promotion of start-ups may improve their chances of survival.

A case can also be made for biasing help for start-ups in favour of the 'wealth-creating' sectors of the economy, such as manufacturing and the more highly skilled areas of the other services sector (e.g., computer software).

Scottish business service companies such as consultants and computer services have had a poorer success rate than their South East equivalents. Scottish industry could help this sector by sourcing even more of its services from within the region.

BIBLIOGRAPHY

Anon (1993a) 'Job creation: The contribution of small and large firms', *Labour Market Quarterly Report*, August: 10–12.

Anon (1993b) 'Scots plan to raise business births', *Employment Gazette*, December: 536.

Brace, E., Robson, G. and Gallagher C. C. (1992) 'The growth of UK Companies 1989–91 and their contribution to job generation', report for the Small Firms Statistics Division of the DTI, Sheffield, Newcastle upon Tyne: Trends Business Research Ltd.

Daly, M., Campbell, M., Robson, G. and Gallagher, C. C. (1991) 'Job creation 1987–89: The contributions of small and large firms', *Employment Gazette*, November: 589–96.

Gallagher, C. C. and Miller, P. (1993) 'The performance of new firms in Scotland and the South East, 1980–87', *The Royal Bank of Scotland Review*, 170: 96–101.

Gallagher, C. C. and Robson, G. (1992) 'Regional variation in the birth and death rates of UK firms', discussion paper, Management Division, University of Newcastle upon Tyne.

Gallagher, C. C., Robson, G. and Kerr, J. (1994) 'Regional variations in the population of small and medium sized enterprises in Britain', in F. Chittenden et al. (eds) *Small Firms Recession and Recovery*, London: Paul Chapman.

Meager, N. (1992) 'Self-employment in the European Community, the emergence of a new institution and its evaluation', The UKEMRA 15th National Small Firms Policy and Research Conference, Southampton, November.

Storey, D. (1994a) 'Should we abandon support to start-up businesses?' in F. Chittenden et al. (eds) *Small Firms, Recession and Recovery*, London: Paul Chapman.

Storey, D. (1994b) *Understanding the Small Business Sector*, London: Routledge.

5 Banks and small businesses
An Anglo-Scottish comparison

Christine T. Ennew and Martin R. Binks

INTRODUCTION

The potential contribution of the small business sector to the economy has been well documented. Thus, for example, small businesses can contribute to economic growth and development through the generation of jobs (Storey and Johnson 1987), by promoting competition (Bolton 1971) and by facilitating economic restructuring (Binks and Coyne 1989). For these positive contributions to be realised, it is important that firms are not constrained by imperfections in either output markets (Mayes and Moir 1989) or input markets (Binks and Vale 1990). One potential imperfection concerns access to capital markets and the potential for finance gaps to constrain growing businesses. The existence of finance gaps is not attributed directly to size; rather, it reflects problems of asymmetric information. Such information problems are not unique to the small firms sector but are considerably more prevalent because of the anticipated higher costs of information collection. While information asymmetries cannot be eliminated, they can be reduced and the nature of the relationship between bank and business is significant in this context. A close working relationship between the two parties can enhance the flow of information and ensure that more efficient decisions are made by both parties with respect to financing.

The quality of the relationship between banks and small businesses will be influenced by a range of characteristics, one of which will be the structures and policies of the bank itself. Anecdotal evidence suggests that there are differences in the ways in which different banks approach the banking relationship and in particular that the larger and highly centralised English banks are in some ways different to the smaller Scottish banks. This chapter seeks to contribute to this discussion by presenting specific empirical evidence relating to the extent to which there are systematic differences in the financing conditions and the banking relationship between English and Scottish banks. The second part of this chapter examines briefly the provision of finance to small businesses while the nature and significance of the banking relationship is outlined in the third part. Empirical evidence on the nature and extent of regional differences is presented next, leading to a summary and conclusions.

THE PROVISION OF FINANCE TO SMALL BUSINESSES

The efficient provision of finance to small firms has long been recognised as a key factor in ensuring that these firms can grow and compete. It is generally accepted that small size may preclude firms from access to certain sectors of the capital markets, particularly where equity finance is concerned. The development of the venture capital market and the experience of the Business Expansion Scheme (BES) improved the supply of equity finance, but recent evidence suggests that the equity gap is still present (Harrison and Mason 1990). With the cessation of the BES, the introduction of a more dilute substitute and the continuing lack of enthusiasm for start-ups on the part of institutional investors, it is unlikely that the supply of equity to small businesses will increase significantly. Access to external equity from venture and development capital firms is typically restricted to projects requiring in excess of £250,000 while informal sources from 'Business Angels' are still embryonic in the UK (Mason, Harrison and Chaloner 1992). Even in cases where projects are large enough to justify venture capital, there is evidence to suggest that a large number of small businesses are resistant to external equity participation (Binks, Ennew and Reed 1992). Consequently, small businesses in the UK rely primarily on debt finance from the banking sector (Keasey and Watson 1992) and it is probably in relation to debt that the issue of finance gaps may be most pertinent.

If businesses experience difficulties in obtaining debt finance for commercially justifiable projects then they may forego potentially viable growth. Such difficulties do not refer simply to the fact that some firms cannot obtain funds through the banking system. Indeed, it would be expected that many applications for funds would be rejected as part of a rational commercial process. Genuine difficulties occur, first, in situations in which a project which is viable and profitable at prevailing interest rates is not undertaken because the firm is unable to obtain appropriate funding, and second, in situations in which viable projects can only obtain funding on apparently disadvantageous terms. Restricted access to finance is not necessarily attributable directly to size, but rather to the costs and difficulties associated with the collection of information for project evaluation and monitoring. These costs and difficulties are considerably higher for smaller projects and smaller firms and, as a consequence, the potential for finance gaps is higher among this group of businesses.

ASYMMETRIC INFORMATION AND THE BANKING RELATIONSHIP

Information asymmetry poses two problems for the provision of debt finance. First, the bank cannot observe *ex ante* certain information which is relevant to the decision to enter into the contract, typically the actual abilities of the individuals applying for finance and the qualities of the project (adverse selection). Second, the risk that the small business will not perform in a manner consistent with the contract necessitates some form of *ex post facto* monitoring procedure (moral hazard). In principle, the information required at a given point could be collected; in practice, it is unlikely that it will be, because the costs of doing so are likely to be prohibitively high relative to the risk and return associated with any given project. Even if a comprehensive information set were available, the bank is likely to encounter difficulties in processing that information, thus limiting its practical usefulness. However, during the lifetime of a firm's relationship with its bank, there exists considerable potential gradually to accumulate and use such information (Sharpe 1989) and this might be expected to ease the problems arising from asymmetric information.

The implications of these information asymmetries for the provision of debt finance have been evaluated from a theoretical standpoint in a number of studies. Thus, for example, in examining capital market failure, Stiglitz and Weiss (1981) identify debt gaps as a result of both adverse selection and moral hazard problems. The adverse selection effect is analogous to that observed in insurance markets and arises because borrowers have different degrees of risk attached to their projects. As interest rates rise, low-risk borrowers (although having viable projects) drop out leaving only high-risk borrowers. This is reinforced by the moral hazard problem associated with the lender's inability to monitor the project undertaken; again it is shown that as interest rates rise the higher-risk projects will be substituted for the lower-risk projects, and there will be equilibrium credit rationing (see also Bester and Hellwig 1989). A contrary view is expressed by de Meza and Webb (1987), who identify adverse selection in the presence of different (but unobservable) entrepreneurial abilities as leading to an oversupply of credit rather than a debt gap.

While there is a need for further work to reconcile these views, it is possible that they may not be mutually exclusive. Berger and Udell (1989) argue that while the macro effects of credit rationing may be small, there is evidence to suggest that when credit is rationed to some firms it may be more readily available to others. In particular, this result may be related to the role of collateral in bonding debt finance. The availability of sufficient collateral can counteract asymmetric information problems; the low-risk borrowers who leave the market in the Stiglitz–Weiss model can signal their status by a willingness to offer appropriate levels of collateral, and the taking of collateral by the banks can provide an incentive to ensure that the firm will perform to the best of its abilities in undertaking the project (Bester 1987).

However, if collateral is in limited supply, debt gaps may still exist. In effect, the information costs associated with the evaluation and monitoring of a project may prohibit an income-gearing or prospects-based approach to project evaluation, thus causing the lender to default to a capital gearing approach which is contingent upon the availability of sufficient collateral. The tendency to value assets at 'carcass value' may limit the ability of a business to raise funds against business assets. The valuation of business assets on a 'gone concern' basis has particular implications for growing firms. For the purposes of collateral, the acquisition of additional plant and equipment typically adds proportionately more to business costs than to the value of business assets. The faster the rate of growth, the greater the gap between capital accumulation costs and business-asset-based collateral value. A likely corollary is that firms with faster growth rates will need to rely more heavily on the personal collateral of the owner/manager. Where personal collateral is required from limited companies there is a direct erosion of limited liability status and the protection it provides. This would be expected to discourage investment at the margin, given the additional personal risk it implies.

Information problems can produce financial constraints either because debt finance is not provided or because it is only available on disadvantageous terms. Although perfect information is an unobtainable goal, the quantity and quality of information available to a bank will be influenced by the nature of the relationship with each business. A close relationship has the potential to provide the bank with a better understanding of the operating environment facing a particular business; a clearer picture of the managerial attributes of the owner and a more accurate overview of the prospects for the business. Thus, from the perspective of the bank, the relationship provides the basis for understanding customer needs and resources and identifying the most appropriate ways of meeting those needs. This relationship is not simply a one-way process. An effective banking relationship requires a positive contribution from both parties. The ability of the bank to meet customer needs requires that the owner/manager provides the bank with appropriate and timely information and is receptive to suggestions and advice provided by the bank. The inability to develop a close working relationship between banks and small businesses has often been identified as a weakness of traditional Anglo-Saxon banking systems (Yao-Su Hu 1984, Edwards 1987) and a comparative analysis of medium sized enterprises in Germany, France and the UK lends some support to this hypothesis (Binks, Ennew and Reed 1992). Some developments in the provision of banking services to small businesses in the UK have attempted to deal with this weakness, particularly through the introduction of specialist small business account managers but the outcome of such initiatives is still uncertain (Binks and Ennew 1991).

As the previous sections have argued, entrepreneurial activity among smaller businesses may be constrained by restrictions on access to finance. Such restrictions may vary from the denial of access to credit through to the availability of credit in insufficient quantities or on inappropriate terms. The previous section has discussed the nature of these financial constraints and has argued that their cause lies with information problems. While recognising that many of these information problems have no practical solution, it also can be argued that the nature of the relationship between banks and small businesses can either ameliorate or exacerbate such problems. Thus, the nature of the banking relationship can be seen as a crucial element in the provision of finance to business in general (Turnbull and Gibbs 1987) and small firms in particular (Watson 1986). A good banking relationship will improve the quality and quantity of information flows and thus may be expected to reduce the extent to which businesses are or feel constrained by banking practices. This does not mean that a good banking relationship leads *per se* to the provision of more finance than a poor banking relationship, but rather that in a good banking relationship the flow of information is such that both parties will have a better understanding of each other; banks will make more informed decisions and firms will be more aware of the reasoning behind those decisions. Thus, the firm that is refused access to finance and has a good banking relationship may feel less constrained than a counterpart with a poorer banking relationship, since the former should have some 'ownership' of the decision.

EVIDENCE ON THE BANKING RELATIONSHIP: THE CASE OF ENGLAND AND SCOTLAND

There is a variety of evidence concerning differences in banking relationships across countries (Bannock and Doran 1991), and variations in banking practices between countries such as Britain and Germany have attracted considerable attention. There are also arguments to suggest that differences in banking practice and banking relationships may be observed even between geographically close regions such as England[1] and Scotland (Dow 1992). Systematic evidence on the presence or absence of Anglo-Scottish differences can be obtained using the survey conducted by the Forum of Private Business (FPB). The survey was conducted among its members by the FPB in spring/summer 1992 (Binks, Ennew and Reed 1993). Approximately 16,000 questionnaires were distributed to the entire membership, along with a follow-up reminder after three weeks. This resulted in 6,101 usable responses, which represents a response rate of 37.5 per cent. A comparison of the sample with the national population of small businesses reveals some biases. Specifically, the sample has a higher than expected proportion of manufacturing firms and a lower than expected proportion of agricultural firms, and there is some bias within the sample towards firms located in South East England and away from firms located in South West England. Neither of these problems was considered particularly significant. The presence of a relatively small number of agricultural firms may actually be desirable given the unique nature of the problems facing farming businesses. Similarly, in the context of the UK market, the uneven distribution of respondents between the South East and the South West is unlikely to cause problems because there are few grounds for believing that the experiences of these two regions would differ significantly. For the UK as a whole, *Business Monitor* suggests that 5.3 per cent of small firms are located in Scotland; the FPB sample is comparable, with 7.6 per cent of respondents being located in Scotland.

Respondents to the survey range from very small businesses through to those which would be considered as medium rather than small. Of the sample, 29 per cent of firms had a turnover of less than £150,000 per year (30 per cent in the case of England and 25 per cent in the case of Scotland). It is noticeable that 17 per cent of respondents had turnover in excess of the £1million threshold which is sometimes used to define the margin between small and medium sized business. The figures for England and Scotland were 16 per cent and 22 per cent respectively. This suggests that Scottish firms in the sample tended to be rather larger than English firms, and this conclusion is supported by data on the average size of firm measured by number of full-time employees. English firms with an average of 11.2 employees were significantly smaller than Scottish firms with an average of 17.1 employees. Furthermore, Scottish firms in the sample are typically older than English firms, with an average age of 28 years compared with 17 years for English firms.

Average profits as a percentage of turnover were not significantly different, with figures of 16.77 per cent for English firms and 16.2 per cent for Scottish firms. Average profit for the sample as a whole was 16.7 per cent, which was significantly lower than an average of 18.2 per cent reported in an earlier survey of a similar group (Binks, Ennew and Reed 1990). Such a fall was to be expected, given recessionary conditions. The fact that the reduction in profitability is relatively small is likely to be a reflection of the loss from the sector of a large number of low-profit firms. Interestingly, there is evidence to suggest that Scottish firms have been affected less by recessionary conditions than English firms. Some 50 per cent of English firms reported a decline in turnover in the previous year compared with around 36 per cent of Scottish firms, and 52 per cent of English firms indicated that they had experienced financial difficulties compared with only 42 per cent of Scottish firms. Interestingly, however, there is evidence of a greater degree of confidence among English firms, with some 16 per cent expecting growth rates in excess of 10 per cent in the coming year compared with only 11 per cent of Scottish firms.

Respondents to the survey could be grouped in two ways: location of firm (England or Scotland) and location of bank (i.e., whether the firm banked with one of the three Scottish banks or one of the four English clearers). While the main focus of our analysis concerns the differences between English and Scottish banks, the differences in the characteristics of the English and Scottish economies (Dow 1992) suggests that the analysis should give some consideration to location of business. Three aspects of the provision of finance by the banking sector were examined for each group of respondents, namely – financing conditions (interest rates, collateral, size of loan), the extent to which the firm perceived itself as being constrained by bank policies and the overall nature of the banking relationship.

The financing conditions for different firms provide the simplest means of examining Anglo-Scottish differences. However, simple comparisons between the groups may be inappropriate because of the different characteristics of English and Scottish firms; to control for such differences, various aspects of financing conditions and the banking relationship are subject to an analysis of variance using a classic experimental approach to accommodate the effects of different cell size.

Interest rates generally appear to be lower among Scottish banks (3.11 per cent over base compared with 2.75 per cent for overdrafts) and Scottish businesses (3.09 per cent over base compared with 2.75 per cent for overdrafts). However, as the analysis of variance in Table 5.1 shows, both age and size effects are important in explaining these differences. In particular, the lower rates for Scottish banks and Scottish businesses reflect the tendency for these firms to be rather larger and older than their English equivalents. Nevertheless, it is interesting to note that even allowing for these factors there is still a significant effect according to location of bank in the case of overdraft rates.[2] That is to say, controlling for age and size, it appears that customers of Scottish banks generally pay lower rates of interest on overdrafts than customers of English banks.

Interest rates are only one aspect of financing conditions; in so far as debt gaps are concerned, the availability of collateral is of relevance (Binks, Ennew and Reed 1993) both in terms of the type of collateral required and the collateral ratio. Other variables of relevance are the level of overdraft usage (since a high level of usage may give some information on the adequacy of existing financing arrange-

Table 5.1 Analysis of variance for interest rates

| | Main effects (F-ratios) | | | |
	Bank	Location	Turnover	Age
Base rate + on overdraft	21.11**	0.37	123.18**	11.40**
Base rate + on loan	2.70	0.08	66.04**	3.02*

Note: * Significant at p = 0.05
     ** Significant at p = 0.01

ments) and the numbers of firms with overdrafts or loans. An analysis of these data is presented in Table 5.2.

The evidence regarding financing conditions is indicative of significant differences between England and Scotland, particularly in relation to size of overdraft, overdraft usage, type of collateral required and collateral ratios. Generally, as was the case with interest rates, financing conditions appear to be more favourable for customers of Scottish banks and Scottish firms. A more detailed examination of these differences suggests that, as was the case with interest rates, the majority of these differences may be due to the size and age of firms rather than their location or bank.[3]

In short, then, the data relating to basic financing conditions suggests that there are few substantial differences between English and Scottish firms that cannot be explained by differences in the size and age distribution of those firms. However, as indicated earlier, one of the key issues relating to the provision of finance is the nature of the banking relationship. Two specific areas will be considered: the extent to which businesses believe they are constrained and the broad, general relationship between a business and its bank.

Table 5.2 An analysis of financing conditions by location of business and location of bank

| | Location of bank | | Location of business | |
	England	Scotland	England	Scotland
% with overdraft	77.2	76.6	76.2	76.1
% with loan	42.3	34.8	41.7	34.7
Average size of overdraft (£1,000)	62.9	78.6	62.8	87.4
Average size of loan (£1,000)	80.3	86.1	80.0	78.9
% of overdraft used	73.9	66.7	73.8	68.1
% required to give personal collateral on overdraft	25.1	20.8	24.8	17.6
% required to give personal collateral on loan	12.0	7.5	12.0	4.2
Collateral ratio on overdraft	3.51	2.59	3.56	2.06
Collateral ratio on loan	2.17	2.50	2.27	2.71
Number	4,954	736	5,448	449

The analysis focuses initially upon the extent to which the owners of small businesses perceive their business to be constrained by existing bank practice. The results of the analysis are presented in Table 5.3.

An initial inspection of Table 5.3 suggested that both Scottish firms and the customers of Scottish banks feel significantly less constrained than their English equivalents. As Table 5.4 shows, these differences are in part due to the effects of differences in the size and age distribution. However, even accounting for these effects there is still some evidence to suggest that bank and location factors have a significant effect on the perceived degree of constraint. In particular, price-based constraints (interest rates and charges) are in part due to bank influences, while quantity-based constraints (collateral and credit availability) are more strongly related to location factors. The results relating to interest rates are consistent with those reported earlier in respect of rates payable on overdrafts for which the bank effect was significant in explaining differences. Bank effects are also significant in relation to speed of service and term of loan. In each case, it is the customers of Scottish banks and Scottish firms who are apparently less constrained that their English equivalents.

The final stage of the analysis focuses attention more specifically on the importance of a well-developed and soundly managed banking relationship. The FPB data-base contained a variety of questions on the nature of the relationship between businesses and their banks. Three specific aspects of the bank–business relationship were measured: the importance attached to aspects of bank service, the quality of provision and the attributes of bank managers. Each aspect of the

Table 5.3 Perceived constraint by location of bank and location of business (figures represent mean strength of constraint with higher scores indicating stronger constraints)

Type of constraint	Location of bank		Location of business	
	England	Scotland	England	Scotland
Collateral	2.75	2.51*	2.75	2.32*
Interest rate	3.24	2.90*	3.19	2.88*
Credit availability	2.69	2.36*	2.68	2.17*
Charges	3.31	2.82*	3.25	2.86*
Competence of manager	2.27	2.03*	2.24	1.99*
Speed of service	2.14	1.91*	2.13	1.89*
Term of loan	2.64	2.31*	2.62	2.28

Note: * Significant at p = 0.01

Table 5.4 Analysis of variance for perceived constraints

Type of constraint	Bank	Main effects (F-ratios)		
		Location	Turnover	Age
Collateral	1.06	34.80**	2.61	127.91**
Interest rates	21.30**	0.14	40.06**	0.05
Availability of credit	0.67	27.42**	3.27	125.98**
Charges	58.74**	0.52	82.01**	1.14
Competence of manager	5.54	3.89	3.00	0.56
Speed of service	8.67**	0.76	0.52	3.72
Term of loan	12.50**	2.11	5.16*	23.59**

Notes: * Significant at p = 0.05
      ** Significant at p = 0.01

relationship was measured using a set of multi-item scales. All these items were measured on the basis of respondents' own perceptions, and a list of these is presented in the Appendix. To identify the underlying dimension for each aspect of the relationship, each set of scale items was subject to a factor analysis using principal components extraction. This resulted in the identification of three underlying dimensions for each aspect of the relationship.

The importance aspect of the relationship measured the respondents' assessments of the value to them of particular aspects of bank service. Factor analysis suggested that three underlying dimensions were present and these three factors accounted for approximately 70 per cent of the variance in the original data-set. The first (IMPK) measured the importance attached to bank knowledge and advice; the second (IMPPE) measured the importance attached to personalisation in the service delivery process; and the third (IMPPR) measured the importance associated with more specific product characteristics such as interest rates, charges and range of services. For a given quality of provision, respondents who identify certain aspects of bank services as important are more likely to feel constrained by the service provided than respondents who identify these aspects as less important.

The quality aspect of the relationship was measured using an identical set of scale items. Again, the factor analysis identified three underlying dimensions based on knowledge (ACTK), personalisation (ACTPE) and product characteristics (ACTPR). These factors accounted for 74 per cent of the variance in the original data-set. The extent to which respondents perceive their businesses to be constrained is likely to be negatively related to their perceptions of the quality of service provided. For each of these six variables, higher values are indicative of higher performance and higher quality.

Finally, the nature of the relationship between the respondent and their bank manager was measured across a range of statements scored on a five-point Likert scale. Factor analysis suggested three underlying factors which accounted for 60 per cent of the variance in the original data-set. The first was concerned with the absence of trust and confidence in the relationship (BMT), with higher scores being indicative of a lack of trust and confidence. The second factor concerned the degree of approachability and equality in the relationship (BMA), with higher scores indicating that managers were more approachable. The final factor concerned information flows (BMI), with higher scores on this factor indicating a reluctance to provide information on the part of respondents.

Table 5.5 presents summary statistics relating to expectations and quality of service delivery. Figures suggest that generally there are no significant differences across the groups in terms of expectations regarding bank services. There are, however, clear and systematic differences with respect to the quality of provision. Once again, Scottish firms and customers of Scottish banks believe that they receive a better quality of service.[4]

A similar pattern is in evidence in the case of aspects of the relationship with the bank manager. Summary statistics are presented in Table 5.6. Customers of Scottish banks and Scottish firms view their bank managers as more approachable and have more trust/ confidence in the relationship. The importance of the bank effect may reflect different traditions and policies and differences in organisa-

Table 5.5 Importance and quality of provision of aspects of bank service

Mean scores on	Location of bank		Location of business	
	England	Scotland	England	Scotland
Importance of				
Knowledge/advice	14.33	14.28	14.31	14.34
Product characteristics	11.95	12.00	11.98	11.92
Personal relationships	15.90	15.77	15.88	15.86
Provision of				
Knowledge/advice	10.11	11.01[*]	10.15	11.42[*]
Product characteristics	8.56	9.62[*]	8.70	9.36[*]
Personal relationships	12.92	13.33[*]	12.66	13.46[*]
Sample size	4,849	727	5,329	443

Note: * Significantly different at p = 0.01

Table 5.6 Assessment of bank manager by bank and location of business

Mean scores on	Location of bank		Location of business	
	England	Scotland	England	Scotland
Approachability	13.6	14.2*	13.6	14.2*
Lack of trust	14.9	13.7*	14.88	13.7*
Information	3.87	3.74	3.87	3.74
Number	4,807	719	5,286	439

Note: * Significantly different at p = 0.01

tional culture and size. The importance of the location effect may be an indicator of the role of expectations in assessing the quality of provision of bank services. It has been argued (Dow 1992) that the Scottish economy may be characterised by more defensive financial behaviour; one possible manifestation of defensive financial behaviour may be different expectations – if Scottish firms have lower expectations about the quality and range of services delivered by their banks then they are likely to be more satisfied with a given level of service than English firms.

However, given that earlier analysis has highlighted the presence of significant differences as a consequence of variations in the age and size distribution of firms, the impact of these variables must also be evaluated in the context of the banking relationship. The results of an analysis of variance for the relationship variables by location, bank, age and turnover are presented below in Table 5.7.

In relation to respondents' assessment of the importance of various aspects of bank service, there is no evidence of any difference according to bank or location, although it is interesting to note that the age variable is significant, with younger firms attaching more importance to both knowledge of business, industry and market and personalisation in the service delivery process. Location effects are significant for each of the variables measuring quality of provision, with Scottish firms generally offering higher assessments of the quality of service provided by their bank. The bank effect is also significant in relation to product characteristics. Finally, there is also evidence of significant bank effects in relation to assessments of bank managers. In all of these cases, the evaluations of Scottish firms/ customers of Scottish banks are the more favourable.

Table 5.7 Analysis of variance for banking relationship

| | Main effects (mean square) | | | |
	Bank	Location	Turnover	Age
Importance of				
Knowledge	1.98	0.65	35.44	189.52**
Product characteristics	0.11	0.18	1.58	19.99
Personal relationships	6.25	2.87	3.7	78.40*
Provision of				
Knowledge	3.44	239.43**	341.26**	106.8**
Product characteristics	466.29**	47.28**	221.37**	0.02
Personal relationships	5.9	86.58*	100.29**	93.33*
Bank manager				
Approachability	54.47*	1.33	879.67**	13.03
Lack of trust	346.94**	6.01	252.99**	172.72**
Information	6.5	0.32	40.31**	0.01

Notes: ** Significant at p = 0.01
* Significant at p = 0.05

CONCLUSIONS

That differences exist in the perceptions held by small businesses in relation to English and Scottish banks is clear. The cause of such differences is less apparent. Where there are bank-based differences (between Scottish and English banks), these may be explicable in terms of internal policies, systems and cultures, particularly given that the Scottish banks are generally smaller than the four clearing banks which dominate the English market. Indeed, it may also be argued that managers in Scottish banks have more experience in dealing with the needs of small firms under depressed economic conditions, and this greater depth of experience relative to English bank managers may enable them to provide more effective services to their small business customers. The explanation of differences due to location is much less clear cut. The evidence suggests that customers whose business is located in Scotland are less constrained in relation to certain aspects of bank practice, perceive a higher quality of provision of bank service and have a better relationship with their bank manager. There are two possible explanations for these observations. The first is that the differences are real and Scottish customers are getting a better service, perhaps because the Scottish economy has been less severely affected by the recession. There is some justification for this conclusion. The extent to which Scottish firms in the sample had experienced financial difficulties was rather lower than their English counterparts and perceptions of the banking relationship and service quality are influenced by whether or not firms had experienced financial difficulties or not. Nevertheless, the generally more favourable perceptions among Scottish firms, noted in Table 5.7, persist, even when controlling for the experience of financial difficulties. This suggests a second explanation for those differences, namely that the actual service delivered to Scottish customers is no different from that delivered to English customers, but that it appears so because of different expectations. Specifically, the presence of defensive financial behaviour of the kind suggested by Dow (1992) may mean that managers of businesses located in Scotland have lower expectations of the quality of service that they should expect from their bank and, consequently, for any given quality of provision a Scottish bank manager will attract a higher level of perceived quality than an English bank manager.

ACKNOWLEDGEMENTS

The authors would like to thank the Forum of Private Business for the provision of the data on which this study is based. The views expressed are those of the authors and not those of the Forum of Private Business.

APPENDIX

Scales used in measuring the banking relationship:

a) Importance attached to dimensions of the banking relationship

How important is each of these services to you? (Ranked on a scale from 1 = not important to 5 = very important.)

IMPK   Knows your business
        Understands your industry
        Understands your market
        Offers helpful business advice

IMPPR   Offers wide range of banking services
        Competitive interest rates
        Competitive/predictable charges

IMPPE   Speed of decision
Tailors finance to needs of business
One person deals with all credit needs
Easy access to loan officer

b) *Quality of service provision*

How well do you think your bank supplies these particular
requirements? (Ranked on a scale from 1 = very poor to 5 =
very good.)

ACTK   Knows your business
Understands your industry
Understands your market
Offers helpful business advice

ACTPR   Offers wide range of banking services
Competitive interest rates
Competitive/predictable charges

ACTPE   Speed of decision
Tailors finance to needs of business
One person deals with all credit needs
Easy access to loan officer

c) *Relationship with bank manager*

The following statements about the bank/small business relationship were scored on a scale from 1 = strongly agree to 5 = strongly
disagree.

BMT   My bank manager is always available to help in a crisis.
My bank manager often comes forward with positive
suggestions to help my business.
I am confident in the advice I get from my bank manager.
I am confident that my bank understands small businesses.
I can rely on my bank manager to find ways of meeting
my business's changing financial needs.

BMA   I prefer to avoid contact with my bank manager.
My bank manager is not really interested in my business.

I feel intimidated when dealing with my bank.
My bank manager is only prepared to offer standard
financial small business products.

BMI   It is important to provide my bank manager with timely
and regular management information.
It is important to discuss in advance potential excesses
over agreed borrowing limits.

NOTES

1 Hereafter the term England is used as a shorthand expression for England
and Wales.
2 The bank effect for loan rates is marginally significant at $p = 0.07$.
3 The results of an analysis of variance by location, bank age and size
suggest that only age and turnover have significant effects in explaining
the variability in the size of overdraft, overdraft usage, size of loan and the
collateral ratios. In the case of type of collateral, crosstabulation suggests
that controlling for size largely eliminates any significant differences.
4 Of course, it is possible that the result could be related to differential
expectations between what the groups consider to be good and bad quality
provision.

BIBLIOGRAPHY

Bannock, G. and Doran, A. (1991) *Business Banking in the 1990s: A New
Era of Competition*, Dublin: Lafferty Group.
Berger, A. N. and Udell, G. F. (1989) 'Some evidence on the empirical
significance of credit rationing', Working Paper, Salomon Brothers Center
for the Study of Financial Institutions, New York University.
Bester, H. (1987) 'The role of collateral in credit markets with imperfect
information', *European Economic Review*, 31: 887–99.
Bester, H. and Hellwig, M. (1989) 'Moral hazard and equilibrium credit
rationing: an overview of the issues', in G. Bamber and K. Spremann (eds)
Agency Theory, Information and Incentives, Berlin: Springer-Verlag.
Binks, M. R. and Coyne, J. (1989) 'The Birth of Enterprise', IEA Hobart
Paper.
Binks, M. R. and Ennew, C. T. (1991) 'Bank finance to small businesses', in
J. Stanworth and C. Gray (eds) *Bolton Twenty Years On: The Small Firm
in the 1990s*, London: Paul Chapman.
Binks, M. R., Ennew, C. T. and Reed, G. V. (1990) *Small Businesses and
their Banks*, Report to the Forum of Private Business, University of
Nottingham.
Binks, M. R., Ennew, C. T. and Reed, G. V. (1992) *Small Businesses and
their Banks: An International Perspective*, London: National Westminster
Bank.

Binks, M. R., Ennew, C. T. and Reed, G. V. (1993) *Small Businesses and their Banks*, Report to the Forum of Private Business.

Binks, M. R. and Vale, P. A. (1990) *Entrepreneurship and Economic Change*, London: McGraw-Hill.

Bolton, J. (1971) *Small Firms*, Report of the Committee of Inquiry on Small Firms, Cmnd 4811, London: HMSO.

Dow, S. (1992) 'The regional financial sector: a Scottish case study', *Regional Studies*, 26, 7: 619–63.

Edwards, G. (1987) *The Role of Banks in Economic Development*, London: Macmillan.

Harrison, R. T. and Mason, C. M. (1990) 'The role of the business expansion scheme in the UK, *Omega*, 17, 2: 147–57.

Keasey, K. and Watson, R. (1992) *Investment and Financing Decisions and the Performance of Small Firms*, London: National Westminster Bank.

Mason, C. M., Harrison, R. T. and Chaloner, J. (1992) 'Informal risk capital in the UK: a study of investor characteristics, preferences and decision making', in Robertson, E. Chell and C. Mason (eds) *Towards the Twenty First Century: The Challenge for Small Business*, Nadamal, Cheshire, 141–61.

Mayes, D. G. and Moir, L. B. (1989), 'Small firms in the UK economy', *Royal Bank of Scotland Review*, December: 15–33.

de Meza, D. and Webb, D. C. (1987) 'Too much investment: a problem of asymmetric information', *Quarterly Journal of Economics*, 102: 281–92.

Sharpe, S. A. (1989) 'Asymmetric information, bank lending and implicit contracts: a stylized model of customer relationships', Finance and Economics Discussion Series No. 70, Federal Reserve Board, Washington.

Stiglitz, J. and Weiss, A. (1981) 'Credit rationing in markets with imperfect information' *American Economic Review*, 71: 393–410.

Storey, D. J. and Johnson, S. (1987) *Job Generation and Labour Market Change*, London: Macmillan.

Turnbull, P. W. and Gibbs, M. L. (1987) 'Marketing bank services to corporate clients: the importance of relationships', *International Journal of Bank Marketing*, 5, 1: 19–26.

Watson, I. (1986) 'Managing the relationship with corporate clients', *International Journal of Bank Marketing*, 4, 1: 19–34.

Wilson, H. (1979) *The Financing of Small Firms*, Report of the Committee to Review the Functioning of Financial Institutions, Cmnd 7503, London: HMSO.

Yao-Su, Hu. (1984) *Industrial Banking and Special Credit Institutions*, London: Policy Studies Institute.

6 Social networking

A comparative behavioural study between would-be entrepreneurs in Scotland and Boston, Massachusetts

Alasdair McNicoll

INTRODUCTION

In recent years we have witnessed a greater interest in, and appreciation of, the importance of networking to entrepreneurial development. Much of the research has focused on established or fledgling businesses and examined the networking behaviour of the incumbent entrepreneurs in order to identify patterns of networking behaviour which increase the chances of ultimate success. Additionally, the research has been directed towards 'business-focused' networks, where the networking activity is initiated solely in response to business requirements.

This study concentrates on entrepreneurs who are at the pre-start-up stage ('would-be entrepreneurs') rather than those who are already in business. This is an important distinction given that this study was part of an overall research programme examining Scotland's low rate of new firm formation; our focus on the pre-start phase allowed us to examine the relevance of networking to new firm formation.

As a consequence of our interest, *social* networking activities, which are broader than but do not exclude business contacts, were the primary focus of this study; it was important that all types of contact, whether formal or informal, be considered because any single one could prove to be important in taking forward the business idea. Indeed, the concept of contact formality is one which is crucial to this study, particularly the degree of formality or informality involved in the initial contact – our evidence would suggest that informal contact mechanisms can add value to the networking process (we will return to this later).

This chapter proposes that social networking is important in the firm formation process, providing a mechanism through which the would-be entrepreneur can access expertise and assistance which will assist in taking forward their business idea. It provides evidence that would-be entrepreneurs in Boston enjoy social networks which are larger, more diverse and of higher value than those enjoyed by their Scottish counterparts.

NETWORKING

As mentioned above, much research has already been carried out on the subject of networking. In particular, interest has focused on identifying entrepreneurial networking patterns, quantitative analysis of time devoted to networking, network diversity and density, networking at various stages of the business life-cycle and international and interregional comparisons of networking.

Many of the issues considered in this research are of relevance to the study reported on here. First, there is the issue concerning our ability to adequately identify and define an individual's networking activities. Johannisson (1986) and Birley, Cromie and Myers (1991) correctly postulate that networks, like organisation structures, are abstract concepts but are even more difficult to analyse because, first, each set of interconnections is unique to the focal person who creates it, and second, because members of networks do not usually disclose their contacts and rarely discuss the nature of their association with others. Further, Johannisson describes networks as loosely coupled systems with fuzzy boundaries which render them elusive to precise definition.

The methodology most commonly utilised to identify entrepreneurial networks is a postal questionnaire sent to (predominantly) small firms. A common difficulty with this approach is that a formal questionnaire, either oral or written, cannot hope to fully uncover the depth and richness within an individual's contacts and can only aim to scratch the surface of what is an extremely complex and interactive process. A further problem lies in the historic nature of many of the responses received. For example, asking the owner of an existing business about their networking activities prior to commencement is fraught with difficulties related to both memory loss and post-event rationalisation.

Ideally, what is required to overcome both problems is an analysis of *current* networking activities, relevant to the current stage in the business life-cycle, and conducted verbally in an interactive manner.

Birley, Cromie and Myers (1991) undertook research which provided a quantitative assessment of the total number of hours spent networking with a breakdown of activity by type. A comparative analysis, their data suggests that Irish entrepreneurs spend less time developing new non-customer contacts than their American or Italian counterparts. Further, American entrepreneurs have larger networks than either the Irish or the Italians.

The diversity and density of networks is a subject which has attracted a great deal of attention. Network density refers to the comprehensiveness of the associations between persons or organisations in a network and is measured by 'comparing the total number of ties present to the potential number that would occur if everyone in the network were connected to everyone else' (Aldrich and Zimmer 1986: 13). Network diversity refers to the kind of people with whom the focal entrepreneur has associations.

Diverse networks lead to more sources of information and provide differing perspectives on given issues. Butler and Hansen (1991) argue that more diverse networks are more likely to provide information which disconfirms the entrepreneur's existing beliefs, while small networks could have much stronger ties and be more likely to provide information which is already known and which merely confirms both parties' existing preconceptions (Granovetter 1973, Nelson 1989).

Birley, Cromie and Myers (1991) contend, however, that a more diverse network may, in fact, be disadvantageous because disconfirming or conflictual evidence may promote uncertainty and caution, thereby destroying the entrepreneur's vital spark.

Where there would appear to be general agreement, however, is on the contention that diverse networks provide more information which could, in turn, generate more opportunities and allow the entrepreneur to better predict their immediate environment. Indeed, Butler and Hansen (1991) conclude that the development of social networks, including friends, family, business acquaintances, etc., is extremely important in the identification of business opportunities at the pre-start-up stage. As the business idea grows, these social networks give way to business-focused networks (lawyers, accountants, bankers, etc.) which assume a greater relevance to the actual start-up of the business and its early development. The final stage of network evolution, according to Butler and Hansen's model, is the development of a strategic network which links the entrepreneur to their competitors and seeks to enhance the competitiveness of all firms in the network. Butler and Hansen's model is shown in Figure 6.1.

Birley (1986) agrees that social networks are most important in providing information and assistance during the start-up phase; they

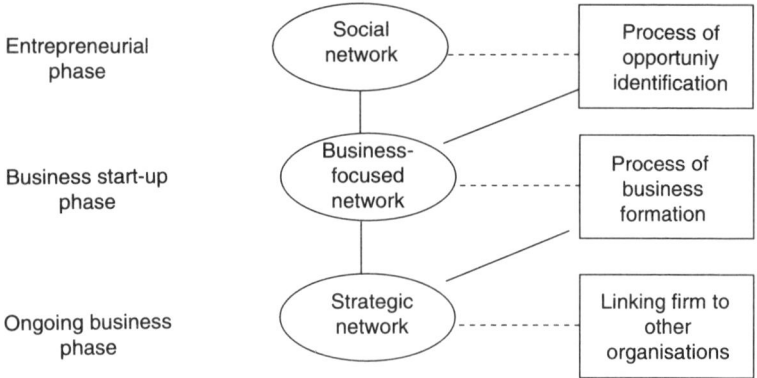

Figure 6.1 The development cycle
Source: Butler and Hanson 1991

then decline as a firm places greater emphasis upon inter-organisational networks to support its strategy. During the early stages, entrepreneurs rely heavily on an informal network of friends, family and other social contacts for support and the provision of information relating to opportunities.

Filion (1990) also hypothesises a three-stage network development model. In the *primary* phase of identifying a business idea, contact patterns are largely based on families, relatives and friends via affective, intellectual and recreational relationships. Filion observed that primary-stage contacts considerably influence the opportunities which emerge at other levels in the relations system. A visionary entrepreneur will proceed to develop many secondary and tertiary relationships. *Secondary* relationships are based upon acquaintances from business, social and political groups; *tertiary* relationships are far more focused and are selected to meet particular business needs. The entrepreneur with a clear vision will build relationships in the tertiary grouping to help to realise their vision. Filion's tertiary grouping also includes the acquisition of know-how and ideas which do not necessarily involve personal contact, e.g., reading a book.

RESEARCH RATIONALE

Many of the above-mentioned studies emphasise the importance of social networking to early-stage development and, given the focus of Scottish Enterprise's (SE) research, it was obviously an area worthy of more detailed consideration. The need for research focused on networking was underpinned by other SE projects which highlighted that networking, or rather the lack of it, might, in part, be contributing towards Scotland's poor rate of new firm formation.

First, the Informal Investors Study highlighted the ineffectiveness of social networks in Scotland with regard to accessing informal sources of finance. Entrepreneurs actively seeking informal investors complained of the difficulty in establishing contact with 'Business Angels', finding that they were rarely part of the same social network; the entrepreneurs tended to rely on introductions by professional advisers such as accountants, lawyers or bankers. However, many professional advisers in this country are reluctant to refer clients onwards, fearing that such referral may be viewed as an endorsement of the proposal; the Financial Services Act, 1986, itself often defers people from so doing. The informal investors themselves rarely actively seek opportunities; proposals arise from business and social contacts but many complained of difficulties in finding proposals suggesting that they are part of the wrong networks and/or that their existing networks are not functioning effectively.

Our research into 'hi-tech' new ventures, which compared the situation in Massachusetts with that in Scotland, found that in Massachusetts chance meetings within social networks together with a willingness to refer individuals and ideas to the most appropriate place played an important role in several of the new starts studied. Informal networks, mutual support and encouragement did not feature so highly in the Scottish case studies. Compared to Massachusetts, there was little networking between industry and research staff in academia and government laboratories, with the consequence that commercial opportunities might be missed.

MORI were contracted to conduct a survey of attitudes towards entrepreneurship and the findings confirmed the importance of the role of contacts. We found that:

- Those who know an entrepreneur are more likely to say that they would like to (and believe they could) run their own business.
- The lowest contact with an entrepreneur is among the group which have considered but rejected the idea of setting-up in business.

Thus, contact with an entrepreneur seems to increase the probability of an individual being in the entrepreneurial pool. Table 6.1 presents the results of the MORI survey and suggests that personal acquaintance with an entrepreneur can act as a motivator for people to take the plunge themselves.

Table 6.1 Percentage of population knowing an entrepreneur

	Scotland	South England	USA
Like to run a business	70	74	72
Not like to	60	66	69
Thought about /rejected	39	51	39
Total population	63	68	71

Source: MORI survey

Table 6.1 shows that Scotland is no different to the USA or the South of England in this regard; however, in nearly every category, the percentage of the population knowing an entrepreneur is lower in Scotland than in the other two areas.

Within Scotland the population has limited personal contact with people in relevant professions with whom they would feel able to discuss their business idea (see Table 6.2). Those who would not like to run their own business have fewer such contacts than other groups. However, even of those who would like to run their own business, only 20 per cent personally know people from three or more relevant professions with whom they would feel able to discuss their business proposition.

METHODOLOGY

Given that one of the purposes of our research programme was to establish 'best practice' in other areas, it was felt important to compare Scotland's performance with an area which enjoys an outstanding track record in entrepreneurial activities and is steeped in the culture of entrepreneurship; the area which best fitted our requirements was Boston, Massachusetts. An added advantage with this selection was that we had built up our own network of contacts

Table 6.2 Scotland: Contacts with relevant professions

	Percentage with range of contacts	
	0	3+
Like to run own business	10	20
Not like to	32	13
Total population	27	16

Source: MORI survey

with support agencies in Boston which would assist us in putting together the American sampling frame.

Quadrangle Consulting Limited was retained to administer the research programme, conduct the interviews, analyse the data and assist in the development of a methodology which would provide detailed information on the networking activities of the case studies selected. In order to avoid some of the problems associated with previous research (referred to earlier) it was essential that the methodology allowed 'real-time' analysis of *current* networking activities and was interactive in that it allowed a dialogue between interviewer and respondent in order to achieve a greater understanding of the subtleties involved in the networking process. The 'real-time' approach overcomes the problems of memory loss and post-event rationalisation, while dialogue enriches the responses in a way which is not possible with questionnaire-type approaches.

The research was to be *exploratory* in nature, which meant that the focus was to be on a qualitative analysis rather than a quantitative one, the latter requiring large sampling frames which would have been both difficult and time-consuming to put together, particularly for the American sample. The Scottish sample of 19 was drawn from people who had responded to Scottish Television's 'The Business Game' (sponsored by Scottish Enterprise); the American sample of 18 was contacted on our behalf by various support agencies, including the MIT Enterprise Forum, the Boston Small Business Development Centre and the Technology Capital Network.

Between October and December 1992, each one of our respondents in both Scotland and the USA was contacted by phone, at a pre-arranged time, once a week over a period of four weeks. The purpose of the interview was to establish who the would-be entrepreneurs had been in discussion with over the previous seven days, thereby obtaining the information while it was still fresh in the respondents' mind. The interviewers were careful to coax as much detail as possible out of the respondents while retaining a sense of informality; it was important that each respondent felt relaxed and comfortable with the line of questioning. Of particular importance was that the respondents were not selective about which contacts they reported, choosing only those which *they* thought were relevant; it was vital that *every* contact was identified so that an accurate picture of social networking patterns could be drawn. The importance of this was demonstrated by the number of informal/casual meetings at which the business was discussed despite the purpose of the meeting being originally non-business-related.

Having collected over 1,200 pages of transcript, the information had to be distilled into a form which would assist interpretation and analysis. A form of mapping incorporating a molecular structure similar to that adopted by Filion (1990) was chosen as this would reflect the breadth and diversity of an individual's network and demonstrate the nature of each contact and report on the outcomes. A second type of map was created for each respondent, this type based on the frequency and value of the respondent's contacts. Each contact was classified according to a typology adapted from Filion (1990):

- *Primary relations* are those relationships that are closest to the individual – mainly family, relatives and friends. Typically, they are linked with more than one aspect of the respondent's life.
- *Secondary relations* include acquaintances – business, social or political – and tend to be linked to a specific activity (e.g., members of sports club, work colleagues, etc). They might include professional advisers (e.g., solicitors, accountants, etc) but are distinguished by the nature of the contact which is always informal. For example, contact might have been made through a social situation or via a friend's introduction.
- *Tertiary relations* are not centred on human relations but are focused on sources of information and stimuli such as courses, books, conferences, exhibitions, etc. They too might include professional advisers but only when these have been contacted purely on a business matter and not as the result of a social situation.

FINDINGS

Central to the research was the following objective:

> *to establish whether issues relating to networking are of any importance in stimulating entrepreneurial behaviour.*

Relative to this, three hypotheses were to be tested:

- that successful businesses operate a different network of contacts from other businesses;
- that formal and informal networks do influence business decision-making;
- that the networking activities of would-be entrepreneurs in Scotland are different from their counterparts in other (more dynamic) regions.

In the event, only the first hypothesis proved difficult to answer during the research programme due to the fact that none of the case studies had, as yet, commenced trading. To test this hypothesis fully, we conducted a follow-up survey in the spring of 1994. A summary of the findings from this follow-on survey are presented later.

Type of contact

Table 6.3 shows both the total number of contacts mentioned by the respondents over the four-week period and the distribution of these contacts between primary, secondary and tertiary relations.

The first observation is that the American sample had one and a half times more contacts than the Scots, thereby revealing a significant difference in the level of networking activity entered into; this means that, on average, each American had 14 key contacts during the research compared to only nine for each Scot. Of greater interest, however, is the breakdown of these contacts between each category of relation. We find that the make-up of the contacts is quite different between the American and the Scots samples. The Scots relied more heavily on tertiary relations (45 per cent) than their American counterparts (28 per cent), which is an indication of more formalised channels being favoured by the Scots. The Scots were also more likely to utilise primary relations, although, as will be demonstrated later, the *quality* of the assistance derived from this source may not have been as high as that for the American sample.

The greatest difference, however, was to be found in the secondary relations category; here, almost half of all American contacts were to be found (47 per cent) compared to less than a quarter of all Scots contacts (22 per cent). It is in this category of relations that the greatest potential for advice and assistance is to be found; like the tertiary category, this type of relation includes professional advisers

Total 6.3 Total contacts over four-week period

Contact type	Scottish sample		US sample	
	No.	*%*	*No.*	*%*
Primary relations	57	33	65	25
Secondary relations	37	22	123	47
Tertiary relations	76	45	73	28
Total contacts	170	100	261	100

Source: MORI survey

and providers of assistance. The informal nature of the initial contact in secondary relations, however, is likely to add value to the interaction. For example, a business adviser (e.g., in a local enterprise company) may be more favourably inclined towards an entrepreneur's idea if he already knows the entrepreneur in another less formal context (e.g., members of the same squash club) and has formed a favourable impression of his capabilities from this exposure. Alternatively, a referral by a friend on to another contact adds value to both the person who is being referred and the person to whom they are being referred, because both will value the opinion of the go-between and both will, therefore, be more favourably disposed towards the meeting before it has even occurred; the same meeting, arranged through formal channels with no go-between to take each partner some way up the learning curve, may still be successful but only after a considerable time has been spent gaining one another's confidence. In essence, networking is a confidence-building exercise and referral is a method which adds value by increasing confidence levels all round.

Primary relations

All respondents mentioned the family and only three did not list it as, at the very least, a source of moral support. However, the extent to which family support could be termed passive or active varies widely between and within both samples.

There were no examples in either sample of family members actively dissuading the respondent from setting up in business. However, in a limited number of cases (four) partners or parents did express some worries and this did seem to be important to the would-be entrepreneurs concerned. In contrast, many entrepreneurs spoke of their partners as offering a rich source of ideas, encouragement and support (both emotional and practical). The Scots in particular seemed to gain most out of this, but the Americans seemed more adept at exploiting the family as a potential source of business assistance. Almost half of the American sample were able to access broader networks via members of their family; further, in half of these cases (i.e., one-quarter of *all* cases) these broader networks extended to links with potential investors. In the Scottish sample, there were no recorded instances of potential investors being accessed via family members.

The American respondents enjoyed greater provision of professional and business advice within the family group than did the

Scots, which may, of course, merely be the result of chance but which may, in part, explain why the US families provided access to better quality networks.

In summary, the families of our Scottish respondents seemed to be involved at a more 'passive' level than those of our American respondents, providing psychological support or general advice rather than professional or entrepreneurial experience.

Much of what has been said about families can also be said about friends. Again, friends were a source of moral support but were perhaps more willing than family to offer criticism of the business proposals. Of most interest in this context was the attitude of the entrepreneurs, the Americans being more likely to accept such criticism in a constructive manner. While the Scots seemed to derive greater benefit from networking with friends rather than family, the Americans still tended to make better use of their friends, being able to use them to access more active and multi-faceted networks than the Scots. Balanced against this higher incidence of networking activity by the Scots were those who deliberately avoided seeking help from friends, or even discussing the business idea, in the belief that this would be an imposition on the friendship. At least a couple of Scottish respondents were afraid that someone would steal their idea or that they would look foolish if their idea failed (the fear of failure was also apparent in other studies conducted for the new ventures research). In contrast, the American sample, almost without exception, saw every meeting as a potential opportunity to get feedback and advice on their business idea.

Secondary relations

It is in this category that the difference between the Scots and American samples is most abundantly clear, with the latter displaying a depth and diversity of networking activity on a scale to which the Scots did not come close. Although a number of Scots developed quite extensive networks they typically did not interconnect or create extended chains of contacts in the way that many of the US respondents did. It was surprising how few of the Scottish case studies were involved in focused activities such as clubs, societies or churches. Table 6.4 shows that only five Scots (26 per cent) belonged to organisations of this type and between them they belonged to only seven different organisations; in contrast, 13 of the American case studies (72 per cent) belonged to secondary-type organisations and between them they covered 21 different bodies.

Table 6.4 Membership of organisations

	Scottish sample		US sample	
	No.	*%*	*No.*	*%*
No. of entrepreneurs	5	26	13	72
No. of organisations	7		21	

Source: MORI survey

These findings suggest that the Americans were more heavily involved in their local communities which, in turn, would provide them with more opportunities to make new, potentially useful, contacts. Nearly all of this group were able to glean information, contacts or advice through the organisations of which they were members.

Roughly half of each sample included in their secondary networks those connected with either their current or previous employment. With only a couple of exceptions, the Scots simply used these contacts as a source of moral support, ideas or general advice. The Americans may have shared the fear that their boss would find out about their plans, but they seemed more willing to accept this risk as necessary in progressing their business idea. A particularly striking example of this involved an American who wanted to establish a 'brew-pub'; he worked as Food Service Director for a Boston law firm. Overcoming his initial fears, he approached his boss who ultimately helped him link up with a venture capitalist, a restaurant backer, a lawyer and other potential investors.

The American respondents tended to either already have, or be able to create, access to secondary networks of a professional or business nature on a much broader scale than the Scots. They also seemed to benefit more from serendipity, perhaps as a result of their more prolific networking generally, and/or a more determined approach to making the most of chance opportunities. Some had the advantage of having an established direct relationship with other professionals, perhaps through social interaction, but others were put in touch with professional assistance via their *primary* network. There were also several American examples of 'chance' meetings, like the entrepreneur who discovered that her local petrol station attendant had a graphic design qualification and was consequently able to offer her some specialist advice. Only one Scottish respondent was similarly 'lucky', meeting someone at a party who was able to offer advice on business administration and marketing techniques.

Five Scots forged secondary-type links with individuals in industries/businesses similar to those which they hoped to establish themselves and two others achieved specialised assistance from 'associates'.

One of the most interesting subjects is how networks are used to access sources of finance. In particular, we are interested in informal sources of finance, which, for this study, we defined as those which were accessed via a primary or secondary relationship. This may include private individuals or organisations or more common sources such as banks and venture capitalists, but they all are regarded as being informal in this context because of the way in which they are accessed by the entrepreneur. Only two Scots accessed finance via social or informal contacts whereas nearly half of the American sample achieved the same goal. While this finding may, in itself, be the result of there being more 'Business Angels' in Boston than there are in Scotland, the research overall does clearly suggest that, to the Scots, 'finance' meant a bank loan, a grant from the public sector or the Enterprise Allowance Scheme.

Tertiary relations

The Scots were much more likely than the Americans to use more 'formal' networking methods as contained in the tertiary category of relations; the Scots made nearly half of their contacts via tertiary networks, compared to less than a third for the Americans. Professional advisers and providers of specialist assistance were much more likely to be accessed via tertiary channels in Scotland; this may be a reflection of poor access to such assistance via primary and secondary networks. Nine (50 per cent) of the Scots respondents included Scottish Enterprise, a local enterprise company or some other public support agency within their tertiary network; these organisations were approached, in the main, for financial assistance or for business training. Both Scottish and American entrepreneurs found course attendance useful from a networking perspective. Five US respondents derived positive benefits from attending trade shows and exhibitions, events which no Scottish respondent even mentioned.

Hardly any of the American respondents made use of formal 'institutionalised' sources of finance, whereas half of the Scottish sample included a bank in their network; a third of Scots respondents sought financial help (usually grants) from other organisations. In effect, the situation for formal finance is the complete opposite to that for informal finance.

Table 6.5 Entrepreneurial contacts

	Scottish sample		US sample	
	No.	%	No.	%
Level of entrepreneurial contacts	13		28	
Individual contact with other entrepreneurs	8	40	13	75

Source: MORI survey

Figures 6.2 and 6.3 are networking maps which summarise and highlight the differences between the two samples. The main findings, once again, are:

- The Americans have a greater number of contacts than the Scots.
- The Americans place more emphasis on secondary relations whereas the Scots favour tertiary relations.
- American contacts, in the main, add more value in that they are not 'dead-end' and often lead to further contacts and/or solutions.
- American contacts tend to be more frequent in nature, i.e., their networks are more active.

Relations with other entrepreneurs

Table 6.5 shows that only eight (40 per cent) of the Scottish entrepreneurs knew at least one other entrepreneur; the corresponding figure for the Americans was 13 (75 per cent). Additionally, between them the American sample knew 28 other entrepreneurs compared to the Scots 13 (mean averages of 1.6 per US respondent and 0.7 per Scots respondent). Given the results of other studies on the importance of role models, this is a significant finding.

GENERAL FINDINGS

One unexpected by-product of the research was information relating to what might be termed 'social and cultural' considerations, e.g., attitudes to risk, motivation, self-esteem, etc. In this section we will examine some of the more interesting observations.

On the basis of this research, the Americans tended to be a lot clearer, more articulate and more purposeful about both the reasons why they wanted to go into business and what they expected to get out of it. Clearly, unemployment was a significant 'push' factor,

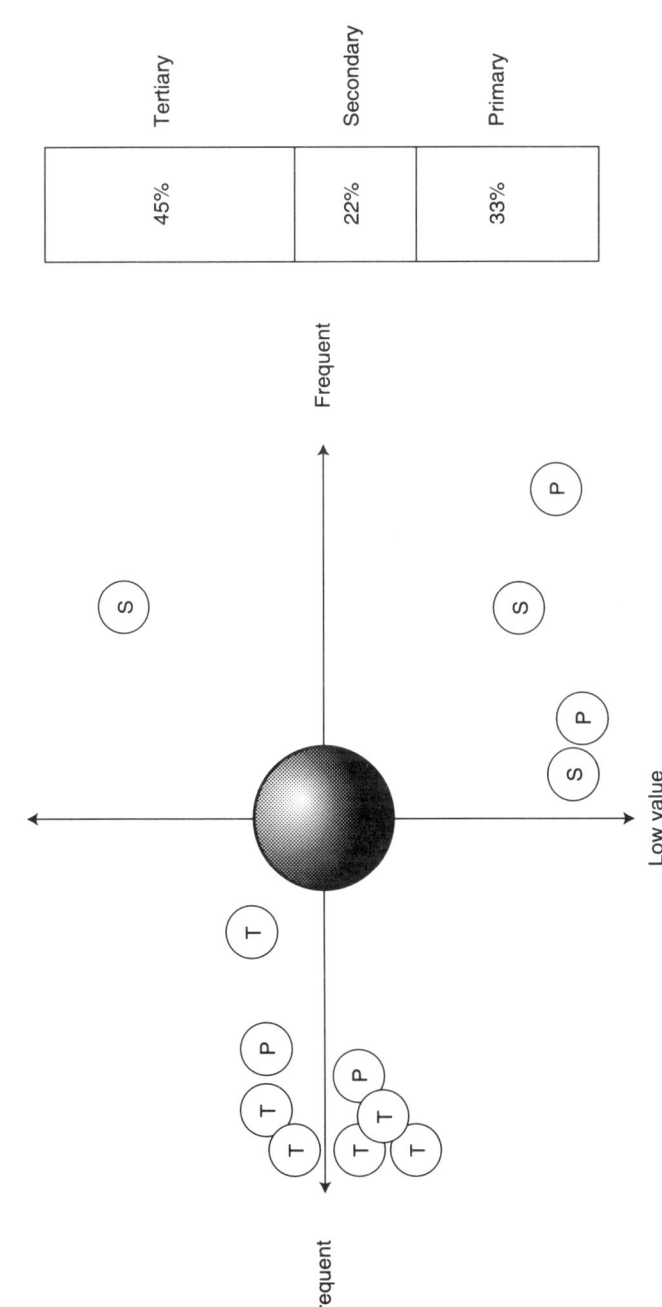

Figure 6.2 Scottish sample

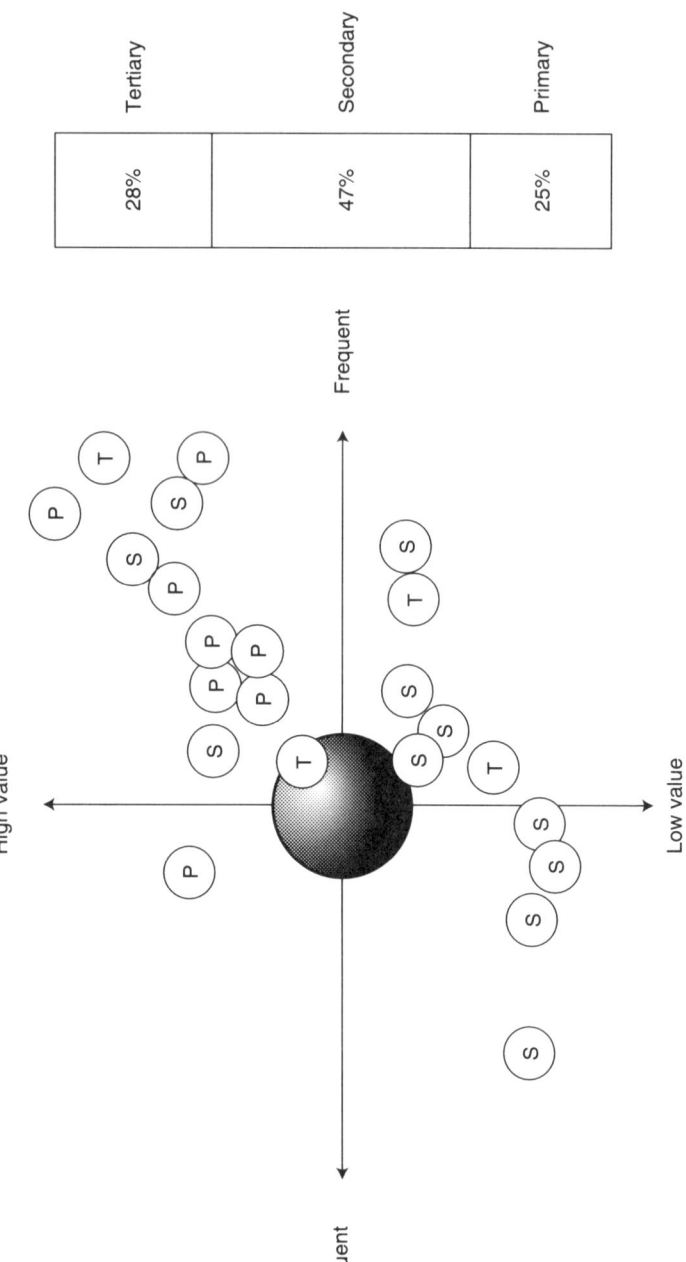

Figure 6.3 Boston sample

particularly for the Scots. There were seven unemployed would-be entrepreneurs in each sample but their attitudes were quite different in each country. The Scots gave the distinct impression that self-employment (note the phraseology) was a last resort and that they would willingly give up on their business idea if a suitable offer of employment came along. The motivation of the redundant Americans, however, was virtually identical to the other American respondents, i.e., desire for self-control, desire to make money, personal fulfilment, belief that they could do a better job than existing businesses. It is interesting to note that none of the Scots mentioned personal fulfilment or the desire to make money as prime motivators.

The Americans were also more ambitious than the Scots. Over half the Scots sample did not, or were not willing to, articulate any substantive growth plans for their business, while others expressed modest ambitions. In comparison, the Americans were both more forthcoming and forthright about what they expected to achieve, e.g., 'going national', dominating a new market. Two quotations from American respondents typify their ambitions:

> Eventually to be one of the largest organic coffee mail order houses. Secondly, to possibly open retail locations. And thirdly, to go public with the company.

> To form a company that services the world, or does business throughout the world.

The Americans had much higher levels of self-belief than the Scots, even to the extent of ignoring advice offered by professional advisers. The Scots tended, in the main, not to view themselves as entrepreneurs, labelling themselves as 'self-employed' or 'freelance'. Another indication of the difference between both groups' self-esteem lay in their willingness to talk about themselves and their business idea; out of more than 1,200 pages of transcript, less than 300 pages came from discussions with Scottish respondents.

Despite the fact that the Americans generally had a greater financial stake in the businesses, they appeared less risk-averse than the Scots. They did not exhibit the same fear of failure.

SPRING 1994 FOLLOW-ON SURVEY

As stated earlier, it was impossible during the course of the initial research to test the hypothesis that 'successful businesses operate a different network of contacts from other businesses'. To address this question and to generally conclude our research, we commissioned Quadrangle to conduct a short telephone survey of our original respondents in order to ascertain what had happened to them over the intervening period in relation to the realisation of their business idea. Only three respondents from each group could not be contacted, which meant that we could obtain a reasonably complete picture of what had become of both groups.

The findings from this survey can be summarised as follows. First, five of the 15 Americans re-contacted had not managed to start their business yet although they still intended to, compared to nine out of the 16 Scots re-contacted. Only two of the Americans had managed to start their business, which is low but still better than the Scots where only one managed this achievement. On the other hand, two additional Scots did set up in business by buying over going-concerns, a route which was never mentioned in the American sample. Two respondents from each sample set themselves up in what would best be described as 'self-employment' rather than a new venture, this description being used to suggest scale rather than inferiority. Taken together, these findings would suggest that our hypothesis that 'successful businesses operate a different network of contacts from other businesses' is unproven because, to prove the hypothesis, we would have expected more Americans than Scots to have established businesses of some form. However, if we consider the networking profiles of the respondents who successfully started up in business we find that these individuals rank as marginally more active networkers than the rest of their own peer group. This, then, may support our hypothesis, albeit tentatively; further research is likely to be required to draw firm conclusions in this area.

Some of our respondents did not proceed with their business proposals because they were offered and accepted employment from another source. An interesting observation is that, of the five to whom this applied (four Americans and one Scot) four of them received job offers as a direct result of their networking activities, an outcome which was not anticipated at the outset.

CONCLUSIONS

Compared to the Scots, the American sample demonstrated a greater understanding and appreciation of the need to network; as a consequence they were more adept and active networkers. They were also much more open than their Scottish counterparts, being totally willing to discuss their activities both with our researchers and also with just about anyone they might meet; they seemed to view almost every meeting as an opportunity to take their idea forward.

The difference in the attitudes of both groups was also quite striking; the Americans were more confident, more highly motivated, less risk-averse and had greater ambition than the Scots; fear of failure, which was mentioned on more than one occasion by Scots, did not seem to be an issue for the Americans.

The research clearly proves that issues relating to networking stimulate entrepreneurial behaviour. Regarding our three original hypotheses, we found that networking does strongly influence the decision process for would-be entrepreneurs in Scotland and Massachusetts; our first hypothesis, that successful businesses operate a different network of contacts from other businesses, remains unproven but there is clear evidence that the more active networkers demonstrate more success at accessing the finance, advice and assistance which they need to help them develop their business idea, and it was the more active networkers in both groups who actually did start up at the end of the day.

BIBLIOGRAPHY

Aldrich, H. and Zimmer, C. (1986) 'Entrepreneurship through social networks', in *The Art and Science of Entrepreneurship*, New York: Ballinger.

Birley, S. (1985) 'The role of networks in the entrepreneurial process', *The Journal of Business Venturing*, 1: 107–17.

Birley, S., Cromie, S. and Myers, A. (1991) 'Entrepreneurial networks: their emergence in Ireland and overseas', *International Small Business*, 9, 4: 56–74.

Butler, J. E. and Hansen, G. S. (1991) 'Network evolution, entrepreneurial success and regional development', *Entrepreneurship and Regional Development*, 3: 1–16.

Dubini, P. and Aldrich, H. (1991) 'Personal and extended networks are central to the entrepreneurial process', *Journal of Business Venturing*, 6: 305–13.

Filion, L. J. (1990) 'Entrepreneurial performance, networking, vision and relations', *Journal of Small Business and Entrepreneurship*, 7, 3: 3–13.

Granovetter, M. S. (1973) 'The strength of strong ties', *American Journal of Sociology*, 78: 1360–80.

Johannisson, B. (1986) 'Network strategies. Management technology for entrepreneurship and change', *International Small Business Journal*, 5, 1: 19–30.

Nelson, R. E. (1989) 'The strength of strong ties. Social networks and intergroup conflict', *Academy of Management Journal*, 32: 377–401.

7 Social networks, entrepreneurship and regional development

Research issues

Ronald W. McQuaid

INTRODUCTION

Much of the research into new firm formation focuses upon entrepreneurs and their characteristics or motivations (Brockhaus and Horwitz 1986) or the external economic environment (Chandler and Hanks 1994). However, theories based upon isolated, independent actors operating in a self-contained manner therefore ignore some of the key influences on their behaviour and are likely to prove inadequate (Cuevas 1994: 82). These theories and research largely ignore the wider network of social relationships between founders and others who influence them and their behaviour. These other key actors, such as funders, critical suppliers and buyers, family, friends, advisers and individuals that serve in leadership or subordinate roles may all have a direct 'strategic' influence on the development of the firm (Gartner et al. 1994).

Theoretically, in order to more fully understand the behaviour of individual entrepreneurs, or the process of new firm formation, it is necessary to understand their relationships with other organisations and individuals as well as their individual characteristics. However, empirically these relationships need to be controlled for in any analysis of the factors influencing firms' start-up and success if they do not play a significant role in the process. Social networks consist of those persons with whom an entrepreneur has direct relations (called personal networks by Dubini and Aldrich 1991) and so may include professional advisers. These are, of course, distinct from networking by companies in order to build competitive advantage (McKiernan 1992).

This chapter reviews the links between social networks and new business formation, the insights that these links offer for policy development and the research questions that they raise. It seeks to team of professional advisers will normally be in place and it becomes important to the entrepreneur to develop contacts with fellow businessmen, i.e., to establish and take part in a strategic network which may even include competitors.

Birley (1985) also found that when entrepreneurs need to secure professional advice, particularly for funding, they turn to formal sources of support. A major problem with start-up businesses is getting funding, and it may be that inadequate networks prevented entrepreneurs from securing the most suitable sources of finance in that a lack of informal contacts may have precluded the establishment of mutual trust, thereby forming another barrier to funding.

Curran et al. (1993) argue that networks are of limited practical use to small business owner-managers. They suggest that while networks may give useful moral support and provide contacts with the environment, they are much more limited than notions of 'networking' would imply. However, this may be explained by the stage of business, with social networks being most significant in the pre-start-up or start-up phases. Also, networks may operate differently in different economic, social or cultural contexts that make up different regions or nations.

Social networks and regional development

While there are many potentially significant factors leading to differences in economic performance and new firm generation between regions, attention has tended to concentrate on industrial structure, markets and direct inputs. The importance of social support networks has received relatively little research attention. Garofoli (1994) found a strong relationship between the socio-economic environment and local economic development and argued that investment in improving the local social and economic 'milieu' was important in fostering new firm formation. Others, such as Camagni (1992) and Reynolds, Storey and Westhead (1994) also show the importance of national, regional and local milieux on the new firm formation rates and economic growth.

On the negative side, Pagden (1988) presents a historical example of how the destruction of social networks can have a profound effect on the development of the economy. Indeed, he argues that the Spanish rulers of Naples in the eighteenth century deliberately sought to destroy trust between the Neapolitans in order to ruin the social bonds holding together their community and so increase Spanish power to control the area. Commerce collapsed and trade became a question of mutual deception. This clearly affected the opportunities for business and the way in which business entrepreneurs would form relations, and arguably there are many similar examples throughout the world today.

Krugman (1991) argues that the concentration of economic activity in space is due to the increasing returns to scale in production. These are due to spillovers from the pooled labour market, externalities relating to inputs from supplier industries etc., and information and technological factors. The question arises, if social networks are important in new firm formation, do these networks and the factors influencing these networks vary systematically across space? The wider literature on conglomeration economies and the concentration of economic activity in space, covering industrial districts (You and Wilkinson 1994), competitive regions (Porter 1990) and innovative regional milieux (Hanson 1992) has relatively little to say on this issue but offers opportunities for more detailed study on the role of social networks.

Lorenz (1988) shows how informal networks have developed in France whereby small companies form relations with larger firms and specialise in one area of production for which there is a ready market. This allows them to invest in current technology and to meet the necessary economies of scale for such an investment, while the larger firms also reap benefit through improved productivity, without having to make the capital investment themselves. These subcontracting markets often involve bargaining, negotiation, mutual adjustment, even when there is no recurrent or continuing relationship, and these relations involve mutual dependency with each firm's actions influencing the other and social contacts also playing a significant role. Hence, while social networks are not always necessary, they may play a significant role in forming the contacts. Networks with overlapping social relations and contacts for contracts may be more likely to be in locations where there are clusters of specialist firms and market opportunities.

The corporate restructuring of large firms during the last two decades may have increased the importance of networking (Halal, Geranmayeh and Pourdehnad 1993). This has often resulted in 'push' factors, where employees are forced or encouraged to set up on their own in order to supply the original employer. This offers the employer a number of advantages, including few overhead costs (in terms of pensions, office costs, holiday pay, etc.), greater flexibility and the ability to bring in competition to keep prices down after the initial contract period. Hence, a number of costs are transferred from the original employer to the former employee who is now the start-up entrepreneur. However, the advantages for the entrepreneur may include the ability to achieve economies of scale by serving a number of customers, financial gain where office etc. expenses previously paid by the employer are now absorbed by the entrepreneur at low cost (e.g., by using their house for an office or having a lower quality of accommodation). Besides the implications of this for the growth in the number of new firms, social networks become more particularly important in the start-up process. This is because the social network incorporating previous work colleagues and associates may be crucial for providing advice, expertise and so on to the entrepreneur on how to start up, and also in gaining important early contracts through networks with decision-makers among former co-workers.

In summary, social networks appear to have an important role in the pre-start-up phases of firm formation in particular, but further research is needed into how this relates to the performance of regions.

NETWORK ANALYSIS

Empirical results

The relative importance of social networks remains an empirical question. Using data based upon the research by McNicoll (Chapter 6 of this volume) the hypothesis was tested that those starting up new businesses had different size and intensities of networks of social relationships. The data related to social networks during the pre-start-up phase. This allows the avoidance of *ex post facto* rationalisation so as to give greater insight into the causal factors influencing the start-ups, and also allowing a comparison between start-ups and those who do not start up. The initial study was taken at a single period over one month controlling for the state of the general economy.

Two samples of pre-start entrepreneurs were taken in Scotland (n = 20) and Massachusetts (n = 18). For each sample the Mann–Whitney test was used to test the hypothesis that the size of networks (median number of relationship) was the same for those starting up (or still seriously trying to start) and those who had given up or were no longer actively pursuing their business idea. In Scotland there was evidence that the two groups did have significantly different network sizes (at the 5 per cent significance level $p = 0.0219$). However, if only those relationships that the entrepreneur considered as being valuable (as measured by them saying it had affected their business plan) were considered, then there was strong support for there being a difference in network size between the two groups (at virtually the 1 per cent significance level, p = 0.0109). In Massachusetts no difference between the two groups was found for valuable relationships. However, when all relationships were included, there was only limited evidence of a positive relationship between network size and start-ups, using a 10 per cent rather than a 5 per cent significance level (p = 0.0412 if two people still seeking to start up are included, or p = 0.0763 if only those already started up are included). In both locations three cases were excluded where their destinations were unknown.

Hence, there is some evidence in Scotland, but less strong evidence in Massachusetts, that those starting firms had larger networks than those not starting. The differences between the two samples may reflect cultural or socio-economic differences. Analysis of the intensity of the relationships proved inconclusive. The results suggest that social networks cannot be omitted from research into new firm formation on the grounds of empirical insignificance. Further research is needed on controlling for various characteristics of the relationships, entrepreneurs (including gender, Aldrich, Reese and Dubini 1989) and businesses. Other approaches to the study of the networks may also prove useful, as is discussed in the next section.

Methodological issues for social network research

Social network analysis considers that individuals are partly characterised by their relationships to one another and the social context within which they operate. Entrepreneurs typically participate in a system which involves many other actors who may influence their decision and the nature of these relations may affect their perceptions, beliefs and actions. Network analysis is concerned with uncovering the patterns of order that underlie the empirical observation of relationships between the various actors (Knoke and Kuklinski 1985), and is therefore potentially useful in improving our understanding of entrepreneurship and regional development.

Curran et al. (1993) argue that much of the theorising and research using the notions of 'network' and 'networking' are conceptually and methodologically poorly realised. They argue that 'networks' are best seen as primarily cultural phenomena, i.e., assets of means, norms and expectations usually linked with behavioural correlates of various kinds and that these, rather than the behavioural correlates, are of prime importance. It is therefore essential that the research methodology of social network studies is given careful consideration. This section discusses some of the methodological issues concerned with network analysis as it may be applied to new firm formation research.

Much research into founders of businesses rely on attribute data which relate to the attitudes, opinions and behaviour of the founders as individuals or as groups, e.g., income, occupation etc. (Scott 1991: 2). However, network analysis considers relational data where other contacts, ties and connections, the group attachments and meetings, relate one actor to another and so cannot be reduced to the properties of the individual actors themselves. Hence these relations are *vis-à-vis* a whole network or system of actors and not of the individual actor. Network analysis can also help to illustrate the various levels of structures within the social systems linking the various actors and so illuminate the entire network.

While each type of data can be collected by similar means (such as questionnaire, observations or from existing documents), the analysis of them tends to vary. The two types of data are conceptionally different approaches to social research; however, they are not opposites or mutually exclusive options for measurement and the use of both can increase explanatory power (Knoke and Kuklinski 1985: 11).

The relationship is not an intrinsic characteristic of either party to the relationship taken in isolation but is a property of the linkage between them with, for example, their individual attributes or characteristics such as age, gender etc. being unchanged. However, the relations are context-specific (e.g., the relationship between an entrepreneur and their bank manager may cease if the firm closes, although most of the characteristics of each actor would be unchanged).

A core theoretical problem for network analysis is to explain the occurrence of different structures of relationships and at a level of individual observation (i.e., individual entrepreneur) to account for variations in linkages to other actors. The empirical task then is to detect the presence of such structures in the network data. The attributes may predict the behaviour of the entrepreneurs only because they are associated with some underlying patterns of relationships, rather than the actual attributes which are important in influencing behaviour. For example, people with higher education adopt innovation sooner, but this may be due to their position within the networks rather than the individual characteristics (Knoke and Burt 1982). The analysis seeks to capture the contextual environment within which actors participate and make their behaviourial decisions.

The analysis can be carried out at a number of levels, the simplest being egocentric network consisting of each individual and all others with which they have a link and the relationship among these links. This has been the type of analysis used in much of the entrepreneurial research into networks. Other levels include dyad level of analysis and triad level which are formed by pairs of actors (nodes) or possible subsets between three actors and their linkages, respectively.

The most important level of analysis is that of the complete network or system. Here the complete information of the patterning of ties among all the actors is used in order to assert the existence of distinct positions or roles within the system and to describe the nature of relations among these positions (Knoke and Kuklinski 1985: 17). This higher level of analysis allows the emergence of structural properties of the network which cannot be deduced from the lower-level types of analysis.

For example, there may be two communities of potential entrepreneurs with similar egocentric, dyadic or triadic structures in their networks for discussing ideas and new business proposals. However, if there are difficulties in the first system in communicating directly or indirectly except among fragmented subgroups, while in the second system there is complete communication among all actors in the system and a high level of integration among the different subgroups, then we would expect to have greater flow of information in the second system. Hence, there is a need for analysis of entrepreneurial networks from the total system's perspective, rather than simply the egocentric perspective of considering individual entrepreneurs. Such a system could perhaps be considered from the perspective of a geographical area over most of the entrepreneurial network, although for many industries, such as computers, the relevant network is international.

A further difficulty of network analysis is in data collection, particularly in sampling (Bernard, Killworth and Sailer 1980). There is a need to specify the boundary as the limits to any network but this may be unclear in reality and there may be no obvious limits to the network. The basis of this boundary will be defined with regard to those relationships which are considered to be significant, others defined as relatively inconsequential in terms of influencing the business.

In summary, a large number of methodological issues need to be taken into account when considering network analysis and the methodological framework for many studies needs to be clarified. However, this is likely to lead to a considerably deeper understanding of the process of new firm formation.

POLICY IMPLICATIONS

There are a number of direct implications of greater understanding of social networks for the development and improvement of policies to aid new firm formation. Implications for team-based new firm initiatives, small business clubs, venture capital and community entrepreneurs are briefly considered here.

A number of policies have been developed specifically to support team-based approaches to new firm formation (for example, through several local enterprise companies in Scotland and elsewhere, although so far the published evidence is very limited). These involve groups of potential new firm founders being brought together and encouraged to build teams with complementary expertise. Interestingly, most of research on social networks and new firm formation concerns those developed by a single entrepreneur and there is little on the development of networks of teams starting up new businesses. More research is needed on the extent to which the separate networks of individuals overlap or are used to complement one another.

In theory, a team-based approach should bring together a number of networks, each skewed towards the expertise or background of each individual team member, and so the value of the network could potentially expand proportionally, after overlaps have been taken into account. However, each member of the team may only allow limited access of the other team members to their own particular network and the potential benefits may not be realised to their full extent. It may be that rather than building teams to run companies, greater effort should be spent on developing the networks among the participants to such programmes, so that even if they start up alone they may still benefit from the full networks of others.

There are many small business clubs, often started up and supported by local enterprise trusts. Their purpose has often been to bring small and new business owners together to exchange experience and to serve as a forum for discussion and presentation by experts on specific issues of concern (for example, tax). It may be that these clubs offer a greater opportunity to systematically expand networking among the entrepreneurs, with less focus on the external speakers and more on developing links within the club and with others outside of the club. In addition, these clubs are often only available to people who have already started up in business, and it may well be that those at the pre-start-up stage may benefit to a greater extent from membership of such clubs, or some other suitable forum at which they can develop networks.

Bygraves (1988) shows that networks provide venture capitalists with information on possible good investment opportunities and may be particularly appropriate in an environment where there is a need to generate a constant stream of new 'deals'. The development of science parks was often accompanied by attempts to create networks among those on the park, particularly as the businesses often shared characteristics of advanced technology (Smith 1991).

Johannisson and Nilsson (1989) argue that personal networks are also useful for the community entrepreneurs (i.e., entrepreneurs who facilitate entrepreneurial events rather than promoting individual business ventures) and their social networks can perhaps help bridge the commercial and social aspects of their endeavour. They argue that for the public sector, as well as for large corporations and small businesses, networking is the main vehicle for venture initiation, development and success (see Thorelli 1986). Hence, they argue that networking is crucial to the success of economic development agencies.

CONCLUSIONS

This chapter has argued that social networks offer important theoretical and empirical insights for research into new firm formation and regional development. Indeed, by ignoring such networks our understanding of the underlying processes will be somewhat limited. However, the approach to analysing such networks is important and a number of methodological issues have been raised. Evidence was presented that suggested that size of social networks was associated with whether or not firms failed to start their businesses and so the role of networks cannot be ignored due to their lack of empirical importance.

The implications for policy in the areas of team-based new firm initiatives, small business clubs, venture capital and community entrepreneurs were briefly analysed. It was argued that greater understanding of the role of social networks could help to develop and adapt appropriate policies.

ACKNOWLEDGEMENTS

I would like to thank Beverley Christy, Alasdair McNicoll, Quadrangle Consulting Ltd and Robin Henderson for their kind help in preparing this chapter. All errors and views expressed remain, of course, those of the author.

BIBLIOGRAPHY

Aldrich, H., Reese, P. R. and Dubini, P. (1989) 'Woman on the verge of a breakthrough: networking among entrepreneurs in the United States and Italy', *Entrepreneurship and Regional Development*, 1: 339–56.

Bernard, H. R., Killworth, P. D. and Sailer, L. (1980) 'Informant accuracy in Social Network Data IV: a comparison of clique-level structure in behavioral and cognitive network data', *Social Networks*, 2: 191–218.

Bhide, A. (1994) 'How entrepreneurs craft strategies that work', *Harvard Business Review*, March–April: 150–61.

Birley, S. (1985) 'The role of networks in the entrepreneurial process', *The Journal of Business Venturing*, 1: 107–17.

Birley, S., Cromie, S. and Myers, A. (1991) 'Entrepreneurial networks: their emergence in Ireland and overseas', *International Small Business*, 9, 4: 56–74.

Brockhaus, R. H. and Horwitz, P. S. (1986) 'The psychology of the entrepreneur', in D. Sexton and R. Smilor (eds) *The Encyclopedia of Entrepreneurship*, Englewood Cliffs, NJ: Prentice-Hall.

Butler, J. E. and Hansen, G. S. (1991) 'Network evolution, entrepreneurial success and regional development', *Entrepreneurship and Regional Development*, 3: 1–16.

Bygraves, W. D. (1988) 'The structure of investment networks of venture capital firms', *Journal of Business Venturing*, 3: 137–57.

Camagni, R. P. (1992) 'Development scenarios and policies guidelines for the lagging Regions in the 1990s', *Regional Studies*, 26: 361–74.

Chandler, G. N. and Hanks, S. H. (1994) 'Under competence, the environment and the venture performance', *Entrepreneurship Theory and Practice* 18, 3: 77–89.

Charan, R. (1991) 'How networks reshape organisations – for results', *Harvard Business Review*, September–October: 104–15.

Cuevas, J. G. (1994) 'Towards a taxonomy of entrepreneurial theories', *International Small Business Journal*, 12, 4: 77–88.

Curran, J., Jarvis, R., Blackburn, R. A. and Black, S. (1993) 'Networks and small firms: constructs, methodological strategies and some findings', *International Small Business Journal*, 11, 2: 13–25.

Dubini, P. and Aldrich, H. (1991) 'Personal and extended networks are central to the entrepreneurial process', *Journal of Business Venturing*, 6: 305–13.

Filion, L. J. (1990) 'Entrepreneurial performance, networking, vision and relations', *Journal of Small Business and Entrepreneurship*, 7, 3: 3–13.

Garofoli, G. (1994) 'New firm formation and regional development: the Italian case', *Regional Studies*, 28, 4: 381–94.

Gartner, W. B., Shaver, K. T., Datewood, N. E. and Katz, J. A. (1994) 'Finding the entrepreneur in entrepreneurship', *Entrepreneurship Theory and Practice*, 18, 3: 5–9.

Halal, W. E., Geranmayeh, A. and Pourdehnad, J. (1993) *Internal Markets*, New York: Wylie.

Harrison, R. T. and Leitch, C. M. (1994) 'Entrepreneurship and leadership: the implications for education and development', *Entrepreneurship and Regional Development*, 6: 111–25.

Hanson, N. (1992) 'Competition, trust and reciprocity in the development of innovative regional milieux', *Papers in Regional Science*, 71, 2: 95–105.

Hutt, R. W. and Van Hook, B. L. (1988) 'The use of outside advisers in venture start-ups', in B. A. Kirchoff, W. A. Long, W. E. McMullan, K. H. Vesper and W. R. Wetzel (eds) *Frontiers of Entrepreneurship Research 1988*, Wellesley, MA: Babson College.

Johannisson, B. (1986) 'Network strategies. Management technology for entrepreneurship and change', *International Small Business Journal*, 5, 1: 19–30.

Johannisson, B. and Nilsson, A. (1989) 'Community entrepreneurs: networking for local development', *Entrepreneurship and Regional Development*, 1: 3–19.

Knoke, D. and Burt, R. S. (1982) 'Prominence', in R. S. Burt and M. J. Minor (eds) *Applied Network Analysis: Structural Methodology for Empirical Social Research*, London: Sage.

Knoke, D. and Kuklinski, J. H. (1985) *Network Analysis*, London: Sage.

Krugman, P. (1991) 'Increasing returns and economic geography', *Journal of Political Economy*, 99: 483–99.

Lorenz, E. H. (1988) 'Neither friends nor strangers: informal networks of subcontracting in French industry', in D. Gambetta (ed.) *Trust: Making and Breaking Cooperative Relations*, Oxford: Basil Blackwell.

McKiernan, P. (1992) *Strategies of Growth: Maturity, Recovery and Internationalisation*, London: Routledge.

Pagden, A. (1988) 'The destruction of trust and its economic consequences in the case of 18th-Century Naples', in D.Gambetta (ed.) *Trust: Making and Breaking Cooperative Relations*, Oxford: Blackwell.

Porter, M. E. (1990) *The Competitive Advantage of Nations*, New York: The Free Press.

Reynolds, P., Storey, D. J. and Westhead, P. (1994) 'Cross-national comparisons of the variation in new firm formation rates', *Regional Studies*, 28, 4: 443–56.

Ronstadt, R. and Peterson, R. (1988) *Networking for Success: KnowWho plus KnowHow*, Natick MA: Lord.

Rush, B. L., Graham, J. B., and Long, W. A. (1987) 'The use of peer networks in the start-up process', in N. C. Churchill, J. A. Horneday, B. A. Kirchhoff, Q. J. Krasner, and K. H. Vesper (eds) *Frontiers of Entrepreneurship Research 1987*, Wellesley MA: Babson College.

Scott, J. (1991) *Social Network Analysis*, London: Sage.

Shapero, A. and Sokol, L. (1982) 'The social dimensions of entrepreneurship', in L. A. Kent, D. L. Sexton and K. H. Vesper (eds), *Encyclopedia of Entrepreneurship*, Englewood Cliffs NJ: Prentice-Hall.

Shaver, K. G. and Scott, L. R. (1991) 'Person, process, and choice: the psychology of new venture creation', *Entrepreneurship Theory and Practice*, 16, 2: 23–45.

Smith, H. L. (1991) 'Industry – academic links: the case of Oxford University', *Environment and Planning C: Government and Policy*, 9, 403–16.

Thorelli, H. B. (1986) 'Networks: between markets and hierarchies', *Strategic Management Journal*, 7, 37–51.

You, J. and Wilkinson, F. (1994) 'Competition and co-operation: towards understanding industrial districts', *Review of Political Economy*, 6, 3: 259–78.

8 The business birth rate, real services and networking

Strategic options

Geoff Whittam and Catherine Kirk

INTRODUCTION

This chapter is an examination of the birth rate strategy employed by Scottish Enterprise which aims to improve the stock of companies within Scotland. The launch of the strategy can be dated from 1993 with the publication of *Scotland's Business Birth Rate* (Scottish Enterprise and Scottish Business Insider 1993). This has been updated to *Improving the Business Birth Rate: A Strategy for Scotland* (Scottish Enterprise 1993). The document identifies three ways in which the birth rate can be increased: first, increasing the number of new businesses created in Scotland; second, increasing the number of new starts that survive; and third, increasing the number of new starts that subsequently achieve significant growth. It is claimed that the relatively low stock of firms within the Scottish economy is one of the major obstacles to the achievement of significant economic growth and job creation within Scotland.[1]

Like other industrial economies the Scottish economy has witnessed an increase in de-concentration over the last two decades.[2] This de-concentration has occurred due to the development of new production methods, such as flexible specialisation, so that new market niches can be exploited (Piore and Sabel 1984).

This decrease in the importance of large firms has focused attention on the small and medium sized enterprise (SME) sector for the generation of economic growth and employment. It is of crucial importance for policy-makers to determine how best to increase the stock of firms. The stock of firms can be increased by accelerating the birth rate, by slowing the death rate, or both. Within the policy statements of Scottish Enterprise there has been a widening of focus from that found in the original document (Scottish Enterprise and Scottish Business Insider 1993) with its emphasis on new firm formation. A much broader approach is to be found in the later statement (Scottish Enterprise 1993) which places a greater emphasis on policy for existing firms.

The first section of this chapter examines the birth rate of firms within the Scottish economy by utilising the 1991 VAT registrations and de-registrations of businesses.[3] What is apparent is the importance that needs to be attached to de-registrations. The second section is a critical analysis of the policy objectives of Scottish Enterprise. While acknowledging the progress that has been made towards developing a strategy for new and existing firms, current policy is still fragmented. The third section examines a case study where a coherent established policy initiative for SMEs has been established. A proposal is given in the conclusion that Scottish Enterprise initiatives could be developed further to achieve an increase in the stock of businesses in Scotland.

BIRTH RATES

We have a problem – too few new companies.

(Scottish Enterprise and Scottish Business Insider 1993: 3)

Scotland has fewer companies per capita than other areas of the United Kingdom. Scottish Enterprise has identified a low company birth rate as one of the contributing factors. The birth rate is low when compared with Southern England.[4] It is claimed that if Scotland's birth rate is not increased, the stock of firms, while rising, will remain lower than other areas, thus impeding potential economic growth. The view of Scottish Enterprise is that:

For some years, perhaps decades, we in Scotland have been aware that as a nation we seem to have lost some of that entrepreneurial drive for which the Scots were once famed. Whether manifested in our obvious lack of privately-run growth companies, or in our failure to generate businesses capable of dominating global markets from a Scottish base, it is apparent we have a fundamental economic problem. The problem can be traced right back to a *simple lack of companies* in Scotland. We do not create as many new businesses as other parts of the United Kingdom, let alone our key competitor nations.

(Scottish Enterprise and Scottish Business Insider 1993: 1; emphasis added)

Table 8.1 examines the data on new firm birth rates. Scotland and the North of England have the lowest rate of new births.[5]

The figure for Scotland and the North of England is 60 new firms per 10,000 of the working population, compared with 103 in the South East and a United Kingdom average of 83. Both Scotland and the North of England, however, have increased their new firm birth rate at a faster rate, achieving a 50 per cent increase over the decade 1980 to 1990 compared with 43 per cent for the South East of England and an average of 38 per cent for the United Kingdom as a whole.

The link inferred by Scottish Enterprise between high birth rates and increasing stocks of firms is questionable. For example, as Table 8.2 shows, the South East, with a high birth rate of 16 per cent,[6] achieved a 46 per cent net growth in its stock of companies between 1979 and 1990. The North West region, with the second-highest birth rate, 14 per cent, achieved net growth in its stock of companies of only 19 per cent. Over the same period, Scotland which had a birth rate of 12 per cent, recorded growth in the stock of its companies of 23 per cent. At a more disaggregated level, Strathclyde region had a birth rate similar to Southern England, 13 per cent, but only achieved a 22 per cent increase in its stock compared with a 38 per cent

Table 8.1 Birth rate of VAT registered firms per 10,000 of the official work-force[a]

Region/area	1980	1990	% Change 1980–90
Scotland	40	60	50
South East	72	103	43
East Anglia	71	86	24
South West	75	94	25
West Midlands	55	75	36
East Midlands	59	78	32
Yorks & Humberside	53	72	36
North West	51	73	43
North	40	60	50
Wales	57	77	35
Northern Ireland	58	50	−14
UK	60	83	38
Great Britain	60	84	40
Southern England[b]	72	100	39

Source: Kirk and Whittam (1994) from Department of Employment (1991, 1992)
Notes: (a) As defined by the Department of Employment (1991, 1992).
   (b) South East, East Anglia and South West

increase in Southern England. At an even more disaggregated level, the birth rate in Glasgow City at 14 per cent was higher than in Southern England, but Glasgow experienced no overall growth in its stock of companies.

Improving the stock of firms may well depend as much on the slowing down of the death rate as to the improvement of the birth rate. A further examination of Table 8.2 reveals that not only does the South East have a high birth rate, but it also has a low death rate. On average across the decade there was a 3 per cent difference between births and deaths in the South East. By comparison, the North West, recorded a difference of just over 1 per cent between births and deaths over the decade. Similarly, Strathclyde Region had a less than 2 per cent difference between the birth and death rates over the 10 years; Glasgow, however, recorded equal rates, indicating turbulence, but zero growth in terms of the stock of firms.

In 1979 the death rate in Scotland was only 9 per cent of its existing stock of companies, by 1989 it was 11 per cent. Had the death rate in Scotland been retained at 9 per cent throughout the decade approximately 20,000 enterprises and 440,000 jobs might still have been in existence.[7] The South East, by comparison, not only increased its birth rate throughout the decade, it also reduced its death rate from 13 per cent of the 1979 stock to 12 per cent of the 1989 stock.

Table 8.2 Average birth, death and growth rates, 1980–90*

Region/area	Birth rate	Death rate	Net growth
South East	16	12	46
East Anglia	12	9	34
South West	12	10	33
East Midlands	13	10	32
West Midlands	13	11	29
Yorks & Humberside	13	11	24
Wales	11	9	23
Scotland	12	10	23
Northern Ireland	7	6	22
North	12	11	21
North West	14	12	19
UK	13	11	33
Southern England	13	10	38
Strathclyde	13	11	22
Glasgow	14	14	zero

Source: Kirk and Whittam (1994) from Employment Department (1991, 1992)
Notes: * (Percentage of previous year's stock)

The above suggests that both the birth and death rate are important when trying to improve the stock of companies. This point is not lost on Scottish Enterprise, whose strategy for achieving economic growth is not only to increase the number of new businesses in Scotland but also to increase the number of new start-ups that survive and to increase the number of new start-ups that subsequently achieve significant growth (Scottish Enterprise 1993). These three objectives are to be pursued via six priorities which are based on underlying principles. The principles include an emphasis on utilising the existing support mechanisms, but: 'Two important working assumptions behind the strategy are that individual action can make a difference, and that change starts with yourself' (Scottish Enterprise 1993: 4).

The first of these priorities is to unlock the potential entrepreneurial talent which has been identified by research undertaken by Scottish Enterprise. The second priority involves improving the business environment and giving more encouragement to new starts by means of formal and informal support networks. The third priority relates to improving access to the available finance. The fourth identifies the necessity of policy specifically aimed at sections of the population underrepresented in terms of business ownership, to encourage them to become small business owners. The penultimate strategy involves policy formulation for ensuring new starts in key sectors. The final priority concerns support for the small number of companies which may achieve substantial growth.

The six priorities can be summarised into two broad categories: the improving of information provision and the development of better institutional arrangements consisting of the establishment of new and the improvement of existing networks.

These broad categories are not mutually exclusive. The improvement of information could for example encourage potential entrepreneurs to set up, inform them of the existing support networks, inform them of the types of finance available and lead to a widening of the entrepreneurial base. An improved institutional framework could lead to an improved business environment which may result in start-ups in key sectors and support for growth companies.

Finance, which is a major problem for SMEs in many economies, is treated separately.

PROBLEMS WITH POLICY ANALYSIS AND DELIVERY

The previous section summarises the Scottish Enterprise strategy aimed at improving the stock of companies. The analysis and proposed delivery of this policy is problematic. Criticism of the analysis relates to the research methodology and directly questions policy delivery relating to point one of the six priorities. Scottish Enterprise found that more people say they would like to start businesses than actually do, and deduce from this that potential entrepreneurship is waiting to be tapped. However, there is often a marked difference between what people say and what they mean. An individual may say they would like to run their own business but this does not mean that they have a sustainable proposal, nor that they would or should do anything about the idea. It is often not advisable to formulate policy on the basis of what people say. The rationale for income tax cuts in the 1980s was based on the premise that individuals would work more hours if the rate per hour were greater. Recent research (Rees and Shah 1993) demonstrates that the self-employed reacted by working fewer hours post tax cuts. This suggests that 'society's interest' is not necessarily served by agencies responding to 'self-interested' groups within society.

There are two main problems associated with finance for small firms. First, access to small sums of capital may have more to do with the cost of processing and monitoring the contract rather than to any adverse reaction from banks towards small firms. As Storey (1994) points out, the costs are similar for small and large contracts, so why should banks bother with the small, less profitable ones. Second, information asymmetries exist due to the lack of information available to the financial sector about specific small firms. Compared with large firms, small firms are more likely to fail, thereby presenting a greater risk, so it is hardly surprising that finance is relatively more expensive for small firms.

Policy delivery is to be achieved through a mixture of formal and informal business support services and contacts. It is argued that these 'networks' which consist of 'family and friends, colleagues and business contacts' will assist in the achievement of some of the priorities, such as improving the business environment (Scottish Enterprise 1993: 9). Other networks are more formal and specific and will be 'ensuring specialist business support networks are available to meet the specific needs of high-tech businesses' (Scottish Enterprise 1993: 15) which relates directly to priority five – developing start-ups in key sectors. These are noble aims but the outcome may be more difficult to realise.

What is missing from the strategy and policy delivery proposals is an identification of the major disadvantage from which small firms suffer, that of scale economies. Starting from this premise, policy delivery should be concentrated on how this fundamental problem can be overcome – the provision of agglomerations. An examination of successful economies based on SMEs, such as, 'the Third Italy' and Baden–Württemberg reveals that their success is based on the provision of intangible investments in a democratic and accountable framework. Scale economies for the SME sector in these regions are achieved via the promotion of co-operation between the firms themselves and the private and public institutions which have been developed to support them. The success of existing SMEs has led to the growth of the stock of firms.

This possible role for government policy is identified in the findings of a cross-national project which examined the variation in new firm formation rates in seven economically advanced countries: France, Germany (West), Ireland, Italy, Sweden, the United Kingdom and the United States (Reynolds, Storey and Westhead 1994). Summarising the conclusions and policy recommendations, Reynolds, Storey and Westhead concluded that three processes have a positive impact on firm birth rates:

> growth in demand, indicated by population growth and growth in income . . . a population of business organizations dominated by small firms . . . a dense, urbanized context, reflecting the advantages of agglomeration, presumably including the benefits of access to customers, sources of supply and capital, as well as awareness of competitors' actions
> (Reynolds, Storey and Westhead 1994: 453)

Clearly, the first of these processes is dependent on government macro-economic objectives. The other two processes, however, deal directly with policy possibilities which may increase firm start-ups. While agreeing with Reynolds, Storey and Westhead that agglomeration resulting from urban development took a very long time to develop, and although the dense, urbanised areas may not be desirable, the *advantages* of agglomeration could be developed through policy initiatives. Economies of scale can result through the promotion of co-operation in the input markets involving such activities as marketing, export promotion and research and development, the type of activities which individual small firms cannot afford in sufficient quantity or quality. Other economies can arise by the provision of infrastructural investments such as transport and training. This type of policy delivery is found at the heart of successful regional economies such as Emilia–Romagna.

POLICY DELIVERY IN EMILIA–ROMAGNA

The region of Emilia–Romagna reflects the de-concentration of firms witnessed in most industrial societies over the last two decades. The economic success of the region can be attributed, in part, to the proactive industrial policy targeted at the SMEs. The objective is to achieve both internal and external economies of scale within the small firm sector. This has been achieved by means of an institutional framework involving all the key players in the region. There are positive incentives to register as a small artisan firm. The most important is having access to loans at favourable rates and the benefits that arise from being a member of the artisan association.

Co-operation between the local authority and the artisan association began with the acquisition of land at favourable prices for the development of artisan parks (Brusco 1982). From this modest beginning, a long co-operative relationship developed between the local authorities, the financial institutions and the artisan associations. By belonging to the association a small firm can make use of the services provided. Typically, these include the supply of administrative services such as, accountancy, financial and marketing activities. This provision of 'real services' is extending economies of scale in administrative activities to the small firm sector. The provision of administrative services by the artisan associations to member firms is likened to the functions provided by the head office of a large firm to its various departments (Harrison 1990).

Other activities by some of the local artisan associations include the operation of a loan guarantee scheme. For example, within Modena, a province within Emilia–Romagna, loans are made available to member firms through a financial consortium. The scheme is administered by a board of representatives from the artisan associations and member firms. The actual loan guarantee fund consists of contributions from member firms, in the form of membership fees, plus funds from local and national government. To obtain a loan a member firm must gain the approval of the local artisan association and the financial consortium. If the firm is successful the report is sent to a bank with a loan guarantee (Best 1990). This approach overcomes the problem of asymmetric information identified earlier and ensures no discrimination on the grounds of scale economies which perhaps occurs within SME sectors faced with a highly centralised banking system. The scheme results in SMEs obtaining loans below the market rate of interest.

The benefits arising out of co-operative external economies can be demonstrated with a game-theoretical approach (Oughton and Whittam 1994). What is crucial for the achievement of the optimal co-operative conclusion to the Prisoner's Dilemma is that enough weight is attached to future games and that there is an effective enforcement mechanism. Within the above loan guarantee scheme there is a dual enforcement mechanism. First, ideas are well vetted by key players from within the region and, second, if firms default from the scheme they can be excluded from future plays. Similarly, within the artisan associations an enforcement mechanism exists. To receive the benefits firms have to be members and firms that abuse the system can be excluded from membership.

Policy initiatives in other areas, such as research and development, training and export promotion, have led to further economies of scale being achieved. These initiatives are undertaken by a service centre system (Cooke and Morgan 1991). At a regional level economic development is the responsibility of the Regional Board for Economic Development (ERVET). ERVET also organises support services for SMEs either directly or through sector specific service centres. These support services include access to new technology and computer-aided design, which would normally be beyond the reach of individual small firms. While the initial cost of the centres is borne by public financing, this is limited to a period of about five years in a movement towards self-financing. So the services to SMEs are not free but are offered below the prevailing market price.

This structured framework geared to enhancing the competitiveness of the SME sector has clear policy implications. The framework is aimed at overcoming the disadvantages which SMEs suffer in terms of economies of scale and, in particular, finance. The achievement of these economies should result in an increase in the survival of the existing stock of firms and ensure that the firms experiencing growth will have access to the necessary support. The democratic framework should ensure good service provision.

CONCLUSIONS AND POLICY RECOMMENDATIONS

As noted earlier, there has been a movement towards the development of a networking system in the Scottish Enterprise strategy. Within certain industries the envisaged policies are already developing. Turok (1993), for example, in discussing the Scottish electronics industry, notes the establishment of the Supplier Development Programme, 'a small team of engineers working to improve the management skills and quality controls in a group of local sub-contractors' (Turok 1993: 415). The objective is to secure more local sourcing for the electronics industry. While this initiative may be limited 'in view of the considerable potential, it ought to be expanded, given a wider remit and a higher profile' (Turok 1993: 415). This is a move in the right direction. The provision of these services should lead to the achievement of some scale economies for subcontracting firms within the Scottish electronics industry.

The emphasis on networking in Scottish Enterprise policy statements is welcome, but the policy recommendations fall short of a comprehensive and effective system of networking. The delivery of 'real services' could lead to SMEs overcoming their fundamental weakness – lack of scale economies. The existing policy recommendations of relying on existing partnerships and networking arrangements could, at best, be described as patchy and undemocratic. The new proposed networking arrangements must seek to provide services required by SMEs. This suggests a decision-making framework which should involve all the key players – the SMEs themselves, the financial institutions, Scottish Enterprise and the local authorities.

The brief case study outlined the type of approach that is required for the achievement of scale economies through the development of a co-operative approach to economic growth and development. The provision of services in this fashion could lead to the establishment of new firms and growth in existing firms once entrepreneurs are aware of the support networks available to them. Existing firms should gain a competitive edge through access to the latest technology, and advantages in advertising and export promotion. This comprehensive package could lead to new firm creation, growth and survival of existing firms, resulting in an increase in the stock of companies within Scotland.

NOTES

1 For impact of this strategy on job creation in the 1980s see Kirk and Whittam (1994).
2 De-concentration is referring to the decline in the number of firms with over 500 employees.
3 Ganguly (1982) explains the validity and some limitations of using VAT data.
4 Consisting of the South East, the South West and East Anglia.
5 Measured as a proportion of the working population.
6 Measured as a proportion of the previous year's stock of firms.
7 Crude estimation retaining death rate at 9 per cent and average size of Scottish firm.

BIBLIOGRAPHY

Best, M. (1990) *The New Competition: Institutions of Industrial Restructuring*, Cambridge: Polity.
Brusco, S. (1982) 'The Emilian model: productive decentralisation and social intergration', *Cambridge Journal of Economics*, 6: 167–84.
Cooke, P. and Morgan K. (1991) 'The intelligent region: industrial and institutional innovation in Emilia–Romagna', Regional Industrial Research Report No. 7, University College, Cardiff.
Department of Employment (1991) *VAT Registrations and Deregistrations: County and District Analyses 1980–1990*, London: HMSO.
Department of Employment (1992) *Employment Gazette: Historical Supplement 3*, 100, 6: 48–53.
Department of Employment *Employment Gazette*, various.
ERVET (1991) *Ervet System's Activities and Structure*, Bologna: ERVET.
Ganguly, P. (1982) *British Business*, 29 January: 204–7.
Harrison, B. (1990) 'Industrial districts: old wine in new bottles?', Working Paper 90–35, School of Urban and Public Affairs Working Paper Series.
Kirk, C. and Whittam, G. (1994) 'Small firms, birth rates and jobs', Discussion Paper No. 23, Department of Economics, Glasgow Caledonian University.
Oughton, C. and Whittam, G. (1994) 'Competition and cooperation in the small firm sector', Discussion Paper in Economics 9401, University of Glasgow.
Piore, M. and Sabel, C. (1984) *The Second Industrial Divide*, New York: Basic Books.
Rees, H. and Shah, A. (1993) 'The characteristics of the self-employed: the supply of labour', in J. Atkinson and D. J. Storey (eds), *Employment, The Small Firm and the Labour Market*, London: Routledge.
Reynolds, P., Storey, D. J. and Westhead, P. (1994) 'Cross-national comparisons of the variation in new firm formation rates', *Regional Studies*, 28, 4: 443–56.
Scottish Enterprise and Scottish Business Insider (1993) *Scotland's Business Birth Rate*, Glasgow.

Scottish Enterprise (1993) *Improving the Business Birth Rate: A Strategy for Scotland*, Glasgow.

Storey, D. J. (1994) *Understanding the Small Business Sector*, London: Routledge.

Turok, I. (1993) 'Inward investment and local linkages: how deeply embedded is Silicon Glen?', *Regional Studies*, 27, 5: 401–18.

9 Networks and new enterprise development in Russia
A case study of the Yaroslavl region

John Struthers, Alistair Young and John Wylie

INTRODUCTION

With the collapse of central planning in Russia, there are undoubtedly opportunities for new enterprise development which did not exist before. These may take the form of the transformation of large state enterprises into entrepreneurial private enterprises, perhaps through being split up into smaller and more economically efficient units; or they may involve the creation of completely new units, possibly in areas of economic activity neglected by the previous system. Unfortunately, it is often very difficult to take advantage of these opportunities. The difficulties are a consequence of the fact that market institutions have not yet taken firm root in the Russian economy; to quote Marx out of context, the new system is 'still stamped with the birthmarks of the old society from whose womb it has emerged' (1875 [1974]: 346).

Because of the uncertainties to which this gives rise, which are detailed in the second and third sections of this chapter, we argue in the fourth section that those entrepreneurs will have the best chance of success who are able to link up with effective networks; these need not have been initially created for the purpose of business development, but must be capable of adaptation to this purpose. In the fifth section we examine the possible networks which might help to promote new enterprise formation in Russia, and develop an argument to suggest that academic institutions may serve as focal points for such a network. The final section tests this proposition against evidence drawn from a case study of the Yaroslavl region.

UNCERTAINTY IN THE TRANSITIONAL ECONOMY

The most obvious source of uncertainty in the process of transition has been macro-economic instability. After decades of price stability, consumer prices rose in 1990 by 5.6 per cent, in 1991 by 92.7 per cent and in 1992 by 1,353 per cent (IMF 1993: Table A13). The real wage index is estimated to have fallen from 100 in 1990 to 50 by April 1992, recovering to 76 by the year end (Blanchard et al. 1993: 162). Real industrial production fell by a quarter between December 1991 and January 1993; real consumer expenditure, by 55 per cent from the first quarter of 1991 to the final quarter of 1992 (Blanchard et al. 1993: 163–4).

Micro-economic uncertainties are also characteristic of the transition. Remnants of the old centralised supply system, based on decisions by ministries, coexist with an inadequately developed market trading system. Blanchard et al. estimate that in mid-1992 40 per cent of inter-enterprise trade was still directed by state orders rather than allocated through the market (Blanchard et al. 1993: 22).

Political uncertainties are also of great significance. One general source of uncertainty, of course, which was exacerbated by the elections late in 1993, concerns the long-run stability of the democratic process. More particularly, there is the question of the degree of political commitment to the economic reforms (see Rutland 1992; Åslund 1993). At the centre, the strongly pro-reform Gaidar administration has been replaced by one which takes a more cautious approach to change. Of perhaps more importance, however, especially for entrepreneurs seeking to create small new enterprises, is the extent to which local authorities are willing to put their weight behind the liberalisation of the economy. As the power of the centre has waned, local governments have begun at least in part to fill the vacuum (Blanchard et al. 1993: Chapter 2). Their inheritance of local public utilities gives them considerable *de facto* power, and they have also claimed the right to exercise some of the control functions over enterprises which formerly resided in the ministries.

Many of the local administrations are unenthusiastic about privatisation, perhaps even to the extent of being prepared to sabotage the attempts of new enterprises to become established. An example is the case of the Smolensk metal recycling co-operative. This was denied supplies by a local official, illegally, as it turned out; but although the decision was overthrown by the courts the co-operative only received compensation for 20 per cent of its losses (*Isvestiya*: 14 December 1991; cited in Rutland 1992: 54 n.155). This example is interesting, not only as an illustration of the ability of local governments to obstruct enterprises, but also because it serves as a reminder of the ill-defined character of property rights in Russia at the present time. The widespread lack of clarity in the definition of property rights in Russia is an aspect of the more general problem of the serious underdevelopment of market institutions. All market activities involve transactions costs: the costs of negotiating, monitoring and enforcing contracts. In the absence of well-established market institutions, such costs are very high.

OPPORTUNISM IN THE TRANSITIONAL ECONOMY

Since the work of Williamson (1975, 1981), building on Coase (1937), economists have attempted to address the efficiency characteristics of different types of economic organisation. The central thrust to these approaches is to view the 'transaction' as the basic unit of analysis and to focus on alternative cost configurations of different types of business organisation.

Williamson's transaction cost analysis is founded on two basic 'behaviourial assumptions' on the part of managers; – *bounded rationality* and *opportunism*; as well as three 'principles of organisational design' – *asset specificity, externality* and *hierarchical decomposition*. Bounded rationality refers to economic decision-making by agents which although supposedly rational, is limited or 'bounded' by incomplete information. Opportunism implies greater uncertainty at the centre as agents pursue their self-interests often in a random and unpredictable way. Asset specificity refers to the end result of the specialisation process (of equipment and labour) in which resources which are utilised in one type of production may have little productive value in another activity. Externality is where individual agents try to satisfy private goals which may not be consistent with the stated goals of the organisation. Hierarchical decomposition refers to the possibility of splitting or subdividing the internal management structure in order to make it more effective.

The consequences of the above characteristics for the transaction costs of any system is summarised in Williamson's term 'information impactedness'. This 'exists when the true underlying circumstances relevant to the transaction . . . are known to one or more parties, but cannot be costlessly discerned by or displayed for others' (Williamson 1975: 31). The end result is the spread of opportunistic behaviour which requires policing or monitoring – an additional cost on enterprises.

The relevance of the above considerations to a transitional economy can perhaps be further highlighted with reference to Principal–Agent theory. Based on the work of Mirrlees (1976), Grossman and Hart (1983) and Jensen and Meckling (1976), the central idea of Principal–Agent theory is that organisations are managed by two separate categories of people: the principal (usually the owner), and others employed by the principal with delegated authority over a particular decision-making activity, the agent(s). In such a set-up, because there is no guarantee that the agent(s) will always act in the best interests of the principal, costs are incurred by the enterprise in obviating possible conflicts of objectives. These costs include the costs involved in restructuring, monitoring and/or the bonding of contracts between, for example, shareholders and managers or employees and managers.

Several analysts have applied Principal–Agent theory to the problems of transition in Eastern Europe. This is especially relevant in the wake of recent privatisation policies, many of which have been facilitated by government-backed voucher schemes. In this context, principals may be seen as those stakeholders whose interests the privatisation scheme is meant to serve: the voucher-holders most obviously, but ultimately the society at large. The agents, by contrast, are the enterprise 'insiders', the managers and workers within the former state enterprises. Frydman and Rapaczynski (1993) highlight both the positive and negative roles of insiders within Eastern European enterprises currently undergoing transformation. According to them, privatisation in Eastern Europe must entail the depoliticisation of economic decision-making: the separation of the enterprise sector from the state apparatus, with the creation of a new institutional structure of corporate governance which assists the privatisation process. Such a delicate balancing act during a period of uncertainty is problematic, especially when set against the backdrop of 'rent-seekers' – whether rent-seeking takes the form of officials who continue to perceive the state sector as a source of patronage or, perhaps more innocently, the continuing demands on the part of state enterprise managers for subsidies from the centre.

Set against this background, any move towards a new institutional structure of corporate governance for enterprises in Eastern Europe will require that the vested interests of the incumbent insiders (in this case management and labour), be challenged. Incentives will need to be changed in order to stifle the presumed entitlements of the insiders to ownership of the newly privatised enterprises. As well as dealing with agency costs, successful corporate governance arrangements accompanying a privatisation programme will facilitate the attraction of external sources of funding necessary for economic restructuring.

To quote Frydman and Rapaczynski (1993: 41), the following are examples of the effects of 'incentives incompatibility' between 'owners' and 'managers' (insiders and outsiders) in enterprises in Eastern Europe – 'shirking' among those agents who can appropriate benefits for themselves; perquisites, empire-building; 'moonlighting', and extreme 'risk-aversion' (or excessive short-termism).

Though these agency problems exist to a greater or lesser extent within every economic system, Frydman and Rapaczynski suggest reasons why the problems may be particularly acute within post-communist economies. First, monitoring is more difficult. In the West it is assisted by proper accounting conventions, an external economic environment against which management performance can be measured (e.g., the discipline of capital markets, share prices and the like) as well as decentralised financial institutions assessing corporate performance. By contrast, in Eastern Europe, not only are approaches to accounting poorly developed, so also is the system for setting prices (including transfer prices within large organisations (equivalent to the Western multinational enterprise – MNE). In such an environment the incumbent insiders will resist forces for change and any attempts by the centre to challenge their pre-eminent position within the hierarchy. Second, of great importance during a period of rapid change in the economy is the role of the external environment in affecting corporate decision-making and the need to eliminate outdated management systems and replace them with new ones. The absence of external monitoring institutions such as those in the West means that incumbent managers who are inept may be able to survive even when they do not display the spirit of entrepreneurship so necessary during the period of transition. Third, agency costs are high due to the unnecessarily short time-horizon under which Eastern European managers operate. Reward (and penalty) systems for managers who adopt a long-term perspective are lacking; there is little innovation and a proclivity towards achieving short-term returns to offset the risk of dismissal.

The final reason is the hangover of overmanning especially in the large-scale enterprises (also noted in Struthers, Wylie and Young 1994). In such an environment the safeguarding of employment and salary levels remains the main priority of stakeholders rather than the overall well-being of the enterprise.

Therefore, although the involvement of insiders in the privatisation of post-communist enterprises appears to be an effective means of offsetting some of the agency costs identified earlier, Frydman and Rapaczynski conclude pessimistically that,

> In the long run, the greatest danger of the mass privatisation plans is that, instead of injecting an element of genuine monitoring and entrepreneurship into the stagnant state sector, they will create powerful new bureaucracies with a permanent hold on the enterprises in their portfolios.
>
> (Frydman and Rapaczynski 1993: 50–1)

In Western societies, a variety of institutions have evolved over long periods to minimise transactions costs: as well as the highly developed accountancy systems noted earlier, these include stock exchanges, laws of contract, and relatively incorrupt enforcement agencies. In Russia, stock exchanges for the trading of ownership titles have been established in the major centres, but they are unsupported by a proper regulatory framework. Commodity exchanges have also been established; these cover a wide range of commodities, but they account for only a small proportion of all industrial purchases and are frequently heavily dominated by the larger former state enterprises. A reduction in the use of these exchanges was reported in 1992, supposedly because firms were finding it more convenient to develop their own direct links with their customers (Rutland 1993: 31).

The inadequacies of the legal system, as a framework for market activity, are two-fold. The first is the complexity (and, sometimes, mutual inconsistency) of the laws regulating enterprise behaviour. This is not least true of the laws which govern small business. An example of this is the recently passed Anti-Monopoly Law in which the definition of a monopoly is deemed to be 35 per cent of the market share. To date, this law has been ineffective with respect to state enterprises, many of whom retain monopoly status. This deficiency also applies to the recently announced Law of Bankruptcy which has left many state enterprises untouched. The second problem concerns enforcement. The weakening of central authority has been accompanied by growing demoralisation and corruption, which make it difficult to enforce legitimate transactions. As legal enforcement agencies have become weaker, illegal ones have become more vigorous. Protection rackets are widespread, not simply covering enterprises which are on or over the frontiers of illegality, but also affecting a mass of perfectly legitimate businesses.

Of course, this uncertain backdrop has to be set against a tax regime in Russia which is hardly conducive to enterprise development,

particularly of SMEs. As far as the official definition of an SME in
Russia is concerned (i.e., for industrial enterprises less than 200
employees, for 'scientific' establishments less than 100 employees),
there exists a plethora of tax arrangements which has intensified
recently as a result of the budgetary constraints which the central
government currently operates under. The following are the key taxes
which many enterprises have to bear:

1 Profits tax	35% (composed of 13% federal tax and 22% local tax)
2 VAT	23% (of turnover)
3 Highways tax	4% (industrial companies – % of turnover)
4 Culture tax	1.5% (of turnover)
5 Municipal tax (e.g. for Police)	Number of employees × minimum wage × 3%
6 Property tax	1%–2%
7 Minimum wage fund tax	35% (if fund exceeded companies pay 35% tax on exceeded amount)
8 Transport tax	1% (of turnover)
9 Education tax	10%

UNDERDEVELOPED MARKETS AND THE ROLE OF NETWORKS

The situation in Russia as described above has aspects which are
peculiar to an economy changing from central planning to a
market form of organisation; but it also has parallels with other
times and places. In Britain, in the early stages of industrialisation, market institutions were similarly underdeveloped, illegality
was widespread and the newly emerging entrepreneurs had to
cope with the resulting uncertainties and high transaction costs.
Such experiences have been repeated many times, as economies at
low levels of subsistence have embarked on the process of
economic growth.

Studies both of business history in the West and of economic
development elsewhere have frequently drawn attention to the fact
that success in the pursuit of enterprise in such situations will become
more likely if the entrepreneur is able to exploit membership of a
network of appropriate contacts. Such networks reduce uncertainty,
both by improving information about the environment and by low-
ering the transactions costs of market relationships through the
fostering of trust.

Networks have been variously defined; a useful definition for present purposes is given by Aldrich and Zimmer (1985), who consider that networks comprise those persons with whom the central character has a direct relationship and those individuals with whom he has an indirect relationship by courtesy of that direct contact.

A number of commentators have emphasised the importance of 'investing in network formation' for the successful establishment of foreign ventures in the republics of the former Soviet Union (Ghauri and Henriksen 1994; de Wit and Monami 1994). Such networks are seen as necessary both to provide sources of information on a complex and rapidly changing environment, and also to develop high-trust relationships with partners or suppliers. Our concern here, however, is with the extent to which indigenous entrepreneurs may be able to take advantage of pre-existing networks.

Frequently, business networks arise out of other, broader social relationships.[1] A very striking example of a set of interlocking networks which fostered new enterprise during industrialisation in Britain is provided by the Quakers, or more correctly the Society of Friends (Prior and Kirby 1993). The Friends' Meeting House served as a focus for commercial as well as for religious activity. Advice was offered to prospective entrepreneurs (who were required to desist from a project if it did not meet with the approval of more experienced members). Finance could also be mobilised in support of promising ventures; not merely from within the resources of the local Meeting, but also from other meeting-houses, sometimes overseas. The very high standards of personal morality accepted by Quakers, and practised as a condition of continuing membership of the community, served as effective guarantees to lenders. The strength of the ties of the network were further reinforced by inter-marriage. As a consequence, Quaker families were overrepresented in the ranks of successful entrepreneurs in the early stages of industrialisation; they were active in banking, manufacturing and in railway development.

In many developing economies, effective networks have been constructed on the basis of ethnic relationships. The success of Asian enterprises in East Africa illustrates the point. However, an interesting comparison between Asian and African businesses brings out an important qualification relating to the role of networks: some types of social network may inhibit the potential entrepreneur. Bosa (1969) has argued that whereas the Asian 'joint family' system successfully fulfilled the functions of managing and financing business enterprise in networks which might span the whole of East Africa, the African 'extended family', by contrast, served as 'a distributive mutual insurance rather than a productive organisation' (p. 93); in consequence, any member of the family who sought to acquire the resources for business formation was liable to be expected to supply them to relatives for consumption rather than investment purposes.

The fact that networks are not always a good thing is, of course, widely recognised – as, for example, in the pejorative use of the term 'old boy network'. Preference for dealing with fellow Freemasons, or with members of one's own golf club, church or ethnic group, may give rise to accusations of nepotism or corruption; indeed, in the labour or housing markets in most Western societies it may in certain circumstances fall foul of anti-discrimination legislation.

Where market institutions are well developed, a preference for trading with members of one's own group may be dysfunctional, if it leads to less efficient insiders being preferred to more efficient outsiders. But this assumes that imperfect knowledge is not a serious problem. More precisely, it assumes some or all of the following:

- the quality of the goods or services to be exchanged is known in advance of the transaction;
- failure to deliver either the quantity or quality agreed can be easily monitored;
- the contract can be cheaply enforced.

Even in Western societies where market institutions have evolved over centuries, these conditions are often not met. In the circumstances prevailing in Russia at present, failure to meet them is likely to be much more frequent, for reasons already outlined. Consequently, a preference for trading with members of one's own network may be 'boundedly rational': a sensible and in some sense 'efficient' response to limited information, and a way of reducing the costs imposed by opportunistic behaviour.

However, as we have also seen, not all kinds of social network are equally supportive of business activities. What are the network characteristics which select for success in this role? This, of course depends on precisely the functions which they are expected to fulfil. In the present context, there are two main ones.

First, there is the function of economising on search costs through the provision of readily accessible information about the business environment. This aspect is particularly emphasised by some writers on small business (Birley, Cromie and Myers 1991). It reflects the need of the decision-maker to keep continually up-to-date with trends in market prices, resource availabilities, relevant technological developments and opportunities for intervention which may result in profits. Published sources are often of limited usefulness, since by the time they are published it may be too late to act on the information; anyway, in the case of the small business in particular, there may be no-one in the company who has time to scan the relevant sources of information. Furthermore, the entrepreneur by temperament may prefer to absorb information through personal contacts rather than from written sources.

A second function has already been emphasised: networks help the entrepreneur to acquire partners whom he or she can trust, thus economising on the transactions costs of entering and enforcing contracts. This is true whether the partnership is one which involves a trading relationship, or a pooling of resources in joint membership of an organisation. These two functions suggest the following list of characteristics of a social network which might allow it also to serve as a business network.

- *Geographical spread* Both the earlier examples of social networks were characterised by the ability to draw on resources or information over a distance, even to the extent of crossing national boundaries.

- *Informational diversity* Although this was less obvious in the examples quoted, it follows from the preceding discussion. Clearly, a network which can supply information about a wide range of potential market opportunities and relevant technologies is to be preferred to one more narrowly focused.

- *Reliability* The reliability of a network depends to an important degree on the opportunity cost of unreliable behaviour. In an impersonal business relationship, unreliability may be punished by any (enforceable) sanctions specified in the contract, and by the loss of future contracts. Where a social relationship is also involved, business unreliability may incur the additional costs of threatened exclusion from that relationship, which may be valued for its own sake. This was a factor in the strength of the Quaker network.

- *Ideology* Finally, if a social network is to be usable for business purposes it helps if it can inculcate in its members an ideology which is supportive of business activity. A religious belief system which emphasises honesty obviously contributes to the reliability criterion. On the other hand, a network based on an ideology which is hostile to the acquisition of worldly goods, or to the profit motive, is not likely to be conducive to the development of enterprise in a market economy, however useful it might otherwise be in providing information to its members or in encouraging high-trust relationships amongst them.

SOCIAL NETWORKS AND NEW BUSINESS FORMATION IN RUSSIA

What social networks exist in Russia which might help to encourage the growth of new enterprise? Quakers, unfortunately, appear to be in short supply. The revival of the Orthodox Church, and the growth of new churches consequent upon the recent invasion of Russia by Western evangelists, might in time lead to the development of church-related business activity, but this is speculation; we have been unable to find evidence of any such development to date.[2]

The Communist Party might serve as a basis for a business network. Although membership has now declined, the personal relationships developed during the years of its dominance are obviously still in place. In terms of the criteria defined in the previous section, this network would obviously score highly on geographical spread; given the close involvement of the Party in the direction of economic activity under central planning, access of former members to diverse sources of information would also be very helpful. The third and fourth criteria, however, are more questionable in this case. The Party was not known for developing high-trust relationships amongst its members; and Party ideology also had a strong bias against private business enterprise and the profit motive.

On the basis of a case study reported more fully elsewhere (Struthers, Wylie and Young 1994) and summarised in the next section, we would argue that higher educational institutions (HEIs) can provide one of the most effective networks for new enterprise development in Russia at the present time. On *a priori* grounds, they would seem likely to perform well in terms of all four of our criteria.

First, HEIs are potentially able to link up with a network across a wide geographical area, transcending national boundaries. Scholarly links developed with the international community can serve as the basis for business contacts. On the second criterion, academic institutions also have notable advantages. Most HEIs are multidisciplinary and, in consequence, are able to offer industry clusters of experts with a wide range of very relevant skills. Since academic researchers are supposedly at the frontiers of their respective disciplines, they will be

as well as of the staff who supervised them. In these cases, the specific expertise of the staff within the University was being used, although the level of technological input was not always high. In another case, part of the premises had been leased by the University to a commercial company which provided financial and marketing services.[4]

In both types of enterprise, it was evident that the relationships which had been developed within the State Technical University of Yaroslavl were being used as the foundation for the business activities observed. In a number of cases, especially in the first type of enterprise which was less 'discipline-specific', it appeared that the staff responsible were drawn from a range of departments. Even in the case of the commercial company, one of the directors was also on the staff of the University.

Lastly, in terms of ideology and organisational culture, the origins and past experience of the University, as a polytechnic institution for training the local labour force to a high level, gave staff a strong orientation towards liaison with industry; very similar, indeed, to that of institutions in the former polytechnic sector in the United Kingdom. Even without the strong incentives provided by erosion of academic incomes through inflation, the development of academic enterprise would have been perceived as a worthwhile activity by many of the Yaroslavl staff encountered during the programme.

CONCLUSIONS

As a consequence of the economic turmoil associated with the transition from a centrally planned to a market economy, the creation of new enterprises in Russia is an activity fraught with uncertainty; and this uncertainty is exacerbated by the underdevelopment of the market institutions which are characteristic of Western economies. In such circumstances, potential entrepreneurs can benefit if they are able to take advantage of pre-existing social networks which can serve as a vehicle for business transactions. Such networks serve two functions: they provide access to information which might otherwise be difficult to come by and they also reduce the cost of transacting by facilitating the development of high-trust relationships.

There are, of course, many serious problems within the Russian economy which effective networking alone will be quite inadequate to solve. Yet every little helps. Even in Western industrial economies, academic institutions are often able to play an important role in encouraging the growth of new business. Often, this is seen in terms of the contribution which they make to the first of the two functions: the spread of information, in particular technology transfer (Segal Quince 1985; Connor, Wylie and Young 1986). We have argued that in the conditions prevailing in Russia at present the role of the academic institution becomes crucial. While its position at the centre of an informational network is important here as in the West, its contribution to the second function, the development of relationships based on trust, may be no less significant. The evidence from our case study of the Yaroslavl Region certainly cannot be said to prove these assertions, but it does seem to us to provide some support for them.

ACKNOWLEDGEMENTS

The authors gratefully acknowledge the advice of Dr Vladimir Petrushansky of Yaroslavl State Technical University. Any errors which remain will of course be entirely their responsibility.

NOTES

1 The incidence of criminal activity within the economic sphere in Russia has been reported on widely. It could be argued that criminal involvement in business represents another example of a network arrangement. This is true. However, a crucial difference is that criminal networks are, by definition, low-trust relationships with high implicit costs manifesting many of the characteristics of a 'contestable market' in which a 'hit and run' mentality is the dominant one! Shleifer and Vishny (1993: 610) have adopted a principal–agent approach to corruption and argue, with reference to Russia and other countries, that ineffective governments who fail to adequately control their agencies experience high corruption levels. They also develop a model which contrasts the bribery prevalent under the old communist 'monolithic bribe collection system' with that operating under the present system in which many more potential layers of corruption exist involving central government officials, local officials, ministry officials and foreign investors. They argue, 'The evidence is strikingly consistent in showing the superiority of monopolistic bribe taking over that by independent monopolists'.

2 Although the Russian Orthodox Church has regained much of its influence in the post-perestroika period, this continues to reside in the spiritual or ecclesiastical domain. The Church, as churches do everywhere, has a wide remit within Russian society and can be seen operating as a galvanising force within some local communities. It also plays an active role in rehabilitation schemes for released prisoners, assistance to blind people, support for veterans of the Afghanistan war and the Chernobyl disaster. However, its contribution to local economies as such is limited, partly as a consequence of directing its energies towards a church rebuilding pro-

gramme. Nevertheless, in the networking sense, it could play a bigger role within the economy just as many religious groups do in the West.

3 In addition to the erosion of the real wage, there has also been a substantial reduction in the social wage provided by many companies. This is explained by the gradual disappearance of many of the fringe benefits enjoyed by state employees, particularly in large-scale enterprises. These include health, education and leisure facilities often provided previously at little cost by the enterprise, or in our case by the University.

4 Further details on these companies can be found in Struthers, Wylie and Young (1994).

BIBLIOGRAPHY

Aldrich, H. and Zimmer, C. (1985) 'Entrepreneurship through social interaction', in D. Sexton and R. Smilor (eds) *The Art and Science of Entrepreneurship*, New York: Ballinger.

Åslund, A. (1993) *Systemic Change and Stabilisation in Russia, Post-Soviet Business Forum*, London: Royal Institute of International Affairs.

Birley, S., Cromie, S. and Myers, A. (1991) 'Entrepreneurial networks: their emergence in Ireland and Overseas', *International Small Business Journal*, 9, 4: 56–74.

Blanchard, O., Boycko, M, Dabrowski, M., Dornbusch, R., Layard, R. and Shleifer, A. (1993) *Post Communist Reform: Pain and Progress*, London: MIT.

Bosa, G. R. (1969) *The Financing of Small Scale Enterprises in Uganda*, Nairobi: Oxford University Press.

Coase, R. (1937) 'The nature of the firm', *Economica*, 4, 16: 386–405

Connor, A. I. , Wylie, J. and Young, A. (1986) 'Academic–industry liaison in the United Kingdom: economic perspectives', *Industry and Higher Education*, 407–20.

Frydman, R. and Rapaczynski, A. (1993) 'Insiders and the state: overview of responses to agency problems in East European privatisations', *Economics of Transition*, 1, 1: 35–59.

Ghauri, P. N. and Henriksen, A. (1994) 'Developing a network position in the Baltic states: the case of Statoil in Estonia', in P. J. Buckley, and P. N. Ghauri (eds) *The Economics of Change in East and Central Europe*, London: Academic Press.

Grossman, S. J. and Hart, O. D. (1983) 'An analysis of the principal–agent problem', *Econometrica*, 51: 7–45.

International Monetary Fund (1993) *World Economic Outlook*, Washington.

Jensen, M. C. and Meckling, W. (1976) 'Theory of the firm: managerial behaviour, agency costs and capital structure', *Journal of Financial Economics*, 3, 4: 305–60.

Marx, K. (1875) 'Critique of the Gotha Programme', in Marx, K. (1974) *The First International and After*, (ed.) Fernbach, D., Harmondsworth: Penguin.

Mirrlees, J. A. (1976) 'The optimal structure of incentives and authority within an organisation', *Bell Journal of Economics*, 7: 105–31.

Prior, A. and Kirby, M. (1993) 'The Society of Friends and the family firm', *Business History*, 35: 66–85.

Rutland, P. (1993) *Business Elites and Russian Economic Policy*, Post-Soviet Business Forum, London: Royal Institute of International Affairs.

Segal Quince (1985) *The Cambridge Phenomenon: The Growth of High Technology in a University Town*, Cambridge: published in association with Brand Brothers, London.

Shleifer, A. and Vishny, R. W. (1993) 'Corruption', *Quarterly Journal of Economics*, August: 599–617.

Struthers, J., Wylie, J. and Young, A. (1994) 'Academic support for enterprise development in the former Soviet Union: a case study', *Industry and Higher Education*, 8, 3: 174–82

Williamson, O. E. (1975) *Markets and Hierarchies: Analysis and Anti-Trust Implications*, New York: Free Press.

Williamson, O. E. (1981) 'The modern corporation: origins, evolution attributes', *Journal of Economic Literature*, 19: 1537–68.

de Wit, A. and Monami, E. (1994) 'Understanding the former Soviet market: an interaction approach', in P. J. Buckley and P. N. Ghauri (eds) *The Economics of Change in East and Central Europe*, London: Academic Press.

10 The use of external advice by new and established SMEs
Some survey evidence

David Devins

INTRODUCTION

The challenge for researchers in the field of enterprise and small business research is to devise and implement methodologies which enable agencies to provide support to those who need it and will benefit from it, at the time it is required. Studies of the characteristics of successful or fast-growing firms (e.g. Storey and Strange 1992) are useful but suffer from the disadvantage, from a policy point of view at least, that they are retrospective. What is required are research methodologies and business development indicators which provide 'real time' systems to enable agencies to effectively develop and implement their services.

This chapter describes the approach undertaken in the Policy Research Unit (PRU) at Leeds Metropolitan University for Leeds TEC. It outlines the policy background underpinning enterprise support. The chapter then describes the research methodology adopted at the PRU based on a combination of primary and secondary research and designed to enable a regular cost-effective monitoring of SME trends to take place. The chapter then outlines results of a key element of the research, examining some of the development characteristics of a segment of SMEs in Leeds before focusing on the use of external advice by new and established SMEs. Finally, the chapter draws on the survey research findings to indicate some lessons for enterprise support policy.

POLICY BACKGROUND

In the late 1980s and early 1990s there has been a shift in enterprise support policy away from a focus on job creation through business start-ups towards increasing the competitiveness of existing businesses with a view to their growth and development. The shift from support for start-ups to support for established businesses is embodied in the major policy initiative of Business Link as outlined in the prospectus issued by the Department of Trade and Industry (DTI) to organisations wishing to develop 'One Stop Shops' in their local area (DTI 1992, 1993). This approach further recognises that enterprise support policy should be led by the needs of businesses in the local area rather than being driven by existing off-the-peg programmes and initiatives at the national level. This has led to an interest in identifying and assessing the multiple and diverse needs of local businesses so that bespoke solutions to business needs can be developed.

There has also been an interest in the contribution of publicly funded enterprise support and monitoring and evaluation of publicly funded enterprise support remains of crucial importance. Researchers have noted traditionally low take-up rates of publicly funded enterprise support initiatives (e.g. Curran 1993, Bennett, Wicks and McCoshan 1994) and this has led to the recognition of the need for a more proactive approach to enterprise support. It is not sufficient to wait for business owners to contact the agency and visit the agency's premises. This has led to the view that support agencies must actively seek out those businesses most likely to need and to benefit from external advice and support of some kind.

There has also been a recognition of the need to target enterprise support so that the greatest benefit, however it is measured (e.g., in terms of value added or additionality), is rendered to the locality. Most commonly in the SME domain targeting is associated with focusing support on the small number of businesses with the greatest potential to grow (e.g., Storey 1994). However, targeting can be viewed from a wide perspective where it involves the identification of market segments based on a variety of business needs and on careful analysis of the market on the one hand and the matching of the objectives of the support agency with the services it offers on the other. Appropriate market segments, can be targeted whether they be high-tech businesses, for example, or those with the potential to grow, those requiring specific technical or managerial skills or those offering a social or cultural benefit to the community.

The proactive, targeted approach presents a major challenge to support agencies given that almost 90 per cent of businesses in a locality can be classed as SMEs. Consequently, the need for a networking approach has been recognised with many existing support agencies (e.g., Local Enterprise Agencies, Training and Enterprise Councils, Chambers of Commerce, Local Authority

Departments) being drawn under the Business Link umbrella. A single Business Link or Local Economic Council (LEC) locality might contain 18,000 VAT registered businesses and a greater number of micro firms and self-employed. It is a dynamic environment with each business facing multiple problem situations, exhibiting a variety of needs and operating in changing economic environments and different markets.

METHODOLOGY

A mixture of qualitative and quantitative research methods are required to assess the dynamics of the SME market in a locality, consequently a combination of primary and secondary sources have been used.

The secondary research was based on the analysis of macro-economic data, namely, the VAT registrations and de-registrations data and the census of employment. The analysis provided broad sectoral changes over the decade and compared the dynamics of the birth and death rates in Leeds with three other spatial areas. A simple forecasting model was used to estimate the changes in the sectoral distribution of SMEs in the Leeds economy. The Census of Employment provided size breakdowns in terms of the industrial units in industrial sector and each spatial area. These analyses provided contextual information on the Leeds economy but they did not provide the information required to develop and implement support policies based on the needs of local SMEs.

The primary survey research contains several elements. The main element was a telephone survey of local SMEs to provide a 'snapshot' of the SME dynamics in the locality based on quantitative information. Second, a series of face-to-face interviews to provide qualitative information to examine some of the key factors in greater depth and to examine the advice-seeking process and experiences in greater depth. Finally a workshop involving researchers, some of the respondents and TEC enterprise staff, to provide a forum for an exchange of ideas based on the research findings and establish further dialogue between the parties. This chapter draws on the primary research and the methodology followed is outlined in greater detail below.

Telephone survey

The survey took place in November/December 1992 and was repeated again at the same time the following year. The survey research focuses upon businesses which currently employ between 10 and 100 employees. This is a group of businesses about which relatively little was known in the Leeds area, and also falls into the target group specified by the DTI for the Business Link initiative.

Using the 'Connections in Business' data-base as the sampling frame, a stratified sample of business establishments in the Leeds area, with 10–100 employees, was constructed. The sample was stratified according to sector (1980 SIC Divisions) and employment size (10–25, 26–50 and 51–100). The data-base identified 3,700 such establishments, of which 2,400 were contacted by telephone. Respondents were asked to confirm their employment size and to indicate the degree of autonomy which the establishment had over business decisions. The sampling strategy deliberately oversampled businesses at the larger end of the scale and undersampled smaller businesses to ensure that the required number of responses to enable meaningful analysis in each sizeband was obtained. The raw data were subsequently weighted to reflect the size and sectoral distribution estimated by the process described above.

Businesses which fell into the required sizeband, and which had some degree of autonomy over business decisions, were asked to participate in a telephone interview. Approximately 35 per cent of establishments were eliminated from the sample through this process, and the results were used to estimate the size and sectoral structure of independent (or semi-independent) businesses. In 1992, 646 interviews were completed, in most cases with the business owner, chief executive or other senior manager. In 1993 the number of respondents was increased to include responses from a total of 870 SME decision-makers (22 responses are excluded from analysis in this chapter due to incomplete details relating to the age of the business). Of the original 646 businesses, 442 (68 per cent) completed the survey enabling a panel to be set up to monitor changes over time.

The interview schedule covered the following areas:

● background details of the business
● changes over the previous year
● training/human resource development
● business planning
● perceived needs for external advice

- use of external advice in the past year
- knowledge of, and use of, TEC services or programmes

The information collected allowed a systematic analysis of SME business characteristics, development characteristics and use of external support agencies in a twelve-month period. A key objective of the research was to enable tracking of SME needs and the demand for services from local business support agencies.

Face-to-face interviews

The telephone survey provided a snap-shot of the situation in Leeds. However, to gain a greater depth of knowledge about a number of issues relating to the development of local businesses and their experiences of dealing with business support agencies, a series of face-to-face (30) interviews were conducted. These interviews were targeted at specific sections of the local SME market based on whether the business had identified a need for external advice and sought advice to satisfy the need, whether the business was involved in an 'innovative' activity (loosely defined as major change in product development, systems development, internal restructuring, export, quality or training) and whether or not the business was independent or with decision-making autonomy but part of a larger group.

Information was collected through face-to-face interviews with a major decision-maker in the business (normally the managing director – MD) using a discussion guide which gave respondents scope to address a wide range of business issues including:

- growth
- organisation
- external advice (barriers)
- attitudes towards external agencies

This provided in-depth qualitative information to supplement the quantitative information collected through the telephone survey.

Workshop

The final workshop element of the methodology provided a forum for SME decision-makers, TEC enterprise staff and the academic researchers, using the research undertaken as a basis for discussion. Presentations by the researchers and the TEC representatives were followed by a wide ranging discussion relating to business practices in SMEs, relationships with support agencies (and in particular the TEC) and the services available to SMEs. The workshop provided a forum to bring together representatives of the business community, TEC representatives and academic researchers and resulted in a useful exchange of information on several key issues such as business planning, human resource development and communication with the TEC.

The research methodology as a whole provided a wealth of information enabling year-on-year comparisons, cross-sectoral analysis and a number of indicators relating to the dynamics of this segment of the SME market in Leeds. The year-on-year comparison indicated was that many of the broad dynamics of the SME market showed little year-on-year change. Consequently, the latest results are presented in this chapter with any key year-on-year differences highlighted in the text. The remainder of the chapter focuses on the characteristics and advice needs of new and established businesses based on results of the telephone study while drawing on the other primary research experience to provide contextual information.

Sample characteristics

Tables 10.1 and 10.2 indicate the number of responses on which the analysis is based, and the breakdown of the weighted sample by sector, age and employment size.

Table 10.1 indicates some differences in the industrial sector breakdown of SMEs employing between 10–100 in Leeds. It indi-

Table 10.1 Sector by business size

Industrial sector	n = 528 10–25 (%)	n = 176 26–50 (%)	n = 64 51–100 (%)	n = 768 All (%)
Production	60	22	11	23
Construction	78	17	5	8
Wholesale	55	29	16	7
Retail	83	14	4	6
Hotel and catering	79	19	2	8
Transport	56	31	13	6
Business services	70	25	5	23
Other services	68	23	8	19
All sectors	70	22	8	100

Table 10.2 Sector by age

Industrial sector	n = 105 0–3 yrs (%)	n = 87 4–6 yrs (%)	n = 163 7–13 yrs (%)	n = 411 14+ yrs (%)
Production	12	7	25	56
Construction	11	9	18	62
Wholesale	13	6	16	65
Retail	10	9	23	58
Hotel and catering	31	16	15	37
Transport	4	3	24	69
Business services	10	9	21	60
Other services	19	23	21	37
All sectors	14	11	22	56

cates the relative importance of 'smaller businesses' in the construction, retail and hotel and catering sectors.

Table 10.2 indicates the considerable difference in the proportion of younger businesses in certain industrial sectors such as hotel and catering and other services. The table also indicates that the sample is heavily biased towards 'older' businesses. It is estimated that 56 per cent of SMEs employing between 10–100 in Leeds are relatively mature businesses.

SOME KEY RESEARCH RESULTS

Policy focus has been placed on the growth of SMEs but there is considerable qualitative evidence that for many SME owner/managers survival, not growth, is the key objective. The dominant leadership ethos of SME managers appears to be one of satisficing not maximising. There is evidence to suggest that the quality of life offered to SME owner/managers and the income their businesses generate compensates for long hours and the financial concerns many of them identified. The benefit of growth is outweighed by the cost of increased time commitments, the cost of formalising systems and of obtaining finance. Although most owner managers were not committed to growth *per se*, most recognised that their organisations needed to change and develop because of changes in the market in which they operate. Consequently, the research investigated a number of broad indicators relating to the development of the business.

These development indicators are included to provide contextual material impinging on the needs of SMEs for external advice and support. The main focus of this paper concentrates on SME use of external advice and/or support on a range of business issues.

The research examines several broad indicators related to the development of SMEs:

- SME decision-makers' perceptions of the growth potential of the business;
- The extent to which SMEs have an entrepreneurial model of organisation or a formalised management structure (existence of a board of directors);
- The extent to which businesses are involved in planning (existence of a formal written business plan which is reviewed);
- The extent to which SMEs are involved in product or process innovation (major changes in product development, systems development, internal restructuring, export, quality or training).

The identification of these factors provide indicators of the propensity for SMEs with these characteristics to identify a need for external advice and to seek a solution to the need. The data are analysed in terms of the age of the business to identify differences attributable to new and established SMEs.

SME growth

SMEs are often suggested as key contributors to the economic growth of a locality. Table 10.3 indicates some of the differences between the characteristics of new and established businesses. It is interesting to examine the potential for growth in relation to the age of the business. Certainly, in terms of employment growth, younger businesses are more likely to expect employment levels to increase in the next 12 months than older businesses. However, there is less of a clear cut

Table 10.3 SMEs with development characteristics

	0–3 yrs (%)	4–6 yrs (%)	7–13 yrs (%)	14+ yrs (%)	All (%)
Employment growth	58	45	40	32	39
Turnover growth	79	70	85	75	77
Board of directors	58	45	65	60	60
Business plan	50	49	46	41	45
Innovative activity	92	74	66	65	71

relationship between the expectation of an increase in the level of turnover and the age of the business. What became clear from the qualitative research was that growth was often a subsidiary objective of the business with survival the key strategy followed in the majority of SMEs.

Decision-making

One of the key stages in the development of the SME concerns the move from an entrepreneurial informal organisational structure to a more formalised management structure. The research indicates the propensity of SMEs to adopt a formalised approach to management by utilising a board of directors.

Table 10.3 suggests that there is little relationship between an increase in the age of the business and the existence of a board of directors. The qualitative follow-up interviews suggested that the existence of a board of directors gives considerable support for the owner-manager providing a sounding board for ideas and/or further skills and experience to supplement the decision-making process. Examination of the existence of a board of directors and the propensity of an SME to have identified a need for external advice reveals that businesses with a board of directors are almost one and a half times more likely than those without a board to have identified a need for external advice.

Business planning

Business planing is a key element in the development of an organisation. It potentially provides a vision for where the business is going and how it is going to get there. The short-term decision-making horizons and the time constraints placed on many owner-managers mean that business planning is often viewed as a luxury rather than a necessity. However, there is evidence to suggest that a substantial proportion of SMEs are involved in the production of a formal written business plan which is regularly reviewed. Table 10.3 examines the extent to which planning is undertaken in the local environment; 45 per cent of SMEs in the sample have a formal written business plan. Furthermore, it is apparent that younger SMEs are more likely to have produced a formal written business plan than older businesses.

Analysis of the relationship between the propensity to plan and the identification of a need for advice reveals that those SMEs with a business plan are more likely to have identified a need for external advice than those without. Of those SMEs with a business plan, 60 per cent have identified a need for external advice as opposed to 48 per cent of those without a business plan.

Innovative activities

Respondents were asked to identify any major initiatives relating to a variety of product and process innovations occurring in the organisation at the present time, and 71 per cent of all SMEs were involved in at least one innovative activity. Table 10.3 indicates that younger businesses are far more likely to perceive that they are involved in major innovative activities than older businesses. There were considerable differences in the propensity of SMEs to be involved with an innovative activity.

Table 10.4 indicates that the dynamics of innovative activities are broadly similar across agebands. Quality and training are the most prevalent major initiatives and export the least in local SMEs. The Table also shows that training initiatives are slightly more prevalent in the younger businesses and internal restructuring more prevalent in older SMEs. This supports at the local level the notion put forward by Hendry et al. (1991) who suggest that after an initial investment in training to establish a work-force competent in the completion of operational tasks, resources for further development are not made available to the same degree in future years. There is also evidence to suggest that as businesses increase in age they become involved in systems development as the business develops and becomes established. The fact that an SME is involved in innovative activities would appear to make it more likely to identify a need for external advice. SMEs involved in an innovative activity are almost one and a half times more likely to have identified a need for external advice than 'non-innovative' organisations.

Table 10.4 SMEs involved in innovative activities

	0–3 yrs (%)	4–6 yrs (%)	7–13 yrs (%)	14+ yrs (%)	All (%)
Product development	17	17	20	22	21
Systems development	16	17	22	22	21
Export	5	5	7	7	7
Internal restructuring	15	32	31	28	27
Quality	43	55	57	56	55
Training	55	49	53	50	52

These findings give an indication of development characteristics of SMEs in the local area and their propensity to identify a need for external advice. An important element of the research methodology was to examine in greater detail the process SMEs went through in the satisfaction of an identified need for external advice. The questionnaire pursued a systematic line of questioning which explored the process through which respondents went in deciding whether to obtain external advice, information or support.

EXTERNAL ADVICE

The remainder of this chapter focuses on the examination of the use of external advice by new and established businesses. For each of eight business task areas (outlined in Table 10.5) respondents were asked to indicate:

- whether they had identified a need for advice during the previous twelve months;
- whether they sought advice, and if not, why not;
- which support agency organisations were contacted;
- whether the required advice was found, and if so from whom;
- whether the business acted on the advice;
- whether the advice had satisfied the need;
- whether the business had paid for the advice, and if not whether they would be willing to pay for the advice.

The reasons were identified if the business had not sought advice, had not been able to find the advice, had not used the advice or was

Table 10.5 Firms identifying needs for external advice by size of businesses

	10–25 employees (%)	26–50 employees (%)	51–100 employees (%)	All (%)
IT/computing	16	25	27	19
Sales/marketing	14	14	16	14
Recruitment	8	6	9	8
Quality	13	18	23	15
Training	13	18	17	15
General business strategy	7	5	9	7
Finance	12	12	10	10
Other	8	12	18	10
Any business area	46	55	61	49

not satisfied with the advice. The survey thus provides a rich source of data through which the process of seeking external advice can be analysed in some detail and disaggregated according to the characteristics of the business, the type of advice sought/found and the source of that advice. In addition, the face-to-face interviews provide some qualitative flesh to add to the statistical bones of the large scale survey.

Identification of advice needs

Table 10.5 illustrates that just over half of all respondents had identified a need for advice relating to at least one business area during the previous 12 months. It also indicates that perceived needs for external advice tend to increase with employment size. Moreover, the pattern of perceived needs varies between businesses of different sizes.

A closer examination of the data reveals that advice needs increase with business size, particularly in the areas of IT, quality and training. For most of the other areas of business activity there is no discernible pattern by business size. Table 10.6 indicates the multiple advice needs of many SMEs and points to a relationship with the size of the business with larger businesses more likely to identify needs in more than one business area.

Sectoral analysis also indicates that external advice needs vary considerably between industrial sectors, being highest in production industries and lowest in hotels and catering. This provides some support for the contention of Curran (1993) that enterprise support should be more sectorally focused. None the less, there is evidence of demand across the sectoral spectrum in specific areas such as quality, training and IT. The age of the business clearly plays an important role in determining the level and pattern of perceived external advice needs (Table 10.7). Businesses which have been established for between four and six years are the most likely to identify advice

Table 10.6 Identification of advice needs by size

	10–25 employees (%)	26–50 employees (%)	51–100 employees (%)	All (%)
One business area only	23	25	23	23
More than one business area	23	30	38	26

Table 10.7 Firms identifying needs for external advice by age

Business area	0–3 yrs (%)	4–6 yrs (%)	7–13 yrs (%)	14+ yrs (%)
IT/computing	18	13	25	19
Sales/marketing	18	15	18	13
Recruitment	6	10	8	8
Quality	7	17	16	16
Training	19	19	14	14
General business strategy	6	8	7	7
Finance	19	10	12	12
Other	10	19	10	10
Any business area	46	56	49	49

needs, notably in the areas of quality and training. It should be noted, however, that half of all long-established businesses (14 years or older) also perceived some needs for external advice.

The very youngest firms (0–3 years) are almost as likely as the longer-established businesses to identify a need for external advice. In comparison with other age groups, the youngest businesses are slightly more likely to identify a need for advice about finance issues, but much less likely to be concerned about quality.

Table 10.8 shows the proportion of businesses within each age group which have identified a need for external advice and indicates that younger businesses are more likely than older businesses to identify needs in a single area of the business.

Reasons for not identifying needs

This is a crucial area for analysis if support is to be developed to meet the needs rather than the wants or demands of SMEs. The research indicates that just under half of all established businesses in the 10–100 size category did not see the need for any form of external advice across the whole spectrum of business areas.

Table 10.8 Identification of advice needs by age

Business area	0–3 yrs (%)	4–6 yrs (%)	7–13 yrs (%)	14+ yrs (%)
One business area only	34	26	21	19
More than one business area	20	30	28	24

The group of businesses which said that they did not identify any need for external advice are of some potential interest to policy-makers and delivery agents. Many of these businesses may indeed benefit from external advice or assistance, although this may not be apparent to the owner-managers. 'Non-identifiers' cited a range of reasons for not seeking external advice.

Just under half felt that they did not need any external advice, due, for example, to the small size of the company or the fact that there have been relatively few changes or new initiatives. One respondent felt that 'the company is too successful to need advice'. One-third thought that they could solve any problems internally, and a further 9 per cent had access to expertise within a group. Only 2 per cent specifically stated that they were not convinced of the benefits of obtaining external advice, and a further 2 per cent felt that no advice was available which would meet their very specific needs.

Table 10.9 breaks down these reasons according to the age of the business. The most striking finding is that more recently established businesses are less likely than others to state that they have no need for external advice. There is an indication of the autonomous nature of new SMEs in that they are more likely to suggest that problems tend to be solved internally. Finally, there is no particular propensity for younger firms to believe that the advice they need is not available.

It is clear, therefore, that the main barrier to the seeking of external advice by SMEs in the size group covered by this study is not cynicism about the benefits of external advice, nor is it a feeling that advice is not available. The main barrier is the feeling amongst a significant proportion of firms that they do not need advice and/or that they have the skills necessary to deal with any issue which might emerge. While this is undoubtedly true in many cases, it is likely that some businesses in this group would benefit from external advice or

Table 10.9 Reasons for not identifying advice needs by age

	0–3 yrs (%)	4–6 yrs (%)	7–13 yrs (%)	14+ yrs (%)	All (%)
Do not need advice	39	40	51	51	42
Problems solved internally	38	23	30	30	33
Problems solved by group	5	11	18	13	9
Not convinced of benefit	2	1	0	2	2
No advice available	1	3	0	3	2
Other	9	9	7	15	10

assistance, leading to improved business performance, development and employment.

The advice-seeking process

Around 90 per cent of those who had identified an external advice need subsequently went on to look for sources of advice, about 80 per cent of whom said they had found the advice for which they were looking. These proportions vary according to the type of advice sought. Table 10.10 suggests that the greatest potentially unsatisfied advice needs relate to sales/marketing, while most of the other needs appear to be relatively well supplied with external advice.

Table 10.10 indicates the propensity to seek advice in terms of the business task environment and the age of the business. It is apparent that an area which is often held up as one of the weaknesses of SMEs (i.e., marketing) is a perceived problem area with all but the youngest businesses. While generally over 90 per cent of SMEs seek advice to satisfy needs in all other business areas, there are a significant portion of SMEs which do not seek sales and marketing advice. The most common reason sighted for this is that they have not got round to seeking external advice but intend to look for appropriate advice in the future.

These figures (some should be treated with caution as they are based on small cell sizes) suggest that, once a business has reached the stage of deciding to look for external advice, there is a good chance that it will subsequently go on to find an organisation to supply that advice.

However, as many as a quarter of 'identifiers' (recruitment) either do not go on to look for advice, or fail to find a potential supplier

Table 10.10 Firms seeking external advice, as a percentage of those who identified a need

Business area	0–3 yrs	4–6 yrs	7–13 yrs	14+ yrs	All
IT/computing	83	91	100	94	94
Sales/marketing	100	76	65	71	74
Recruitment	100	100	89	99	97
Quality	100	100	93	87	91
Training	97	90	97	86	91
General business strategy	100	100	84	94	93
Finance	88	100	100	95	95
Other	94	100	100	98	98

Table 10.11 SMEs finding external advice as a percentage of those identifying a need for advice

Business area	0–3 yrs	4–6 yrs	7–13 yrs	14+ yrs	All
IT/computing	85	100	92	91	92
Sales/marketing	77	68	90	81	81
Recruitment	51	77	86	77	75
Quality	62	100	90	89	88
Training	100	97	95	89	93
General business strategy	100	100	92	82	88
Finance	90	78	84	91	88
Other	90	78	80	88	85

despite looking. This suggests that there is some role for policy in assisting firms to locate appropriate advice. Table 10.11 clearly demonstrates that in some task areas (e.g., sales and marketing, recruitment, quality) the youngest businesses are much less likely to go on to seek and find advice after having identified a need.

Those businesses which did not go on to seek advice were asked to articulate the reason in a free text field. The reason was then coded into the broad categories outlined in Table 10.12.

Over half decided to pursue an internal solution, for example, by training staff or utilising the expertise of directors or other members of the business. Twenty-five per cent felt that they did not have the time to look for sources of advice or intended to look for advice and 8 per cent cited cost as the main barrier. Older businesses are slightly more likely than younger to pursue an internal solution, and do not appear to view cost as a major barrier.

A large minority of businesses had identified a need and sought advice but, because of their internal decision-making processes, they were still considering the advice (40 per cent) or they were still looking for advice (9 per cent). A further 37 per cent suggested

Table 10.12 Reasons for not seeking advice by age

	0–3 yrs (%)	4–6 yrs (%)	7–13 yrs (%)	14+ yrs (%)	All (%)
Did not have the time to look or intend to look	22	44	19	23	25
Found an internal solution	34	38	67	61	62
Financial considerations (cost)	13	0	16	7	8
Not known	22	18	0	7	9

that there was a lack of specific advice available. However, while the results provide broad indications related to the age of the business, some of these percentages are based on low cell counts as the majority of SMEs are able to successfully proceed through the advice seeking process.

Sources of advice received

There has been considerable interest in the contribution of 'public' agencies such as local authorities, libraries, government departments and more recently TECs and LECs in the enterprise support environment. The research enables examination of the support network to investigate where businesses look for external advice and which agencies provide the advice.

For analysis purposes it is useful to view the support networks in terms of public sector organisations (libraries, educational establishments, government departments, TECs) and private sources of advice (suppliers, customers, independent consultants, banks, solicitors, accountants). The numerous diverse sources not taken account of by the public and private networks (friends, relatives) are amalgamated into a catch-all 'other' category.

The research is consistent with the findings of Smallbone, North and Leigh (1993) that chambers of commerce, local authorities and enterprise agencies have made relatively few inroads into the provision of advice for small businesses. The TEC emerges as an important source of advice on training and, to a lesser extent, recruitment. The Department of Trade and Industry supplies some advice in the sales/ marketing and quality areas, and may have provided subsidies for some of the advice provided by private consultants (this was not specifically explored in the survey). It is also worth noting that the advice role of banks and other financial intermediaries extends beyond the financial area into issues relating to business planning and other business areas.

Table 10.13 summarises the nature of the organisations from which respondents ultimately received some form of external advice.

The most striking aspect of Table 10.13 is the central role played by private sector organisations, who provided the majority of advice sources for all business areas apart from training and recruitment, which tend to be serviced through public agencies such as Job Centres, educational establishments, TECs. Further analysis suggests that agencies (such as banks and accountants) provide advice in a variety of business areas not solely related to finance and in certain

Table 10.13 Sources of external advice used by businesses identifying a
need for external advice

	Private sector (%)	Public sector (%)	Other (%)
IT/computing	78	12	10
Sales/marketing	65	21	14
Recruitment	49	35	16
Quality	63	28	8
Training	42	48	10
General business strategy	60	21	9
Finance	85	10	5
Other	66	25	9

sectors trade associations (particularly in relation to quality, training
and business strategy) are the first port of call for a large number of
established SMEs, reinforcing the calls of many commentators (e.g.,
Curran 1993) for a clearer sectoral dimension to small business
support policies. The qualitative interviews suggested that the
advice-seeking process involved dealing with agencies with which
the business had already built up a relationship in the course of
trading.

Younger businesses are more likely than average to have received
advice from the TEC and less likely to have been helped by the DTI.
This may reflect the fact that the TEC has only been operating for
four years, and the fact that older businesses are more likely to be
involved in technology or marketing initiatives, for which, until
recently, help has been available under the DTI Enterprise Initiative.

Impact of advice received

The research indicates that when a business has identified a need for
external advice, sought and found the required advice then it will
(perhaps unsurprisingly) act on the advice it has received. Table
10.14 indicates the likelihood of a business acting on the advice by
the business task area and the age of the business.

In the vast majority of cases respondents who received advice took
action as a consequence. The most common reason for not implementing the advice received is the cost of implementation (31 per
cent of non-implementors), with a further 26 per cent feeling that the
advice they had been given was unsuitable in some way. The remainder had not decided yet whether to implement the advice, or felt that

Table 10.14 Acting on external advice by age

Business area	0– 3 yrs (%)	4–6 yrs (%)	7–13 yrs (%)	14+ yrs (%)	All (%)
IT/computing	100	100	91	95	95
Sales/marketing	90	100	84	97	94
Recruitment	100	100	85	98	96
Quality	100	88	94	88	90
Training	95	100	94	82	90
General business strategy	100	100	100	91	95
Finance	100	100	82	97	95
Other	73	90	100	94	92

the circumstances of the business had changed to such an extent that the advice was no longer relevant.

Table 10.15 shows that the majority of businesses were satisfied with the advice they received. Those who were not, indicated that the advice had satisfied the need for which it was sought but suggested that it was too early to assess the impact of the advice they had received. Other reasons for dissatisfaction focused upon the unsuitability of the advice or (in a small number of cases) the cost of implementing the suggested course of action. The results suggest that changes in circumstances or difficulties in implementation are more of a problem for younger businesses than more established firms who tend to emphasise the cost and/or suitability of the advice.

Willingness to pay

A final issue which is of some interest to policy-makers, particularly in the light of the exhortation to Business Links to become

Table 10.15 Satisfaction with advice received by age

Business area	0–3 yrs (%)	4–6 yrs (%)	7–13 yrs (%)	14+ yrs (%)	All (%)
IT/computing	100	87	95	94	94
Sales/marketing	100	100	87	89	91
Recruitment	100	77	100	100	97
Quality	100	90	93	96	95
Training	85	84	91	95	90
General business strategy	61	100	58	91	83
Finance	100	100	84	98	96
Other	80	91	100	89	90

self-financing, is the willingness of SME owner-managers to pay for advice received. This is a notoriously difficult area to investigate, but the survey approached it by asking respondents whether they had paid for the advice which they had received. If they had not paid, they were asked if they would be willing to pay for the advice in future. Clearly, this only gives a general indication, as we did not collect information about how much respondents had paid, or how much they would be willing to pay. Moreover, although some respondents said that they would be willing to pay, it seems certain that a proportion would not do so when faced with a real rather than a hypothetical choice. Nonetheless, the responses (summarised in Table 10.16) provide some indication of the relative fee-earning capacities of different types of service, and Table 10.16 suggests that younger businesses are just as likely to have paid for advice in most business areas. Finance, sales and/or marketing advice and assistance with quality are the areas for which it appears to be most feasible to charge for the provision of advice services. At the other end of the scale, only half of respondents paid for the advice they had received regarding training issues, with the lowest proportion of non-payers stating that they would be willing to pay for such advice in the future. Recruitment is another area where businesses tend to expect (and receive) free advice. These statistics are not encouraging for agencies such as TECs, who tend to specialise in labour-market-related issues.

Those businesses which did not pay for the advice were asked if they would have been willing to pay for it and their responses are recorded in Table 10.17. There appears to be a considerable willingness to pay for certain types of advice (IT, finance) and in many cases younger businesses are more likely to exhibit a willingness to pay for what was 'free' advice than the average business.

Table 10.16 Paid for advice by age

Business area	0–3 yrs (%)	4–6 yrs (%)	7–13 yrs (%)	14+ yrs (%)	All (%)
IT/computing	70	61	68	78	73
Sales/marketing	69	100	81	82	81
Recruitment	20	0	65	71	55
Quality	70	61	72	82	76
Training	66	51	66	55	58
General business strategy	39	82	63	82	75
Finance	82	90	88	84	85
Other	55	60	54	66	62

Table 10.17 Willingness to pay for advice by age

Business area	0–3 yrs (%)	4–6 yrs (%)	7–13 yrs (%)	14+ yrs (%)	All (%)
IT/computing	33	88	39	61	57
Sales/marketing	47	0	42	19	33
Recruitment	73	0	0	73	37
Quality	50	70	40	41	47
Training	60	30	17	54	45
General business strategy	66	0	43	0	25
Finance	65	74	0	66	68
Other	0	41	48	57	45

Notwithstanding the comments made relating to the difficulty of charging for 'public sector' enterprise advice, it does appear that there may be some scope for at least partially covering the costs of providing advice services through some form of charging policy, although it remains to be seen how successful such approaches would be in practice.

LESSONS FOR POLICY

This paper has presented some results from a large-scale detailed investigation of the use made by established SMEs with 10–100 employees of advice services provided by organisations external to the business. The research has provided a large set of timely data suitable for use at both the operational and the strategic levels of the commissioning agent, Leeds TEC. The research has raised several issues of relevance to TECs and other organisations planning the development of advice services through 'Business Links' or similar arrangements.

SME needs

There are a multitude of SME business needs contingent on a variety of internal and external factors which SMEs may choose to address through the use of external agencies. In the absence of an encompassing explanatory framework to map the needs of developing SMEs, the research outlined in this chapter draws on the PRU approach to addressing the needs from a variety of perspectives. This chapter has focused on the needs associated with broad task areas in the SME. However, the research also investigated other dimensions such as key problem areas or barriers to growth facing the SME (usually macro-economic) and specific innovation opportunities.

There remain significant issues as to whether enterprise support services should be based on the needs of SMEs (by adopting a marketing-led approach) or the wants of SMEs by adopting a customer-led approach. The former approach involves ascertaining and understanding the underlying problems facing the business rather than the symptoms which SMEs often require addressing in the short term. This is a challenging domain and it remains to be seen whether researchers, support agencies or SME decision-makers themselves have the skills, abilities and/or resources to adequately recognise, define and address the business needs of SMEs in the long term.

Monitoring and evaluating services

It is vital to ensure that the services provided or supported by public agencies are effectively monitored and evaluated. There are several problems associated with evaluation of enterprise support. One problem is that the impact of support is usually not immediate or direct. The benefits to a business of effective business planning may only emerge over a period of months and years. Contact with a TEC or other agency may lead the business to think positively about the potential benefits of seeking external advice and support. This support may alternately come from a private consultant or other agency, but the TEC (or Business Link) will have played some role in prompting this move.

This suggests some of the problems associated with evaluation. Nevertheless, it is crucial if the services offered by Business Link, for example, are to be developed and implemented to meet the needs of SMEs. Evaluation should be a positive organisational change force. It must take account of criteria such as value for money and accountability but its focus should be as a tool to be used in informing the development, evolution and marketing of the services offered by the agency clearly focused on the needs of its SME customers and achievement of the agencies' objectives.

Proactive approach

It is clear from the research that established businesses face a multiplicity of business problems and issues which arise in different combinations and at various stages of the business life-cycle. Most problems are (at least in the mind of the owner-manager) unique to the individual business and require bespoke rather than off-the-shelf solutions.

Clearly, therefore, a proactive and flexible approach is necessary to ensure that information, advice and support services reach those businesses which can benefit, in the form which is most beneficial and at the time when it is needed. With the exception of a few very specific issues (e.g., the introduction of new legislation into specific sectors) it is unlikely that a general seminar or course will meet the needs of sufficient numbers of businesses at one time, to enable such provision to be cost-effective. A much more varied approach, drawing on specialist advisers, seems to be the most viable option. This type of approach is clearly more resource-intensive than the type of courses generally provided for start-up businesses, but if targeted effectively will have a significant pay-off in terms of growth and jobs.

Defining and segmenting the market for SME support services

Along with other studies (e.g. Curran 1993; Bennett, Wicks and McCoshan 1994) the research suggests low take-up of publicly funded enterprise support initiatives. However, while this may be the case in the potential market for SME support services, i.e., all SMEs, a clearer definition of the market in terms of the available market as a set of consumers who have interest, income and access to a particular product or service may lead to a different view of the take-up rate.

Leeds TEC provided the first clarification of the market they were interested in when they commissioned the research to address businesses employing between 10–100. However, commentators (e.g. Gibb 1993; Vyakarnam and Jacobs 1994) have argued that this is only the beginning of defining the market for SME support services. There are many proponents of a sector-based approach to SME support. The approach adopted by the PRU (Devins 1994) enables the support agency to segment the market in a number of ways based on a variety of variables. This is relatively easy, given the advances in computer and data-base technologies which has made the storage and processing of market information so much more accessible. This chapter has focused on the needs of SMEs based on their age and the 'market' has been analysed in terms of the following variables:

- rational management approach (existence of formal written business plans, linking of training plans with business plans, management structure);

- innovation (involvement in innovative activity);
- 'growth' expectations (expected turnover or employment growth, planned growth, growth strategy);
- task environment (e.g. IT, sales and marketing etc.).

The market can be further broken down by the successive application of the above attributes. The approach offers the opportunity to break down the market based on the needs of SMEs and to target segments on this basis. There appear to be significant readily identifiable segments of the market which may be addressed. For example:

- Businesses which do not identify any needs for external advice. In most cases this is because of a feeling that problems can (or should) be dealt with internally. Approaches to such businesses should emphasise the potential benefits of external advice in a way which does not threaten deeply held feelings of independence or self-reliance. Sectoral factors are important here. Working with trade associations in sectors such as hotels and catering, which have a very low propensity to seek advice, would be a potentially fruitful strategy, as would the provision of a diagnostic service which aided businesses to recognise different needs.
- Those who identify advice needs, but cannot find suitable suppliers. These are clearly important potential customers for a One Stop Shop (or 'First Stop Shop') advice service. The evidence suggests that such businesses are disproportionately 'first time' advice seekers, probably having been established for between three and six years and looking to grow or change in some way. Agencies need to find ways of targeting such businesses, for example, through the monitoring of information on new businesses, and approaching the cohort of businesses which has survived to three years. While our evidence suggests that this is a relatively small group in numerical terms (less than 10 per cent of businesses in the 10–100 size category), they are potentially very important for the performance of the local economy.
- Businesses with multiple advice needs. A significant proportion of longer-established businesses tend to look for advice across a number of business areas (e.g., marketing, quality, training and finance). It is important for policy-makers and delivery agents to recognise that one source of advice or one particular programme is unlikely to meet all of the complex needs of the established, growing business. This has important implications for 'One Stop Shop'-type approaches. The role of the Business Link cannot (and should not) be to provide all the necessary information, however it

may provide a means to provide an overview in order to bring the different sources of advice and recommendations together. Businesses which do recognise advice needs appear to have very little problem with seeking out sources from a number of possible providers – the problems come in trying to implement the solutions in a coherent way.

● Dissatisfied advice seekers. Businesses which have gone through the process of seeking and obtaining external advice, but have not been satisfied with the outcome represent an important group. Agencies need to establish why businesses are dissatisfied and look for ways to improve the 'market' for external advice, to avoid potential disillusionment.

Targeting the market and positioning services

Segmentation is the first step in breaking down the 'homogeneous' SME market. The information can be used to inform the development of a strategic approach to the development of services to meet the needs of SMEs and the targeting and positioning of its services. Targeting implies a more commercial approach to the development and provision of SME support services. It involves the evaluation of each of the market segment's 'attractiveness' and the selection of one or more segments to enter. This approach is dependent upon the recognition of the specialised needs of the SMEs. The PRU research can be used to target a variety of market segments. The indicators offer the potential for agencies to proactively target products and services to aid SMEs' development on the basis of business need. For example, the market can be segmented into those SMEs which require information and advice to develop more formalised systems and those SMEs which already have formalised systems which require external information and advice to service them.

The evidence suggests that a 'scatter-gun' approach to promoting the benefits of external advice, information and support is unlikely to bear fruit. SME owner-managers differ in their approach to external advice, and it is important to target promotional activities appropriately. The market information has to inform the marketing mix adopted by the support agencies in the market if a business-needled policy is to be developed. Decisions have to be made relating to the marketing mix associated with the service to be offered. What price will it be sold for? How will it be promoted? What is the best way to package it? The service needs to be differentiated in order that it has a clear distinctive place in the market. PRU research along with others (e.g. Bennett, Wicks and McCoshan 1994) suggest that many of the services offered by the support agencies are not clearly differentiated at present.

Network linkages

It is very clear from the research that businesses which do look for and use external advice are well used to using a wide range of sources. Very few respondents stated that they were confused by the large number of available providers and services. Business owners and managers seem to be able to cope with the fact that they need to look to different providers for services relating to different areas of businesses.

On the face of it, these findings appear to negate many of the arguments for the development of 'One Stop Shops'. Indeed, the research does suggest that it is very difficult to envisage a single organisation which could directly provide all of the information and assistance needs of every growing business. The Business Links clearly need to work very closely with specialist agencies such as trade associations and need to promote awareness of these sources amongst providers such as enterprise agencies and local authorities.

The research also suggests that large numbers of businesses approach financial and professional advisers about issues outside the purely financial area of the business – particularly business planning. There is clearly an opportunity here for agencies to work closely with the banking sector to ensure that clients are guided towards advice which takes an holistic rather than a purely financial view of the business planning process. Business plans can only be truly effective if, for example, managers have the skills necessary to implement them and to communicate effectively with the work-force. There is evidence to suggest that positive steps have been taken in some Business Links to address the public–private sector organisation linkages in the support system (Gunn 1994).

CONCLUSION

This chapter has outlined some of the results of the research undertaken by the Policy Research Unit. The methodology draws on a combination of quantitative and qualitative information to gain an insight into the dynamics of the SME market in Leeds. The methodology described in this paper provides one way of keeping track of overall trends in the attitudes of business owner-managers and their use of external advice. Not only does this allow the public agency to take stock of whether its activities are meeting the needs of the market, but it provides a valuable tool for evaluation of direct and indirect impacts of activities in a locality.

However, there remains a need to further develop the indicators used in the PRU research to take account of SME needs on the one hand and the economic and social objectives of each locality and those of the agencies operating within it on the other. This will help agencies develop their networking roles in the business support environment and inform the development of services and a proactive, flexible approach to enterprise support. The research has demonstrated that it is possible to obtain meaningful information from local businesses in a timely manner to aid the development and implementation of enterprise support services. The research has provided information which has been used to inform decision-making at the operational and strategic levels of Leeds TEC in both the planning of support services and the targeting of specific initiatives. Furthermore, there appear to be some valuable lessons to be learned for the development of Business Links and agencies involved in the development and implementation of business advice and support if the needs of SMEs are to be met.

ACKNOWLEDGEMENTS

This chapter is based on a research project funded by Leeds Training and Enterprise Council and I would like to extend my thanks to them for their support. The conference paper was joint authored with Steve Johnson and I would like to acknowledge his role in the preparation of the original paper.

BIBLIOGRAPHY

Bennett, R. J. , Wicks, P. and McCoshan, A. (1994) *Local Empowerment and Business Services*, London: UCL Press.
Curran, J. (1993) 'TECs and small firms: can TECs reach the small firms other strategies have failed to reach?', paper to All Party Science and Policy Group.
Department of Trade and Industry (1992) *A Prospectus for One Stop Shops for Business*, London: HMSO.
Department of Trade and Industry (1993) *Business Link: a Supplement to the Prospectus*, London: HMSO.
Devins, D. (1994) 'Segmenting the SME market: survey indicators', paper

presented at the 17th ISBA Small Firms Conference, 16–19 November, Sheffield.

Gibb, A. (1993) 'Key factors in the design of policy support for the small and medium enterprise (SME) development process: an overview', *Entrepreneurship and Regional Development*, 5: 1–24.

Gunn, S. (1994) 'The impact on small business development of the policies and practices of a dedicated intermediary networking resource within TECs', paper presented to the 17th ISBA Small Firms Conference, 16–19 November, Sheffield.

Hendry, C., Jones, A., Arthur, M. and Pettigrew, A. (1991) 'Human resource development in small to medium sized enterprises', *Employment Department Research Group Research Paper No. 88*.

Smallbone, D., North, D. and Leigh, R. (1993) 'The use of external assistance by mature SMEs in the UK: some policy implications', *Entrepreneurship and Regional Development*, 5, 3: 279–95.

Storey, D. (1994) *Understanding the Small Business Sector*, London: Routledge.

Storey, D. and Strange, A. (1992) 'Fast Growth Businesses in Cleveland', Department of Employment Research Paper.

Vyakarnam, S. and Jacobs, R. (1994) 'A new framework for enterprise support', paper presented to the Small Business and Enterprise Development Conference, Manchester.

11 New software companies in Scotland
Growth constraints and policy implications

Tony Clarke

INTRODUCTION

This chapter reports some of the findings of research in progress on the growth prospects of new and established firms in the software and computer services industry in Scotland. On a global and UK scale, this sector has taken on particular significance in the 1980s and 1990s, largely due to the shift in value-added and activity within the information systems or computer industry from hardware to software and services. Falling margins in computer hardware and peripherals pose a particular threat to the Scottish economy, given that its employment profile in high-tech industry is heavily influenced by its position as a base for computer and electronics assembly operations. In this context, Scottish economic development agencies have begun to target the software industry as a focus for policies directed towards inward investment, indigenous start-ups and 'growth companies'. Scottish Enterprise National established a small project team in 1990 with a specific focus on software, and interviews in the policy network indicate that at least three local enterprise companies have developed initiatives specifically targeted on software companies.

What are the characteristics and origins of indigenous software and computer services firms in Scotland? What are the major constraints on the growth of established and new firms? What conclusions can be drawn regarding economic development policies in relation to this sector?

Two theoretical perspectives have informed the tentative answers to these questions framed in this chapter. The choice of these perspectives reflects the fact that the software industry can be analysed both as part of a wider complex of producer services industries and as a site of research-intensive high-tech based firms.

There is a growing body of literature on the role of producer services in regional development (cf. Howells 1987, and the wider surveys by Marshall and Jaeger 1990, O'Farrell and Hitchens 1990, and Wood 1991). In the UK, this literature emphasises the concentration of producer services growth in Southern England, in response to spatial patterns in the location of corporate headquarters and administrative functions of government, and to a tendency to agglomeration through the co-location of suppliers of complementary services. 'Peripheral' regions which are less well-endowed with higher corporate functions are viewed sceptically with respect to the prospects for the formation of strong complexes of producer service companies (Massey and Allen 1988). Supplier–customer linkages within a particular region, and especially the presence or absence of customers with a demand for sophisticated services, are viewed as critical to growth and innovation within such complexes (O'Farrell, Hitchens and Moffat 1992). Access to such customers is a key source of technical information for the development of innovative services which contribute to the competitiveness of indigenous companies in both local and extra-regional markets. This literature suggests that indigenous companies in 'peripheral' regions may be confined to market niches and customers which are unattractive to major service providers. This could constitute a source of cumulative disadvantage which would be heightened by the growing internationalisation of producer services. In consequence, extra-regionally based or foreign suppliers would tend to win the larger and more sophisticated client contracts within the region, thus closing off a key source of competitive advantage from indigenous firms.

By contrast, the literature on high-tech-based firms, innovation and regional development is more attuned to research-based, product-oriented companies, and to the funding and other constraints which might inhibit their growth (Oakey 1984, Oakey et al. 1990). The mobilisation of resources for product development is seen as a central focus for constraints on company growth. Although this work is sensitive to the importance of linkages to other organisations, particularly for purposes of technical information exchange and product development, it emphasises that such linkages are not necessarily localised in particular regional complexes. The geographical dispersal of such linkages is more likely the closer one gets to the frontier of scientific research, where relationships need to be forged with major international companies and research organisations.

The relevance of these perspectives to the questions posed earlier will be addressed below. Their fruitfulness depends in part on the specific relationships between products and services in the software industry, both in general and specifically in Scotland. To begin to assess this relationship, this paper will be organised as follows. First, it will profile the origins and activities of companies, drawing on data from a postal survey of software and computer services establishments in Scotland which was conducted in June/July 1993. This survey produced 122 useable responses, from a population of 278 companies and business units, compiled from relevant trade and business directories. This represented a response rate of 43 per cent. Second, findings from the survey will be presented regarding constraints on company growth. These findings will be interpreted in the light of the theoretical considerations posed above. Finally, conclusions will be drawn regarding policies for promoting the development of the software and computer services industry in Scotland and other 'peripheral' locations.

The central argument in this chapter will be that new and established software and computer services companies in Scotland reflect elements of, and experience problems diagnosed by, both perspectives. However, the precise nature of these problems is mediated by the specific relationships between products and services, and the particular trends in markets, technology and user requirements in the sector in question. This supports the need for a sectoral focus in the development of policy on the part of economic development agencies.

SOFTWARE AND COMPUTER SERVICES COMPANIES IN SCOTLAND

A definition of the sector

It is difficult to operationalise a definition of the software and computer services industry, due to the diversity of activities and types of participating companies which it entails. New sources of competition have entered the field of software-related services over the past 10 years, including computer hardware companies, management consultants, retailers of computer hardware and software (Value Added Resellers or VARs), and spin-offs from the IT Departments of non-IT companies seeking to market expertise developed for in-house use. For the purposes of the research reported here, the sector was defined in terms of companies or separable business units located in Scotland and either producing software products for sale or providing marketed services involving a software development function or software-related consultancy. Companies or business units involved solely in the sale of third-party hardware and software, or in routine service functions such as hardware maintenance and training, were excluded. The focus on software-related functions was adopted in part to ensure a match with the efforts of economic development agencies in this sector and with data from earlier surveys commissioned by these agencies.

In the UK, the software and computer services industry is characterised by somewhat contradictory trends. On the one hand, there has been a tendency towards the internationalisation of the sector, with the growth of large computer service firms and an internationalisation of ownership. These tendencies are favoured by the internationalisation of user companies and the shift in user requirements towards single sourcing for international operations. There has been a concomitant growth in demand for 'total solutions' which has increased the pressure on suppliers to be capable of accessing a range of complementary services. For instance, the boundaries between management consultancy and services related to information technology has been blurring, and computer services companies have increasingly required specialist knowledge of the business area of their clients in order to service their IT requirements. These factors are enhancing the significance of internal economies of scale and scope within computer services companies. On the other hand, the rapid pace of change in technology and user requirements, particularly with the advent of smaller computer systems and computer networks, has continued to provide a range of market niches for the entry of new start-ups and the survival of small, regionally based firms. The industry structure appears to show a growing polarisation between large, generalist, computer services conglomerates and smaller companies serving localised or specialist markets.

Origins and character of software companies in Scotland

The structure of the Scottish industry reflects these trends. Most software companies are small, independent Scottish-owned companies, founded within the past decade. Independent Scottish-owned companies represented 94 (77 per cent) of the 122 respondents to the survey. However, branches of largely UK and overseas companies were significantly larger than these indigenous companies. Only 21 (24 per cent) of 87 independent companies reported a turnover in excess of £1 million in the most recent financial year, as compared to eight (47 per cent) of 17 branches. Moreover, some of these branches had expanded particularly rapidly, making a disproportionately large contribution to the growth of aggregate revenue in the respondent companies. Turnover in the three years to 1992/3 had increased by 45 per cent in cash terms, taken as the aggregate change for 88 respondent companies. It is notable that two UK-owned branches alone accounted for about one-third (31 per cent) of this increase in turnover. It is unclear how far the rapid growth of such branch establishments has been at the expense of indigenous Scottish companies. It is likely that this growth is due in some measure to the expansion of outsourcing by IT user organisations, as in the development of facilities management services, and to the rapid growth of scale intensive markets such as systems integration.

Turning to examine the nature and origins of indigenous software and computer service companies in more detail (Table 11.1), these were primarily young, with 70 per cent founded after 1983, and only 14 per cent founded prior to 1981.

The survey generated data on the employment status of founders of these companies immediately prior to their establishment and on the factors which were reported by founders as having initiated the founding of the company (Table 11.2). Data on founders was provided by 86 independent companies, covering a total of 143 individuals.

Founders came from a range of backgrounds, but notably from other software and computer services companies and from positions in other organisations which involved responsibilities for managing or delivering IT services in-house. The small proportion of founders (4.9 per cent) who came directly from an academic post is notable. Most Scottish software companies have been formed by personnel with close past relationships with IT users, and few are start-ups derived directly from expertise gained in academic research. Such academic spin-offs are rare in proportion to the software industry in Scotland as a whole.

Table 11.1 Year of foundation of Scottish-owned independent companies (n = 93)

	Pre-1981	*1981–3*	*1984–6*	*1987–9*	*1990–*
No.	13	15	18	27	20
%	14	16	19	29	22

Source: Postal survey June/July 1993

Table 11.2 Prior employment position of founders (n = 143)

Position of founder	No.	%
Proprietor/director	24	16.8
Sales/marketing	20	14.0
IT management	12	8.4
Software engineer/analyst	20	14.0
Other management	12	8.4
Consultant	16	11.2
Engineer	11	7.7
Academic post	7	4.9
Student	9	6.3
Other	13	9.1
Total	143	100.0

Source: Postal survey June/July 1993

Respondents were also asked to indicate from a list of factors those which 'helped to stimulate the decision to start the company'. Founders' lack of satisfaction with their previous posts or career prospects was the most frequently cited factor, followed by the existence of ideas for products or services generated in the course of previous employment (Table 11.3). Comparing newer companies, founded after 1987, with those founded before this date displays some change in the factors behind start-ups. Redundancy or closure on the part of previous employers appears to have increased in importance, although numbers were too small to permit of reliable tests of significance. However, a statistically significant difference did emerge in the extent to which product/service ideas from prior employment played a part in the decision to establish a company. Companies founded after 1987 were significantly less likely to cite product or service ideas from previous employment as a factor (chi square: $p = .034$).

Taken together, Tables 11.2 and 11.3 suggest that most start-ups have arisen from personnel in IT functions, and from management personnel, in companies engaged commercially or in-house in IT related activities, with little input from academic research. There are worrying signs that the stimulus behind the formation of more recent companies may have shifted somewhat in relative terms from factors based on commercial ideas generated in employment to 'push' factors associated with career dissatisfaction and corporate retrenchment. This concern is strengthened given that formation dates for responding companies incorporate both the recession of the early

Table 11.3 Factors cited as stimulating start-up ('established' and 'new' companies) (n = 93)

Factors in start-up	Year of formation	
	Pre-1988	1988–
Dissatisfied with post/career	28	24
Redundancy/closure	7	13
Product/service idea from prior employment (*)	31	14
Customer contacts from prior employment	14	13
Opportunity to work independently for previous employer	5	8
Other reasons	10	11
Total	95	83

Source: Postal survey June/July 1993
Note: Numbers in the table are numbers of companies responding. Some respondents cited more than one factor.
(*) denotes a statistically significant relationship at the 5% confidence level between the frequency of citation of the factor and the period in which the company was founded.

1980s and to a lesser extent that of the early 1990s (see Table 11.1 above).

Products and services in the activities of software-related companies

The product–service distinction is a necessary but problematic starting point in discussing the character and origins of software-related companies. The software and computer services industry in Scotland and the UK as a whole is primarily service oriented. Although a large proportion of companies in the survey reported some revenue from software products developed in-house, very few companies can be portrayed as primarily product-based. Only 13 (14 per cent) of 93 independent Scottish-owned companies derived more than half of their revenue from software products. By contrast, 81 or 87 per cent of these companies reported that they had developed software products for sale over the preceding five years.

In most cases, these products have taken the form of applications software, generally tailored to particular types of user in specific vertical market segments. Such products are often developed from bespoke programming work for a particular client, by subsequently developing and repackaging the code for wider sale. In this respect, products and services are interdependent in a manner which reflects the specific character of software development. The centrality of software development to IT services, and the nature of software, create opportunities for product development which are not available in some other business services.

The interdependence between software products and related services has increased due to a further trend, namely, the increasing service content involved in the supply of products. Software products are more readily exportable than many services, since they can be marketed through third parties (distributors, VARs) and in some cases direct to customers without a direct presence in the target market. However, profit margins on software products are tending to fall, following the trend in hardware. As with computer hardware, software product sales are increasingly functioning as a vehicle for the sale of value-added services (consultancy, system modification, installation and training, for instance). For this reason, the development of applications software products is now more important to the competitiveness of software and computer service companies than is reflected in the share of such products in company revenue. Such products function in part to access a wider customer base.

The final point above indicates that many applications software products developed by small companies share key characteristics with services, in that close knowledge of customer requirements is a key to competitiveness. Thus, in the Scottish survey data, the bulk of companies sell software products directly to end users, and specify customers as important sources of technical information for product development. Eighty five (87 per cent) of 98 responding companies (including both branches and independent companies) used this sales route. The next most frequently mentioned route was the use of VARs or distributors (18 companies, or 19 per cent of respondents). Customers were also the dominant source of technical information for the development of new products and services, referred to by 81 (79 per cent) of 103 companies, followed equally by hardware vendors and other software houses, each cited by 27 (26 per cent) of respondents.

Links with customers for technical information enabling the development of new products or services were significantly more common among companies founded prior to 1988. This appears to reflect the time required to develop relationships and technical contacts with customers, rather than any major difference in the activities of companies founded before or after that year. The data have not revealed significant differences in the range of activities between newer and more established companies.

In summary, the data on the origins and character of software and software-related computer service companies in Scotland indicates a sector which is intermediate between the two theoretical models discussed in the Introduction. The potential for product development inherent in the software development function indicates the relevance of themes from the literature on high-technology small firms. However, the small independent companies in the sample are closer on balance to the concerns of the literature on producer services. In particular, many have originated from a service base and continue to depend on revenue from services in order to fund product development (see IDA 1992). Thus, relatively few Scottish software companies are leading edge, research-intensive concerns with origins in or links to academic and other research institutions. However, such companies are represented in the survey, particularly by a small minority of companies engaged in the development of systems or utilities software, necessitating geographically dispersed linkages with leading hardware or packaged software developers. Issues regarding constraints on company growth and policy implications need to be interpreted in the light of the particular mix of characteristics examined above.

GROWTH CONSTRAINTS AND POLICY IMPLICATIONS

Given the profile of the sector in Scotland provided above, one would expect to find that the implications of the producer services literature on constraints on the growth of indigenous companies are borne out. In particular, small independent companies should be constrained particularly by the lack of access to sophisticated customers within the regional economy. This would then inhibit their ability to develop products and services which are competitive in wider markets. A full test of this hypothesis would require a comparative dimension to the research and a direct examination of customer requirements in different regions. However, the data from the survey does provide some insights into this argument. In particular, the survey indicates that only a minority of companies aim their services or products wholly or partially at small businesses (35 or 33 per cent of respondents). 'Blue chip' clients figure prominently for many companies. Nevertheless, for the small independent companies, there are strong indications that they are unable to compete with larger UK and international organisations in terms of scale and access to the prime contractor role in large systems development contracts. Such companies may not lack technical sophistication, but may have a tendency to be confined to servicing the needs of larger organisations on smaller contracts. The survey provided some data on contract size which supports this conclusion. Only 12 of 75 independent companies specified an average contract size of more than £50,000, as compared to 12 of 15 branch establishments. The scale factors referred to above appear particularly significant as a constraint on the growth of service-oriented indigenous companies. This would suggest that Scottish software companies, many of which occupy sophisticated but small market niches, would need to broaden the geographical scope of their markets early in their life-cycle in order to grow. Information on constraints on company growth perceived by companies tends to bear out the salience of this need to a significant proportion of companies.

Respondents to the survey were asked which, if any, of a list of factors had proven to be 'serious constraints' on company growth over the past three years (Table 11.4). Over 40 per cent of respondents specified resource constraints inhibiting their ability to research new markets and a similar proportion identified constraints on their capacity to achieve entry to new markets. The most commonly cited constraint, however, was the lack of resources to develop new products and/or services, which was indicated by 71 or 67 per cent of respondents. Responses to a further question, which examined resource constraints on companies which had plans to develop new software products, found that independent companies were significantly more likely to cite product development funding constraints than branch establishments (chi square: p = .012). Newer companies founded after 1987 were also significantly more likely to report this constraint (chi square: p = .042).

Constraints on funding the development of new products and services need to be interpreted in the light of the low capital intensity and human-resource-intensive character of software development. In

Table 11.4 Frequency of citation of 'serious constraints on growth' (independent companies and branches)

Growth constraint	Nos	%	n
Policies of parent	7	6.5	107
Availability of investment funds	33	31.7	104
Lack of suitable premises	13	12.4	105
Distance from markets	12	11.3	106
Limited Scots customer base	35	33.3	105
Lack resources to research markets	46	43.8	105
Lack resources to enter markets	48	45.3	106
Lack resources for product/service development	71	67.0	106

Source: Postal survey June/July 1993

specific relation to the development of new software products, qualitative responses by companies to questions in the survey indicate that staff time and the quality of staff were important problems. Resources to free key personnel to undertake development work appear to be a specific need. The problems of small software companies in this regard are heightened by their relative lack of fixed assets, which renders some potential funding sources, such as bank loans, difficult to access.

The data in Table 11.4 suggest the relevance of some themes from literature on new-technology-based firms. In particular, Oakey (1984) identified the difficulty which companies have in freeing resources for further product development over the short life-cycle of existing products, leading to recurrent funding problems at the end of each life-cycle. In addition, in an industry characterised by rapid change, particularly in user requirements, this point may have relevance to the resources required to diversify and update services, rather than applying primarily to product development. Public sector funding for innovation, for instance through innovation grants and awards administered in Scotland by the Scottish Office Industry Department, is generally available only for the development of tangible products. Public sector support for service development and diversification is not well-developed.

What policy implications can be drawn from the above? The applicability of themes from the producer services literature to software and computer services in Scotland suggests the importance of measures to develop more sophisticated forms of customer demand and to strengthen local linkages between customers and suppliers. Programmes such as the Forum for Open Systems, sponsored by Scottish Enterprise, embody such objectives. This programme is one of a number which seek to strengthen technical and commercial contacts between software developers and user organisations in Scotland and, in the process, to encourage suppliers to upgrade their technological capabilities. Conversely, literature on new-technology-based firms may also have relevance. Oakey (1984, and Oakey et al. 1990) favours a strategy of supporting growth companies through public sector equity investment. However, the research reported in this paper suggests a shortage of leading edge, product-based software companies in Scotland. Key economic development agencies (for instance, Scottish Enterprise and Local Enterprise Companies) are already targeting product-based, export-oriented companies in high-tech sectors. Such companies are not numerous, at least in the software field, and it is not easy to see how the policies of development agencies can rapidly increase this stock through a higher rate of successful high-tech based start-ups. There may be a case, however, for the extension of innovation grants to address the specific problems of small software firms in product development and service diversification. The survey data indicate that a substantial proportion of companies perceive themselves as constrained by a lack of available funding for these purposes. If public sector funding is confined to a small minority of established, export-oriented and product-based firms, the most likely outcome is an intensification of competition between economic development agencies to attract and support them.

CONCLUSIONS

The software industry in Scotland does not fall neatly into one or other of the two theoretical frameworks outlined briefly in the introduction to this chapter. The specific technology and market trends applicable to software and computer services mediate the effects of the more general regional development tendencies derived from these literatures. In particular, the nature of software development and the complex relationship between software-related services and software products imply that the industry cannot be conceived exclusively either as a component of producer services or as a product-based high-tech sector. The current policy mix contains elements which can be related to each of these perspectives, although the dominant emphasis is on support for a minority of export-oriented product-based companies. The survey data provides support for the extension of funding assistance in the light of the more general problems faced by small software companies in funding product and service development. One positive aspect of the current policies of economic development agencies in Scotland has been the development of sector-specific programmes. Given the specific characteristics of the software and computer services industry reported above, this sectoral focus needs to be retained and developed.

ACKNOWLEDGEMENTS

The research reported here was supported by the funding of a research assistantship by the University of Paisley. Thanks are due to Alison Carnichan for her contribution to the research project and comments on an earlier draft of this paper.

BIBLIOGRAPHY

Howells, J. (1987) 'Developments in the location, technology and industrial organisation of computer services: some trends and research issues', *Regional Studies*, 21: 493–503.

IDA (1992) *The Software Industry in Ireland: A Strategic Review*, National Software Directorate, Industrial Development Authority of Ireland: Dublin.

Marshall, J. N. and Jaeger, C. (1990) 'Service activities and uneven spatial development in Britain and its European partners: determinist fallacies and new options', *Environment and Planning A*, 22: 1337–54.

Massey, D. and Allen, J. (eds) (1988) *Uneven Redevelopment*, London: Hodder and Stoughton.

Oakey, R. (1984) 'Innovation and regional growth in small high-technology firms: evidence from Britain and the USA', *Regional Studies*, 18: 237–51.

Oakey, R., Faulkner, W., Cooper, S. and Walsh, V. (1990) *New Firms in the Biotechnology Industry: Their Contribution to Innovation and Growth*, London: Pinter.

O'Farrell, P. N. and Hitchens, D. (1990) 'Research policy and review 32. Producer services and regional development', *Environment and Planning A*, 22: 1141–54.

O'Farrell, P. N., Hitchens, D. and Moffat, L. (1992) 'The competitiveness of business service firms: A matched comparison between Scotland and the South East of England', *Regional Studies*, 26: 519–33.

Wood, P. (1991) 'Conceptualising the role of producer services in economic change', *Area*, 23: 66–72.

12 What is the role of new firms in a local economic development strategy?
How the issue was tackled in developing Forth Valley Enterprise's business strategy

Richard Holt

INTRODUCTION

This chapter considers whether new firms have any special role to play in a local economic development strategy. The chapter is in three sections. The first draws on the theoretical economics literature to consider whether new firms have a special contribution to make to economic development, and whether in principle new firms require special help from government. The conclusion is that the literature provides little firm guidance. Accordingly, the second section discusses an approach which side-steps many of the conventional problems and uncertainties, and which has been used by one development agency, Forth Valley Enterprise, in deciding how large a role to ascribe to the encouragement of new firm formation in its local economic development strategy. The third section looks at that example in detail, while the final section draws some conclusions about the approach and the case for generalising either the methodology or the policy conclusions to other local economies.

SOME THEORY

New firms and economic growth

Much of the academic writing on new firms is concerned with identifying the factors which favour the inception and (to a lesser extent) the survival of new companies. These are perfectly reasonable subjects to investigate but there is a prior question, discussed elsewhere in this volume, of whether new firms have a special contribution to make to economic development. It is too easy just to assume that new firms are desirable, without considering why that should be.

Many commonplace claims exist about the special qualities of smaller – and by extension, new – firms. Small firms are supposedly leaner, less bureaucratic, more entrepreneurial and more innovative than larger firms and, as a result, it is supposed that they grow further and faster than established firms. Small firms are thought to be especially important as wealth creators and job creators, and they are also considered to be more committed to their local communities than large firms, both in the sense of sourcing and recruiting locally and in the sense of being less geographically footloose than large companies.

Even if small firms in general and new firms in particular really do possess these or other special qualities (itself a matter of dispute) the question remains as to why that should be so. Ordinary economic growth theory provides little insight, focused as it is on a neoclassical production function that is blind to institutional structure. At best, it might be argued that the entrepreneurial and innovative qualities of smaller firms are represented in neoclassical theory by the ubiquitous third term in the growth equation. However, that term already does duty as a measure of the effects of R&D, technical innovation, education, and so on, and it would be far-fetched to use estimates of the size of this term as a justification for ascribing a key role to small firms.

This is especially true if, as Scott suggests, the third term is little more than a measurement error arising from too narrow a definition of capital formation (Scott 1989). Scott defines investment very broadly as expenditure devoted to changing existing arrangements in the economy. Creating a new firm seems to be a clear case of changing such arrangements, but still perhaps only one of many such cases.

An alternative approach is that of Schumpeter (1934), who argued long ago that new firms are important because they innovate; in particular, they adopt new products or processes that are better than those of existing firms, and hence they grow faster. However, product and process innovation can and does occur within existing large firms, and there is a strong sense in which, for example, the large pharmaceuticals firms regularly reinvent themselves when they launch major new products. So there is no immediately obvious reason for assuming that new firm formation might be better or worse than other types of structural change such as, for example, its near opposite, merger activity. Furthermore, the available empirical information on new firms such as Acs and Audretsch hardly makes one confident about the Schumpeter story (Acs and Audretsch 1989).

A less ambitious theoretical justification for new firms is not that they are especially dynamic and innovative, but simply that they are cheap and efficient. Strictly speaking, this argument, which largely hinges on the relationship between technical economies of scale and managerial diseconomies, is about the merits of small firms relative to large firms rather than new firms relative to existing ones (Stigler 1951). However, the argument may be particularly apposite to new firms, since one source of new firm formation is the contracting out of activities from existing firms. The theory of vertical integration suggests that subcontracting will occur when market transaction costs are lower than a firm's internal bureaucratic costs and when the information provided by price signals is at least as good as the information available within an organisation. However, company insiders may be able to conceal their relative inefficiency from their colleagues and employers, and thereby obtain a rent. Less tendentiously, inertia will generate the same result. That suggests that if new firms have the effect of stripping activities away from existing firms, then they may generate an increase in overall efficiency.

It is possible, however, that the key difference between firms that win subcontract work and the organizations which contract the work out is not relative productive efficiency but relative wage rates. That is indeed a common suspicion, and it is possible that small firms (new or otherwise) use low wages to compensate for their inability to exploit economies of scale. To the extent that such firms are nevertheless able to win business from elsewhere, there may still be net gain to the local economy, especially if overall employment rises. Ultimately, however, the conclusions are ambiguous.

Alternatively, subcontracting may be essentially a device for shifting risk. If small firms are less able to spread risk than large firms, that may imply an overall loss of efficiency. Finally, shifting some activities out of a firm may reduce the viability of other activities, as internal economies are turned into external economies. Training, an activity commonly associated with large firms more than small ones, might, for example, be reduced as a result of any growth of small firms at the expense of large firms. Also, small firms may be less able than large firms to obtain supplies and recruit staff from far afield because they cannot afford the search costs. If so, then the tendency for small firms to source and recruit locally may be a sign of inefficiency and not, as is commonly assumed, a clear advantage from a local development perspective.

For many people, the key measure of the usefulness of new firms is that they create significant additional employment. For example, research by Scottish Enterprise on employment changes and VAT registrations in Scottish regions between 1980 and 1990 suggests that 'Having allowed for other factors which could generate employment growth, the analysis confirms that new firms have a significant effect on job creation' (Scottish Enterprise 1993: 12). It is not clear, however, what the policy implications of that should be. The results may be a sign that policy initiatives are needed to strengthen the performance of medium sized or large firms, to bring them up to the standards of new firms. Also, if the high rate of job creation is an indication of a low ratio of capital to labour, it may be more a sign of capital shortage than anything else. This can bring with it a range of other possible problems such as poor investment in human capital, to which development agencies cannot be indifferent.

A further clear difficulty with policies to encourage new starts is the high failure rate of new businesses: official estimates from the Employment Department (1992) suggest a 36 per cent mortality within three years. How problematic that is depends of course on the counter-factual: a one in three chance of losing your job within three years may be better than having no job at all – unless, as is often the case, the whole experience imposes great psychological and financial hardship on the person concerned. Conversely, if support that was withheld from new starts was provided instead to existing firms, then on average the consequence might be stronger and more sustained growth rates for output and perhaps employment – see (Storey 1992).

Even that is not certain, however. It is possible that government support for new starts is genuinely additional, and allows activity to take place that would not otherwise occur, whereas support to existing firms may simply displace inputs (managerial, financial, or whatever) that would otherwise be bought in the usual way. If that is true then, given the multitude of linkages, it rapidly becomes impossible to establish the overall economic impact of such measures.

MARKET FAILURE AND SOCIAL ARGUMENTS

Although it is not clear whether new firms really do have any special contribution to make to local development strategies, it may still be appropriate for public policy to provide special assistance to new firm formation, and to provide a degree of post-natal care, if for some reason market failures generate problems for new firms that do not exist for established companies.

The most compelling example of such a market failure is the difficulty that small firms face in raising finance. The problem is well-known: lenders want a track record to examine before they will provide funds, so either finance is rationed and new firms just cannot get funds, or in the absence of a track record lenders impose borrowing terms that undermine the viability of the new firm. Whereas the remedy for the general failure is likely to be Keynesian demand management, a macro answer will not deal with the specific problems of potential new starts.[1] Hence, there is a policy case for giving special help to new starts.

Furthermore, although this financial example is the most widely discussed, it probably has several counterparts. For example, new firms may have difficulty in recruiting the kind of managerial or professional staff whose reputations are influenced by the reputations of their employers. New firms may also have difficulty getting sales because potential customers are worried about the reliability of such firms as suppliers. More generally, new firms may have to spend heavily on establishing brand awareness, something which is already a sunk cost for established firms.[2]

However, the case of sunk costs draws attention to a theoretical difficulty. Sunk costs are often described as a powerful, even if perhaps unintentional, barrier to entry. The same is true for advertising, although in that case the degree of intention is likely to be higher. That suggests that the dividing line between a problem of market failure on one side and a characteristic of market structure on the other side may be difficult to discern. That in turn implies that the 'market failure' arguments for intervention to help new starts may be less straightforward than is sometimes suggested.

Admittedly, that is not a problem if one accepts a general public policy case against all market concentration and in favour of promoting highly competitive market structures. If so, the case for policy to promote and support new firms can be subsumed under a larger industrial and competition policy. Some of the popular arguments for new firms do indeed seem to be part of a larger pro-competitive structure agenda, and indeed the poor survival rate of new firms may well be partly the result of anti-competitive activities on the part of larger rivals with more market power.

The difficulty with this approach is that market concentration may not be universally undesirable. If market concentration means that firms invest more, perhaps because they capture consumer surplus, perhaps because they face less uncertainty than firms in less concentrated markets, then the consequence may be faster economic growth and a net welfare gain. In such a story there are likely to be casualties, and new firms are obviously at risk. This may imply that policy to help new firms is pointless and wasteful. Less harshly, it may imply that policies to help small firms perhaps have more in common with social policies than with purely economic development strategies. Social policies arise in response to market failures, and such policies may be legitimate even if they will do nothing to transform the general state of the economy.

A NEW APPROACH: THE FORTH VALLEY METHODOLOGY

Two broad points were made in the previous section. First, neither theory nor evidence provides general and conclusive answers to the question of under what circumstances a faster rate of new firm formation will cause faster economic growth and increased economic welfare. Second, help for new firms may nevertheless be defended on the same grounds that are used to support social policy interventions, which is that new firms are discriminated against by the market mechanism, and hence there is a role for public policy.

In practice, local development strategies rarely take the latter approach. Instead, they seek to defend support for new firms, either idealistically or cynically, in terms of their potential contribution to local economic development. So if those are the terms on which the argument must proceed, a new analytical framework is needed to help answer the question of what should be the role on new firms in a local development strategy.

Such a framework has been developed for Scotland's Central Region, or 'Forth Valley' as it is otherwise known. Forth Valley comprises a region to the north of Edinburgh and Glasgow which includes the towns of Alloa, Falkirk and Stirling, plus a large rural area including Loch Lomond and the Trossachs – see Figure 12.1. For several years Forth Valley has experienced higher unemployment rates than the Scottish average, and in the recent recession it appeared to be suffering more heavily than many other parts of the nation. The reasons for this underperformance are, as always, open to debate. At least until recently, the area has lacked particular strength in Scotland's fastest growing sectors such as electronics, support for North Sea activities, distilling and financial services. However, sectoral reasons cannot entirely explain Forth Valley's apparently poor

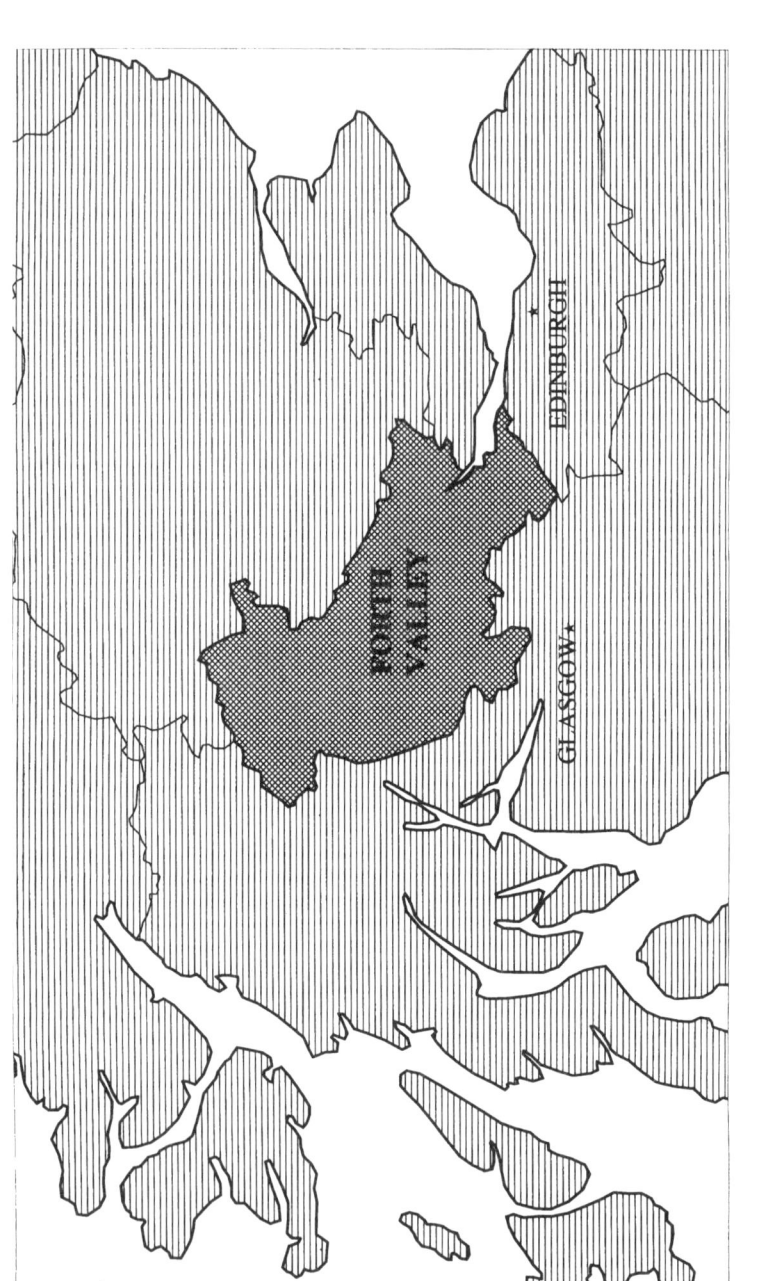

Figure 12.1 Scotland's Forth Valley

performance, since the region does have its own sectoral strength in the form of the giant petrochemicals complex at Grangemouth, where half of Scotland's North Sea oil is landed and where major employers such as BP and Zeneca are located. Accordingly, Forth Valley Enterprise suspected that a low rate of new firm formation might be an important part of its problem, and thus wanted a feel for whether it should focus more of its resources on promoting new starts.

The approach developed during 1993 on behalf of Forth Valley Enterprise (FVE), the local economic development organisation for the region, involved the following steps:

- quantify what the development strategy is trying to achieve over the long term;
- derive the implications of that in terms of output (GDP) for the initial year or years;
- derive what has to be achieved in terms of the number of new starts if they are to contribute a particular share of that output;
- similarly derive what has to be achieved via other measures such as export promotion to contribute the same share of the total;
- compare those against existing rates of new firm formation, exports etc.;
- also compare them against the track records of local development agencies at helping new starts, supporting exports etc.;
- iterate towards a policy mix which provides the best combination of what the agencies are trying to achieve and what in practice they can deliver.

The following section describes the approach in detail, while the final section considers the possibility of adapting and transfering the approach to other regions.

LONG-TERM OBJECTIVES

In 1993 Forth Valley Enterprise had already identified four long-term objectives – raising real incomes, encouraging inward net migration, achieving low unemployment and helping to create a distinctive regional identity – tied together by a declared vision of Forth Valley as 'a prosperous area with a high quality of life' (see Forth Valley Enterprise 1993: 1). One way to quantify what these aims meant in practice was to consider the scale of increase in local output (gross domestic product or GDP) that would be needed to reverse Forth Valley's relative decline, and attain levels of income per head equivalent to those prevailing elsewhere in the United Kingdom (or alternatively in Scotland alone or in Europe as a whole).

Baseline projections using Business Strategies' national, regional and local area models suggested that, in the absence of policy initiatives from Forth Valley Enterprise, the local economy would experience average annual growth rates over the period 1993 to 1997 of 1.9 per cent. That compared with 1.8 per cent for Scotland and 2.2 per cent for the United Kingdom.[3] Thus, Forth Valley would recoup only a little lost ground against Scotland and would not grow relative to the United Kingdom. Indeed, given existing disparities between income levels, and assuming the same rate of productivity gain and the same capital/labour income distribution as in the baseline forecast, the projections implied that it would be necessary to raise Forth Valley's growth rates by 0.75 per cent a year over the next decade, to reverse fully the previous decade's decline in Forth Valley's share of the Scottish economy.[4]

In the light of that, Forth Valley Enterprise decided to adopt a target of adding, on average, an extra 0.75 per cent a year of output to the local economy. Since the 0.75 per cent extra growth would be in addition to the forecast of annual growth of 1.75 per cent growth over the period, it would mean a growth rate of 2.5 per cent a year, or about the historical average for the United Kingdom. In those terms it seemed a reasonable target at which Forth Valley Enterprise could aim – and anything less would imply an acceptance that the agency could not succeed in its fundamental objectives of helping to create a prosperous area with a high quality of life.

Calculations suggested that over a decade the additional 0.75 per cent a year of output would result in Forth Valley GDP attaining a level £200 million higher at constant 1993 prices than in the baseline forecast. Put another way, it would be consistent with Forth Valley achieving average pay levels, outside the well-paid chemicals sector, roughly equal to the average levels in the United Kingdom as a whole, while also achieving a significant increase in employment in the region.[5] In the baseline forecast Forth Valley would continue to have quite a loose labour market over the coming decade, particularly for men. However, if the output target was achieved within a decade, that might create some 10,000 jobs, assuming that the current productivity mix applied. If Forth Valley Enterprise chose to go for low-productivity jobs, perhaps in tourism, then many more jobs would be created.

Of course, if employment goes up 10,000, unemployment will fall by considerably less. This is because some of those obtaining work will come from outside the currently available local labour force, either through an increase in the participation rate or through immigrants or in-commuters. Nevertheless, since in 1993 there were about 12,000 men without jobs (either on the basis of registered unemployment or those who are really looking for work) and 12,000 women, it can be seen that hitting the output target would solve a large share of Forth Valley Enterprise's unemployment problem, without particular recourse to low-productivity jobs designed simply to empty the unemployment register as quickly as possible.

SHORT-TERM TARGETS

Since the long-term target implied that, by 2004, Forth Valley GDP at constant 1993 prices would need to be £200 million higher than in the baseline forecast, it follows that a smooth profile would suggest targets of generating an extra £20 million in the first year, £40 million in the second year, £60 million in the third year, and so on. However, it seemed more sensible to think in terms of a logistic or lazy S-shaped curve involving a slow start, rapid increases during the middle of the period and a slowdown at the end: the slowdown reflecting either exhausted opportunities or a risk-averse policy of not leaving too much work to be done in the last few years of the strategy. That implied a first year target for extra output of perhaps £7 million.

POSSIBLE WAYS TO ACHIEVE THE TARGETS

At the time Forth Valley Enterprise had in place a range of 10 initiatives, plus various support and development activities, intended to contribute towards the development of the local economy. Table 12.1 summarises these initiatives and their attendant funding. It can be seen that the plan included £0.8 million to be spent in 1993/4 on assisting new starts in the region, or 4 per cent of the total, followed by £1 million in 1994/5 and £1.2 million in 1995/6.

These various initiatives could directly raise activity in the region via four different routes:

- helping people within Forth Valley to set up new firms;
- helping existing firms to increase sales outside Forth Valley;
- encouraging firms from elsewhere to locate within the region;
- increasing sales to people within Forth Valley via import substitution.

Table 12.1 Forth Valley Enterprise strategy, 1993/4

	Initiatives and attendant cash bids, £m		
	1993/4	*1994/5*	*1995/6*
Company growth	1.7	1.9	2.1
High-growth small company	0.3	0.5	0.7
High-growth start-up	0.8	1.0	1.2
Stirling initiative	1.0	1.4	2.0
Loch Lomond and Trossachs	0.8	1.2	1.7
Inward investment	1.0	1.3	1.6
Access to improved skills	0.5	0.7	0.9
Higher level skills	1.1	1.3	1.6
Quality of education and training	0.3	0.5	0.7
Industrial and commercial property	1.9	2.2	2.5
Support and development	9.5	9.9	10.5
Total	18.9	21.9	25.5

Source: Forth Valley Enterprise (1993)

In addition, there would be multiplier effects attendant on all of these, which might vary case by case.

The question that we posed was what would need to happen in practical terms in order to generate a given amount of additional output – say £5 million – in the local economy via each of these four different routes.

The potential contribution of new starts to the local economy is relatively easy to assess. For example, if an extra 100 people could each be encouraged to start businesses, if they each succeeded in generating revenues in the year of £100,000, and if the value-added component of revenue was 50 per cent (a number consistent with that implied in Scotland's input–output tables) then the direct increase in the region's output would be £5 million. It is similarly easy to assess the direct impact on the economy of an increase in sales beyond Forth Valley, or a rise in import substitution: in either case, if sales rise by £10 million, output will rise by about £5 million.

In contrast, it is much more difficult to assess the scale of inward investment required to generate the same increase in output. Little information exists on either capital stocks or investment rates by sector, and capital output ratios are likely to differ substantially across sectors, making generalizations potentially misleading; for example, that the construction sector generates a particularly large amount of output from the capital that it uses. Thus, the effectiveness of an inward investment strategy in generating extra output within an economy is likely to depend heavily on the sectors within which the new enterprises operate.

In the absence of any better information Forth Valley Enterprise used broad capital output ratios for the UK to assess how much inward investment Forth Valley would need to attract. The best estimate was that on average the region would need to attract net inward investment of £16 million in order to raise output by £5 million.

There are also problems involved in judging the size of the multiplier. This is important partly because the multiplier associated with new starts may be higher or lower than that associated with export promotion, import substitution or inward investment. For example, new starts may generate a larger multiplier than existing larger firms if they make more use of local suppliers. Local sourcing is certainly something that varies greatly by sector: evidence, again from the Scottish input–output tables, suggests that of Forth Valley's ten largest sectors, the share of *Scottish* input ranges from 78 per cent for retailing to just 5 per cent for oil processing.

Small firms may also be more inclined to employ local people than large firms, or may simply employ more people to generate the same amount of output, and that too will tend to imply a larger multiplier. This too varies a lot by sector; of Forth Valley's ten largest sectors, the number of people needed to produce £5 million of output ranges from 35 for oil processing to about 500 in the health sector. A further influence on the size of the multiplier is differences in pay levels; the average wage of a male manual worker in Forth Valley varies from £216 in retailing and in education and health to £317 in the chemicals sector, and it is possible that wage rates in new starts are lower than in established companies.

The need to combine these factors makes it very difficult to assess differences in the likely values of multipliers in different sectors, let alone for new starts compared with other forms of new development activity. Tourism, for example, may be particularly important in terms of its employment creation and its local inputs but since it tends to be a relatively low pay sector its local multiplier may be less than is often assumed. In general, however, sectors which are likely to have particularly high multipliers are:

- Oil and gas extraction
- Sanitary services
- Business services
- Other services

- Light manufacturing
- Construction

In contrast, sectors with low multipliers are:

- Footwear and clothing
- Leather goods
- Air transport
- Electrical/electronics
- Oil processing
- Forestry

Business Strategies' econometric modelling suggests that at the Scottish level very few sectors have a multiplier much higher than 0.5, while quite a few have a much smaller multiplier (0.3 would not be unusual). In this exercise for Forth Valley, a small initial multiplier of 0.3 was assumed. That partly reflected the existing underperformance of the Forth Valley economy, and it was assumed that in time the multiplier might increase, partly thanks to efforts by Forth Valley Enterprise itself. For example, a weak entrepreneurial tradition might have depressed the local multipler, but that might change thanks to the efforts of Forth Valley Enterprise and others.

PRACTICAL CONSIDERATIONS

The next steps in the methodology involved the directors and staff at Forth Valley Enterprise deciding what they thought the organization could achieve, in the light both of its resources and of the existing state of the economy. Could it, for example, reasonably expect to help 100 people successfully start their own £100,000 businesses, or only a fraction of that number? Or, what impact on firms' exports could Forth Valley Enterprise expect to have, and how many such firms could it assist within a year? Also, as part of that investigation, Forth Valley Enterprise consulted with other local organisations, particularly the regional council, to discover what contribution they could make.

It quickly became clear that there were serious doubts about the possibility of achieving a transformation in the local economy that was primarily driven by *new starts*. The point has been made that an extra 100 successful business start-ups, each generating annual revenues of £100,000, would raise local output by £5 million. Judging by VAT statistics, that would mean a substantial increase in the rate of new firm formation. Table 12.2 shows VAT registration and de-

Table 12.2 VAT registrations and de-registrations, Forth Valley

	Registrations	De-registrations	Net change
1985	526	533	−7
1986	640	500	140
1987	663	522	141
1988	729	567	162
1989	816	546	270
1990	846	553	293
1991	706	613	93

Source: NOMIS (National On-line Manpower Services)

registration figures for Forth Valley, from which it can be seen that in 1990 846 new firms were set up and in 1991 706. After allowing for de-registrations the net gain in the number of firms was just 293, and in 1991 the number was 93. In previous years the net increases were much smaller.

It is thus clear that, over a decade, 100 successful extra new starts a year would imply a major transformation in the rate of new firm formation. That is especially true because of the difficulty of picking winners; if a small minority of new firms account for most of the output growth, then either there has to be a method of identifying those firms, or a much larger number of starts has to be stimulated than the number expected to succeed. Furthermore, despite the common view that start-ups can transform a local economy and that a cluster of thriving small firms will support and encourage one another, the alternative possibility remains compelling: that small firms depend on larger firms. Only 10 per cent of Forth Valley firms have output of £500,000 or above compared with nearly 13 per cent for the UK. Similarly, the general weakness of the local economy may be a problem for potential start-ups. The implication of that might be that small firms should play a small role early in the strategy and a larger role later, as the general state of the economy picks up.

In contrast to pessimism over the opportunities provided by help to new starts, there was considerable confidence over the possibility of markedly raising local output via more *sales beyond the region*. In terms of exports beyond the United Kingdom, survey data from the Scottish Council Development and Industry suggest that in 1991, the latest year for which information was then available, Forth Valley's non-chemical manufactured exports were worth £150 million – a gross revenue measure which, on the basis of the 1989 Input Output tables, translates into £100 million of net output at current prices. (These figures exclude chemical exports from Grangemouth, since such exports are unlikely to be sensitive to the sort of measures that Forth Valley Enterprise might bring to bear.) Thus, an increase of £5 million in the region's output as a result of increased exports beyond the UK would represent a fairly modest 5 per cent boost to what would already be happening. Furthermore, the figure of £150 million represents a low export propensity by Scottish standards, implying scope for improvement.

From the local perspective, 'exports' could mean sales to other parts of Scotland and the United Kingdom, strengthening the opportunity available to local firms: in terms of output and jobs, an extra sale to Cardiff is as desirable as an extra sale to Cincinatti. However, thanks in part to the sterling depreciation which had occurred only recently before, it seemed feasible that the fastest market growth would come from overseas. Furthermore, Forth Valley firms were already highly dependent on sales to the rest of the United Kingdom rather than to markets abroad, and a high dependency by Forth Valley firms on the rest of the UK represents an imbalance that may be problematic. Not only does such an imbalance increase risk, but a low propensity to export may reflect weaknesses on the part of local firms of a kind that Forth Valley Enterprise ought not to encourage. In contrast, raising the ability of Forth Valley firms to compete internationally ought to raise their ability to compete domestically.

On the downside, it seemed possible that Forth Valley's poor non-chemicals exports reflected the lack of large firms in the region, raising concerns that the number of suitable companies might become exhausted fairly quickly. The implication was possibly that exporting should play a large role early in the strategy and a smaller role later, as the supply of suitable firms becomes exhausted.

Forth Valley Enterprise also argued that *import substitution* has a lot of potential, given that a very large proportion of Forth Valley incomes are spent on goods or services imported from outside the region. In arithmetic terms, therefore, a small degree of success in import substitution would be associated with a significant impact on the local economy, which is one reason why encouraging import substitution is a common candidate for a key position within any development strategy. However, basic trade theory warns against the risk that the crude promotion of import substitution will result in firms purchasing goods or services inferior to those imported from outside the region. In those circumstances there may be temporary output and employment gains, but there are also likely to be problems with resource misallocation and lost competitiveness, leading to longer-term losses of output and employment. Accordingly, the decision was taken not to include this as an explicit feature of the strategy.

Finally, Forth Valley Enterprise recognised that a strategy that relied heavily on *inward investment* would clearly involve high risk, given the difficulty of predicting success in this activity. Nevertheless, £16 million of investment represented only a tiny 0.02 per cent of all inward investment into the United Kingdom. Forth Valley had not been as successful as some regions such as Lothian, and the Renfrewshire area of Strathclyde, at attracting inward investment, despite what seemed to be a favourable location, implying scope for significant gains. The main potential constraint appeared to be floorspace, of which there was a lack in the region, and the need for a strongly positive attitude from the local planning authority, Central Regional Council, which is itself a key property owner. The latter's positive attitude toward inward investment suggested that, on balance, Forth Valley Enterprise could reasonably factor in expectations of some significant achievements in this respect.

THE DECISION

In the light of these considerations, Forth Valley Enterprise opted for a target of £8 million of inward investment in 1993/4, translating into an output target of £2.75 million, and set a target of 5 per cent increase in exports in the year, which appeared to be within the capabilities both of Forth Valley Enterprise's business support initiatives and of the local economy. Thus, Forth Valley Enterprise decided to seek extra export revenues of £4.6 million, implying an increase in output of £2.3 million. Finally, Forth Valley Enterprise decided that new firm formation should lose the distinct role in the strategy that it had hitherto been given. Instead, it opted to seek an increase of £0.5 million from high-growth small companies, as a result of generating turnover in 40 firms of an average of £25,000, with no presumption that the firms involved would be new starts.

Table 12.3 summarises these decisions, and the numbers for the subsequent two years, while Table 12.4 expresses them in percentage terms. On the basis of the latter, Forth Valley Enterprise made the financial bid shown in Table 12.5. A general feature of this table is the reduction that has taken place in the number of initiatives, with the merging of start ups into the small company initiative being of special importance.

Table 12.3 New split between priorities for Forth Valley Enterprise

	94/5	95/6	96/7	97/8	98/9
Start-ups	4%	5%	6%	7%	8%
Exports	32%	31%	30%	29%	28%
Inwards	43%	43%	42%	42%	41%
Multiplier	21%	21%	22%	22%	23%
Total	100%	100%	100%	100%	100%

USING THE FORTH VALLEY METHODOLOGY IN OTHER REGIONS

Thus, a key result of this particular exercise was that Forth Valley Enterprise reduced the importance that it attached to new starts within its strategy. However, it is important not to assume that the same would be true for any local area. In other regions, for example, an existing stock of thriving small firms in particular sectors might provide scope for networking, or the existence of thriving medium sized firms might provide a strong local market in which to sell. Thus, the conclusions are not readily transferable; the method, however, is.

The method is rather different to that which is usually used in assessing the possible role of new starts (or any other measure) to a regional development strategy. The normal approach starts from the proposition that it is possible to identify a general set of key features of a successful local economy. The strategic approach is then to identify which of the features is missing from a given area and then fill the gap, either directly or by encouraging others to do so. The key features are often said to include a high rate of new firm formation, but others include a highly skilled labour force, a broad mix of industrial sectors, a focus on high-technology activities and a strong export performance.

In comparison, the Forth Valley methodology compares the *difficulty* of achieving a certain increase in output via the promotion of

Table 12.4 Detailed targets (£ million)

	94/5	95/6	96/7	97/8	98/9
Start-ups	0.3	0.5	0.9	1.4	2.0
Exports	2.2	3.1	4.5	5.8	7.0
Inwards	3.0	4.3	6.3	8.4	10.3
Multiplier	1.5	2.1	3.3	4.4	5.7
Total	7.0	10.0	15.0	20.0	25.0

Table 12.5 Forth Valley Enterprise strategy, 1994/5 (funding £ million)

Initiative (brackets denote initiatives discontinued)	Priority	Old strategy	New strategy	Output target
Company growth	Exports	1.9	2.7	1.5
High-growth small company	Exports	0.5		
(High-growth start-up)	New Starts	1.0	1.0	0.5
Stirling initiative	Exports	1.4	2.4	0.5
Loch Lomond and Trossachs	Inward Invest	1.2	0.8	0.5
Inward investment	Inward Invest	1.3	1.5	2.5
(Access to improved skills)		0.7		
High level skills		1.3		
(quality of education and training)		0.5	3.1	
(Industrial and commercial property)		2.2	–	
Support and development	Multiplier	9.9	9.5	1.5
Total		21.9	21.0	7.5

new starts, with the difficulty of achieving that success by other means. Thus, the unsurprising inability of most research to identify the contribution of new starts to economic growth does not have to be the end of the story.

It is essential, if this approach is to be useful in any particular case, that the relevant development agencies feel comfortable with the methodology. In that context two points merit attention. First, an essential feature of the methodology is that it relies on comparisons between different ways in which a development agency can impact on a local economy. In the case of Forth Valley the comparison was made in terms of output, but that is not the only possibility.

It might, for example, be appropriate to focus on job creation. Such an approach would be consistent with the way in which many people think about local development efforts. However, there are arguments to be made in both directions. In the Forth Valley case the focus was placed on output, partly from a desire to avoid problems over the difference between 'real' jobs and some other form of job. For example, the promotion of new starts is often rejected summarily because most of the jobs created do not last, and inward investment is widely criticised on the basis that the jobs are low-skilled. More importantly, the focus on raising output as an objective provided a strong and self-evident link between the activities of individual staff at Forth Valley Enterprise, such as helping a client company to develop a marketing strategy, and hence increase its turnover, and an overall objective for the region and all its people. Thus, the use of an output target related directly, both to what companies do, and to what Forth Valley Enterprise staff might seek to achieve. That in turn made it easier to decide what could or could not be expected of the latter, and it also meant that Forth Valley Enterprise's own assessment of what role to ascribe to new starts within its development strategy was one of which it had 'ownership'.

A broader objection that might be offered against the Forth Valley methodology is its focus on quantification. The results of the work lend themselves to regular monitoring and evaluation, which is an aspect of local development that is rapidly increasing in importance, but there is also widespread suspicion that this approach sometimes means quantifying the unquantifiable. However, the real need is to strike a balance. For example, it would be absurd to stick to the detailed numbers set out in Tables 12.3 to 12.5, irrespective of what is happening to the local, national and international economies, and it would also be absurd to extend these detailed numbers forward beyond two or three years. The idea of the approach is not to make premature or excessively detailed commitments, but to devise policies that are fully consistent with a longer term strategy and yet which still mean something in practical terms.

A related concern is that quantification cannot fully encapsulate the distinctive and special contribution of new starts, and that the approach is therefore implicitly biased against a smaller firms strategy. The point remains that if new firms are small, which in most cases they are, then by definition their direct impact on the local economy will be small. They may still have an indirect impact because of the special qualities of new and small firms but, as the first section of this chapter argued, those special qualities are themselves somewhat open to doubt, so that even if a high rate of new firm formation is a sign of a vibrant and successful economy, it is unlikely to be an important *cause* of that success.

ACKNOWLEDGEMENTS

The work discussed in this chapter was developed jointly by the author and Charles Burton, also of Business Strategies, and Stuart Ogg and Peter Swinson of Forth Valley Enterprise. Responsibility for any opinions expressed in this chapter and for any errors remains that of the author.

NOTES

1 Lack of information on the part of the potential lender may not be the only problem. Cressy (1993) offers an explanation of why small firms may be reluctant to borrow from banks that relies on attitudes to control rather than asymmetric information and credit rationing.
2 The opposite arguments may also be true, however. For example, potential employees may be attracted by new small firms because they perceive them to be less bureaucratic and more entrepreneurial.
3 The forecast was based on a model of the Forth Valley economy which uses non-linear shift-shares to convert Scottish level forecasts to Forth Valley levels. The Scottish forecasts are generated using an integrated econometric model of the UK standard planning regions. That model generates class level forecasts by regions and industry, as well as detailed income and expenditure and income disaggregations. The details of the forecast and the methodology are not important to the present discussion, although clearly a different underlying forecast would have different implications for the scale of improvement the Forth Valley needs to achieve. The model is reviewed in Hughes and Hunt (1994).
4 Some of that reversal has already occurred, and further gains in Forth Valley's share of Scotland's GDP will probably occur, even in the absence of action by Forth Valley Enterprise, since other parts of Scotland have problems which do not directly affect Forth Valley to the same extent. Rosyth's loss of the Trident contract is a recent example. However, that effect is likely to be very modest.
5 In April 1992, average earnings of men in the Forth Valley were £324 a week. That was almost the same as the Scottish figure of £325 but well below the Great Britain figure of £340. Indeed, in underlying terms the gap between Forth Valley and the UK average is likely to be larger, reflecting the cyclical effects of the recession hitting the main employment areas of the UK, especially the South East, much harder, an effect that will at least partly reverse itself as the recovery gathers momentum. For women, the Forth Valley, Scottish and Great Britain figures were £210, £222 and £241 respectively.

BIBLIOGRAPHY

Acs, Z. and Audretsch, D. P. (1989) 'Small firm entry in US manufacturing' *Economica*, 56: 256–66.
Amin, A. and Pywell, C. (1989) 'Is technology policy enough for local economic revitalisation? The case of Tyne and Wear in the North East of England', *Regional Studies*, 23, 5: 463–76.
Cressy, R. (1993) 'Small businesses borrowing and control: a theory of entrepreneurial types', *Working Paper*, Small and Medium Enterprise Centre, Warwick Business School.
Employment Department (1992) *Small Firms in Britain Report*, London.
Forth Valley Enterprise (1993) 'Business Plan 1993–96', Forth Valley Enterprise, Stirling.

222   *Richard Holt*

Gripaios, P. et al. (1989) 'High-technology industry in a peripheral area: the case of Plymouth', *Regional Studies*, 23, 2: 151–8.

Hughes, L. S. and Hunt, L. C. (1994) 'The BSL UK econometric model: a user's perspective', *Regional Studies*, 28, 8: 859–66.

Keeble, D. and Walker, S. (1993) *New Firm Formation and Small Business Growth in the United Kingdom: Spatial and Temporal Variations and Determinants*, Employment Department Research Series 15, Employment Department: Sheffield.

Schumpeter, J. A. (1934) *The Theory of Economic Development*, Cambridge, MA: Harvard University Press.

Scott, M. F. G. (1989) *A New View of Economic Growth*, Oxford: Clarendon Press.

Scottish Council Development and Industry (1992) *Scottish Manufacturing and Exports in 1991/92*, Scottish Council Development and Industry: Edinburgh.

Scottish Enterprise (1993) *Scotland's Business Birthrate*, Scottish Enterprise: Glasgow.

Stigler, G. J. (1951) 'The division of labour is limited by the extent of the market', *Journal of Political Economy*, 59: 256–66.

Storey, D. J. (1992) 'Should we abandon the support to start-up businesses?', *Working Paper*, Small and Medium Enterprise Centre, Warwick Business School.

Swales, K. (1989) 'Are discretionary regional subsidies cost effective?', *Regional Studies*, 23, 4: 361–7.

13 Whatever you hit call the target
An alternative approach to small business policy

Richard T. Harrison and Claire M. Leitch

INTRODUCTION

The link between business dynamics, in terms of the birth, death, expansion and contraction of firms (in the conventional components-of-change job accounting framework) and economic well-being at national, regional and local levels, has been widely accepted as important, at least since the publication of Birch's (1979) original influential study in the United States (Reynolds and Maki 1990). In general, although the details of Birch's results have been debated, the significant role of new firms in job generation, innovation and economic change has been widely demonstrated (Loveman and Sengenberger 1991; Stanworth and Gray 1991; Storey 1994). However, the simple association of new and small firms with employment generation has recently been subject to increasingly rigorous scrutiny, and the policy options available and appropriate to maximise both the employment impact of the sector (particularly at local and regional levels) and the value for money and effectiveness of public sector support have been the subject of increasing debate. It is our purpose in this chapter to review the current debate on small firms, new firms and growth firms as the basis for reviewing the operation of a policy initiative targeted specifically at supporting the establishment of high-growth potential ventures.

SMALL FIRMS, NEW FIRMS AND GROWTH FIRMS

As research in the field has expanded, two major areas of differentiation within the population of new and small firms have become increasingly important. First, it has become increasingly clear that the economic impact of new and small firms, particularly on job creation (which has been the policy-inspired focus of much of this research), is uniform over neither time nor space (Keeble, Walker and Robson 1993). In particular, the pattern of business dynamics differs considerably between countries and regions (Illeris 1986; Keeble and Wever 1986; Keeble, Potter and Storey 1990), and although empirical research has progressed significantly since Bruno and Tyebjee's (1982) review of the regional characteristics influencing business dynamics, new firm formation and its impact, rather than other aspects of business dynamics, remains the major focus of attention (Davidsson, Lindmark and Olofsson 1995; Mussati, Fumagalli and Vivarelli 1994). The dominant approach in this emerging literature is a focus on the relationship between the structural characteristics of regions (in terms of demographics, socio-economics and industry structure) and new firm formation (Westhead and Moyes 1991; Fritsch 1992; Garofoli 1992; Keeble, Walker and Robson 1993), although formal analyses based on survey generated data have been used to test the relationship between entrepreneurial characteristics and aspects of the new firm formation process (Barkham 1994; Barkham, Hanvey and Hart 1993).

One limitation of this style of research is that it tends to view the new/small firm as a 'black box', concentrating on the specification, measurement and analysis of external influences on the formation process rather than on the internal processes and characteristics of the enterprise. As Jennings and Beaver (1993) have pointed out, however, the small business venture (and in particular its formation and growth) can be viewed as a response to four sets of influences: *demographic*, in terms of the background and lifestyle of the entrepreneur and the nature of the trigger event for self-employment or venture creation (Cooper 1981; Birley 1989); *psychological*, in terms of the personality traits of the entrepreneur (Chell 1985; Chell, Haworth and Brearley 1991); *sociological*, in terms of social and contextual variables such as ethnicity, gender, education, social role and network participation (Johannisson 1990; Gibb 1993); and *environmental*, in terms of the physical and situational circumstances in which the new enterprise is founded.

While the emerging body of research on business dynamics and regional economic performance, using aggregate data and multivariate analyses (normally in cross-sectional rather than time-series form) falls clearly into the fourth of these categories, it is premature to argue that this approach represents a more constructive and informative line of enquiry than does the study of entrepreneurial characteristics (Davidsson, Lindmark and Olofsson 1994). As in studies of the specific link between unemployment and new firm formation, there are strong arguments for pursuing a range of methodological approaches, including time-series, cross-sectional and survey-based approaches using both aggregate and disaggregated data, to increase the range of questions which can be asked and issues explored (Storey 1991; Vivarelli 1991; Harrison, Leitch and McGuigan 1994).

The second area of differentiation within the population of new and small firms is more central to the argument in this paper. It has become an increasingly important feature of the debate on the relationship between new and small firms and economic development, particularly as it applies to policy, that the population of new and small firms must be differentiated into those that start small and remain small and those, a minority, which may start small but which have significant growth potential that is subsequently realised. In short, investigation of the role and potential of new venture development as a transformational mechanism for less developed and restructuring local and regional economies (Storey and Johnson 1987; Mason and Harrison 1990) has been accompanied by a growing recognition that the job-creation/economic development impact first identified by Birch (1979) is not universal within the new/small business sector, but is instead confined to a small proportion of start-ups, perhaps no more than 4 to 5 per cent of the total, which have high growth potential (Storey and Johnson 1987). The challenge, therefore, for analysts and policy-makers involved in local and regional economic development is not necessarily one of encouraging the development of small firms *per se*, nor is it one of encouraging business venture start-ups, which has been a predominant emphasis for much of the 1980s (Harrison and Mason 1991). It is, rather, a challenge to create the conditions for the development and growth of those high-growth potential businesses which can make a sustained difference to regional economic development in the medium term.

In the remainder of this chapter we briefly review and illustrate the argument that it is growth firms rather than small or new firms *per se* which contribute to job generation and regional economic development, assess in the light of this the extent to which it provides the basis for a selective approach to small business policy and summarise one attempt to develop an approach to small business development support which can contribute to the establishment of a higher proportion of growth businesses. There is some evidence to suggest that, while the influence of business assistance programmes on new firm formation rates varies throughout the start-up gestation process, such programmes play an important role in the transformation of nascent entrepreneurs into new business owners (White 1994) and thereby enhance the extent to which entrepreneurial follow-through (Katz 1990), from intention to action, occurs. Accordingly, the design of effective programmes of training and development intervention at the pre-start-up phase may make a significant contribution to improving the regional economic impact of the small firm sector.

SMALL FIRM GROWTH

Attempts to produce, define and measure criteria for identifying successful entrepreneurial ventures, and to produce explanations of business success and growth are numerous (Storey et al. 1987; Foley and Green 1989; Jennings and Beaver 1993). As already discussed, part of the motivation for this comes from evidence, largely from studies of the employment performance of small manufacturing firms (e.g., Gudgin et al. 1989; Hart et al. 1993) reinforced by more general evidence on spatial variations in the formation rates of new enterprises (Hart, Harrison and Gallagher 1993), that:

> one of the major problems with depressed peripheral regions in the UK lies in their inability to generate sufficient numbers of *successful* small firms. Increasing the levels of enterprise formation rates does not on its own provide the necessary platform for economic regeneration.
>
> (Barkham, Hanvey and Hart 1993: 2)

The nature of the distinction drawn by Barkham, Hanvey and Hart (1993) can be illustrated with reference to data for Scotland and Northern Ireland within the UK. Table 13.1 indicates that in the enterprise decade of the 1980s, the rate of new firm formation in

Table 13.1 New firm formation rates, 1980–90

Northern Ireland	Gross	22.2	(rank 6 of 11)
	Net	7.5	(rank 4 of 11)
Scotland	Gross	17.1	(rank 10 of 11)
	Net	3.7	(rank 10 of 11)
UK average	Gross	28.2	
	Net	5.3	

Sources: Hart, Harrison and Gallagher (1993)
Notes: (a) 'Formation' is defined as new production sector registrations for VAT.
     (b) Rates are per 1000 manufacturing employees.

the production sector in Scotland, measured in terms of gross business births or in terms of the net addition to the stock of businesses registered for VAT, was significantly below the UK average. In Northern Ireland, despite the initial diagnosis of a low business start-up rate as a key regional economic problem in policy documents (DED 1987) and a gross formation rate below the national average, net formation rates were in fact above average.

More detailed research on the Scottish data, however, suggests that the low business birth rates experienced were exacerbated by poor subsequent growth performance in surviving businesses (Kidd and Gallagher 1994): using performance data for businesses started in the period 1980–2 which were still in existence in 1990, Kidd and Gallagher (1994) suggest that, relative to population, Scotland produced fewer significant growth businesses (at less than half the rate in the South East of England). Furthermore, these businesses remained smaller in employment terms and in terms of both total turnover and turnover per employee (Table 13.2). While this in part may reflect sectoral composition effects, in that the Scottish service sector performs particularly poorly in this comparison, these figures suggest that a regionally unfavourable growth performance compounds the effect of low business start-up rates (Scottish Enterprise 1993).

Evidence on job creation in Northern Ireland in the period 1973–90 makes a similar point (Gudgin et al. 1989; Hart et al. 1993, 1993b; Hart and Hanvey 1994). As Table 13.3 makes clear, the job-creation performance of the small indigenous sector in Northern Ireland in the period 1973–86 was significantly poorer than that in Leicestershire, and this was largely attributable to the greater relative contribution of

Table 13.2 Firm performance[a] in Scotland and the South East

	'Flyers'[b]		*'Sinkers'*[c]	
	Scotland	*South East*	*Scotland*	*South East*
No. of firms	215	1687	125	4300
No. per million population	42	97	77	251
Employment	160	348		
Turnover per employees (£1,000)	103	146		
Turnover per firm (£m)	16.4	50.6		

Source: Kidd and Gallagher (1994)
Notes: (a) Business starts in the period 1980–2 still in existence in 1990 (total: 2600 in Scotland, 20000 in South East)
 (b) Firms with turnover >£3.5m and employment >50 in 1990.
 (c) Firms with turnover <£0.25m and employment <10 in 1990.

employment in survivors in Leicestershire. However, in the period 1986–90 there appears to have been a significant change in employment performance in the small indigenous manufacturing sector in Northern Ireland (Table 13.3): not only did total employment in the sector increase by 11 per cent, compared with a fall of 2 per cent in Leicestershire, but employment change in surviving establishments was the major contributor to this, and in relative terms exceeded the contribution of surviving plants to employment change recorded in Leicestershire. However, this change may simply reflect an increase in the survival rate of plants in Northern Ireland relative to Leicestershire, rather than their growth, which may in turn be a consequence of an increasingly active small business support policy in the region; NIEC (1986), for example, had earlier suggested that one consequence of the operation of small business policy in the region was the deferral of firm closures by around two years compared with national cohort studies. Hart and Hanvey (1994) confirm this indirectly in suggesting that for the 1986–90 Northern Ireland data, 82 per cent of the companies had fewer than 10 employees by 1990, and 77 per cent of start-ups in the period employed less than 10 at start-up. The evidence suggests, therefore, that businesses in Northern Ireland start small and stay small, while those in Leicestershire were starting bigger and staying bigger. Accordingly, Hart and Hanvey (1994) conclude, the *quality* of the start, and not just the number of starts, is important for regional development impact.

Although not comprehensive, these two regional cases do provide supporting evidence for the assertion, based on analysis of employ-

Table 13.3 Employment change in small indigenous manufacturing firms

| | Northern Ireland | | Leicestershire | |
	1,000s	*%*	*1,000s*	*%*
(a) *1973–86*				
All established small firms (<50 employees)	−7.5	−42.4	+1.5	+7.4
Survivors	+3.1	+44.4	+10.0	+86.4
Closures	−10.6	−59.9	−8.5	−42.2
(b) *1986–90*				
All established small firms (<50 employees)	+2.9	+11.1	−0.6	−2.0
Survivors	+6.3	+28.2	+5.0	+19.1
Closures	−3.5	−13.3	−5.6	−17.7

Source: Hart, Harrison and Gallagher (1993); Hart and Hanvey (1994)

ment trends in a number of European countries, that significant employment creation takes place in relatively few but growing firms (Storey 1988) and that from a policy point of view, the best way of generating employment in the longer term is to focus policy on those firms with the greatest growth potential (North and Smallbone 1993).

This conclusion is supported by the growing attention being given by governments world-wide to the issue of how to stimulate early corporate growth (Gibb and Davies 1990). However, the extent to which it is, in practice, possible or desirable to adopt a 'picking winners' policy towards young growing firms is the subject of considerable debate, polarised between the advocates of a *laissez-faire* policy and supporters of selective interventionism of various kinds (see e.g. Storey 1982; Birley 1987; Storey and Johnson 1987; Hakim 1989; Jennings and Beaver 1993; Levie 1993). Part of the difficulty in resolving this debate on the extent to which policy can or should be selective lies in the lack of clarity in the definition of the concept of business growth itself (Hanks and Chandler 1993, 1994): business growth has variously been defined in terms of size (Steinmetz 1969; Mueller 1972; James 1973), business structure (Greiner 1972; Churchill and Lewis 1983; O'Farrell and Hitchins 1986) or entrepreneur development (Stanworth and Curran 1976). However, 'it would seem that the volume of research on small business performance, particularly growth, has yet to produce any widely-accepted insights into why some firms grow more than others when confronted with a roughly equivalent set of circumstances' (Tuck and Hamilton 1993: 12). While it is possible, therefore, to establish *a priori* a valid basis for selectivity in channelling public funds into the small firm sector, there is a continuing lack of any adequate theoretical basis for being selective which provides a framework 'to understand why firms grow or not, and to be able to differentiate between their needs for support and assistance' (Horne et al. 1992: 65). In similar vein, Robson and Gallagher have argued that:

> small firms can play a leading role as a test bed for new ideas, new innovations and new technologies. Therefore those firms in which new innovations, ideas and technologies are likely to be developed should be at the top of the list for receiving aid. Also, to further encourage those small firms which can grow independently of large firms, or whose growth can be complementary to large firm

growth. The practical problem in this case is that of our inability to successfully identify these firms.

(Robson and Gallagher 1993: 35–6)

One characteristic of the venture start-up process which is receiving growing attention as a possible indicator of subsequent business growth and success is the involvement of a venture team rather than an individual in the start-up process. The need for a balanced venture team in the start-up process has long been recognised (Hoad and Roskoe 1964; Cooper 1973; Cooper and Bruno 1977; Timmons, Smallen and Dingee 1977), although often no distinction was drawn between post-start-up team building and development and team-based, or collective, entrepreneurship itself. Recently, however, the involvement of venture teams, rather than individuals, in the start-up process itself, and the link to venture success, has become the focus of increasing attention (Harvey and Harrison 1992; Kamm and Aaron 1993; Vyakarham and Jacobs 1993). This increasing attention is in response to two sets of influences. First, as we discuss below, there is increasing evidence of the link between team-based venture creation and subsequent business success. Second, the argument that prior work experience in the business area is one of the most important influences on the subsequent success of a new business (Vesper 1980; Cooper 1981) is well accepted: by extension, if prior start-up experience, whether as a multiple entrepreneur with simultaneous involvement in a number of entrepreneurial ventures (MacMillan and Katz 1992) or as a sequential or habitual entrepreneur founding a number of businesses over time (MacMillan and Low 1986; Kolvereid and Bullvag 1992; Birley and Westhead 1993), increases the likelihood of the foundation of a growth-oriented business, then so will joint or team-based entrepreneurship (on the assumption that the team dynamics are adequate rather than dysfunctional – Kamm and Aaron (1993)).

In a recent case study paper, Vyakarnam and Jacobs argue that:

discussion about how to "pick winners" . . . carries with it an underlying assumption that by picking winners, i.e. individuals, growth businesses are likely to result. However, there is evidence to suggest that growth businesses are started by teams and not by individuals . . . it is time to take another look at the start-up process and see if it is possible to redesign the delivery of support.

(Vyakarnam and Jacobs 1993: 3)

In the following section, therefore, we review the available, albeit fragmentary, evidence on the link between team entrepreneurship and business growth before summarising one recent initiative designed specifically to develop a team-based venture creation process.

TEAM ENTREPRENEURSHIP

As Vyakarnam and Jacobs (1993) have recently suggested, the concept of team entrepreneurship, that is, the establishment of a venture by a team rather than by an individual entrepreneur, is not a new one. It is, however, almost entirely neglected in the entrepreneurship and economic development literature. This reflects, *inter alia*, the dominance within entrepreneurship research of an implicit paradigm of individualism which makes difficult the development of alternative explanations of the new firm formation process.

As in other areas of management research, notably leadership studies, with which entrepreneurship as a field of study shares many characteristics in terms of intellectual evolution (Carsrud and Johnson 1989; Chell, Haworth and Brearley 1991; Harrison and Leitch 1993, 1994), entrepreneurship research was initially grounded in trait-based approaches. As this approach has proved to be less informative than was anticipated (Aldrich 1992), it was supplemented with a situational approach and, as in leadership studies, one would expect that a contingency model will eventually be adopted (Carsrud and Johnson 1989). However, while these theories may be useful in contributing to an increased and improved understanding of the motivations and behaviours of entrepreneurs, there is still a tendency to focus on the individual aspect of entrepreneurship. As Kamm et al. (1990) indicate, the entrepreneurship literature reflects, and in fact may have contributed to, the myth of the lone entrepreneur, as most literature reviews, conceptual frameworks and empirical studies refer to individual entrepreneur's traits and behaviours (Gartner 1985; Hofer and Sandberg 1986). Indeed, heroic individualism is a characteristic of much of the recent writings in both entrepreneurship and leadership studies. Reich (1987) terms the behaviour of those individuals whose exploits have either saved an ailing firm or led to the rapid growth of another as traditional individualism and contrasts it with the Japanese concept of collective entrepreneurship (Kenny and Florida 1993).

This general recognition of the importance of collective entrepreneurship as a systematic economic phenomenon corresponds with the renewed attention being given to the importance of teamwork and team-based leadership. Companies who wish to remain competitive do so by drawing on the talent and creativity of all their employees, recognising that the collective capacity to innovate becomes greater than the sum of its parts. Team or collective entrepreneurship, however, goes further than the view of top management teams, rather than significant individuals, as the driving force in entrepreneurship venture creation and growth (McMullan, Kulow and Khoylian 1988). Stewart has pointed out that team entrepreneurship must include, indeed must be centrally based on, the concept of entrepreneurial teams of employees in which:

> individual leadership is a crucial part of the entrepreneurship process . . . [and] . . . the team as a whole must act so as to grasp emerging opportunities . . . Because it must continually create its own resources, it parallels both entrepreneurship and WCM efforts to learn to continually improve.

> (Stewart 1989: 16)

One of the least researched areas of entrepreneurship is that of teams and team behaviour. One recent study has attempted to redress this balance. Sapienza, Heron and Menendez (1991), in response to the current concern within entrepreneurship regarding its theoretical underpinnings, have attempted, by analysing in-depth interviews with 17 new venture founders, to confirm, refine and extend empirical and theoretical work within the discipline. They believe that the traits, motivations, attitudes, values and beliefs which emerged from the case interviews illuminate and were illuminated by much of the prior research. Solo founders of new ventures and those firms established by partners were both included in the investigation. The results reveal that those who favoured going solo seemed to have difficulty sharing ownership or decision-making and expressed a general scepticism about partnering. Interestingly, these individuals stressed the negative aspects of multi-partnering rather than the benefits of going solo, while those involved in partnership stressed the benefits of teaming up as well as the negatives of solo efforts. The sharing of rewards in addition to sharing psychological risks were particularly stressed as benefits by those involved in a partnership. This study is of particular interest as the researchers have begun the process of addressing a particular area of concern in the entrepreneurship literature as highlighted by Kamm et al.:

> Although new ventures are commonly started by entrepreneurial teams, relatively little has been written about the process of

effectively assembling and maintaining them. Systematic, descriptive research is needed to define the dimensions of entrepreneurial teams, to identify the costs and problems of assembling teams, and to identify successful strategies for resolving problems.

(Kamm et al. 1990: 7)

The role of entrepreneurship teams as a success factor in new firm formation is not a phenomenon which has been systematically researched in the past; instead any information which has been generated has generally been incidental to the main focus of research. Reviewing the literature, it is evident that new ventures established on a co-founder basis are not only common in practice (Obermayer 1980; Teach, Tarplay and Schwartz 1986) but also tend to be growth businesses (Cooper and Bruno 1977; Timmons 1979; Obermayer 1980); this fact appears to hold irrespective of geographic location, type of industry or gender of founders of a new venture. Thus, teams are highly significant for researchers and entrepreneurs for two reasons; first, they occur more frequently than was previously thought; and second, in the majority of cases they have a positive effect on a firm's subsequent performance.

In a qualitative study of 33 successful high-tech companies in Boston, San Francisco and Milwaukee conducted by Obermayer (1980) it was discovered that 23 of them were founded by teams. In another survey of 237 microcomputer software entrepreneurs Teach, Tarplay and Schwartz (1986: 550) reported that 'only 68 followed the mythology of the individual entrepreneur, and over two-thirds of the firms had two or more principals'. In a study conducted during the 1960s and 1970s, Cooper (1973) found that 48 per cent of high-tech firms in Austin, 61 per cent in Palo Alto and 59 per cent of 955 geographically dispersed firms were started by groups of two or more members. As Gartner (1985) points out, it is not surprising that new firms created in high-tech industries are established by teams, as a wider and more complex range of skills than one individual is likely to possess is required. However, teams are responsible for new venture creation in low-tech fields also. Approximately half of the top 25 fastest-growing small companies in 1983, many of which could not be considered high-tech, were started by two or more people ('Inside the Inc. 500' 1983). Evidence that team-based new venture formation is not a gender-specific phenomenon is provided in the study managed by De Carol and Lyons (1979) of 122 female entrepreneurs. They found that 38 per cent of the respondents started their businesses with partners, and few of these ventures were in high-tech.

Thus, it would appear to be clear that co-founded ventures are of consequence. As has already been stated, investigations have also established that teams impact significantly on their firm's performance. Cooper and Bruno (1977) found that over 80 per cent of the high-growth companies they surveyed had been founded by teams, while Teach, Tarplay and Schwartz (1986: 561) concluded that 'larger venture teams were more successful, on the average, than individual entrepreneurs'. In the investigation conducted by Obermayer (1980) it was discovered that three out of the 10 individually founded firms had an annual sales volume of $6 million or more, while on the other hand 16 of the 23 team-founded firms reached this level. Further evidence to support high performance ratings of team-founded firms comes from a 1988 study of the 100 best-performing firms that sold their stock publicly for the first time (Initial Public Offerings) during the period 1985 to 1987 ('IPO' 1989). The survey indicates that 56 per cent of these were team ventures, and in 56 of them between two and four of the stock-owning founders were still actively involved in the running of the business. The remaining 44 per cent were headed either by solo entrepreneurs or one remaining team member. Statistically, the team ventures were significantly more successful than their non-team counterparts in terms of market capitalisation (stock price multiplied by number of common shares outstanding). Team ventures also tended to have higher revenues and net income than their counterparts, but the differences were not statistically significant.

Additional, if incomplete, evidence on the link between team entrepreneurship and venture growth performance comes from studies in the USA and the UK. In the USA, Brockaw (1993, quoted in Vyakarnam and Jacobs 1993) states that during the 1980s, of the 306 of the Inc. 500 companies which were founded in 1985, 1986 and 1987, almost two-thirds were started by teams. In a separate study of 1,709 businesses, only 6 per cent of 'hypergrowth' businesses were founded by a single person; 54 per cent had two founders and 40 per cent had three or more founders; 42 per cent of low growth companies, by contrast, were started by individuals. Brockaw (1993, quoted in Vyakarnam and Jacobs 1993) concludes that 'after stripping away the folklore, it is apparent that companies that grow begin differently from the ones that do not, in a handful of starkly identifiable ways. One of these is that they rely on team effort'.

In the UK, a recent study of multiple entrepreneurship suggests, first, that businesses established by habitual entrepreneurs are more likely to have teams than are ventures established by novice, or first time, entrepreneurs and, second, that businesses set up by groups rather than individuals will have, *ceteris paribus*, a greater than average chance of survival and a greater ability to achieve fast growth (Birley and Westhead 1993; see also Storey, Watson and Wynarczyk 1989). In similar vein, research into the link between entrepreneurial characteristics and new firm size and growth performance (Barkham, Hanvey and Hart 1993; Barkham 1994) suggests that the number of founders of the venture is significantly and positively associated with start-up size (they establish larger firms) and growth performance (their ventures grow more quickly). As Barkham (1994), drawing on the arguments of McGuire (1976), points out, the performance-enhancing effect of team entrepreneurship is not simply a matter of empirical observation, but may reflect the operation of a number of fundamental economic factors. First, team entrepreneurship increases the stock of skills and expertise available to the business (Stewart 1989). Second, team entrepreneurship may significantly increase the supply of capital to the business in circumstances in which personal sources of capital are often the most important (Walker 1989). Third, entrepreneurial teams may form 'to reduce the cost of labour in the start-up period. Owners of the firm will work for below the opportunity cost of their labour so as to earn a capital reward at a later date' (Barkham 1994: 121). Fourth, multi-founder firms are likely to be attracted to the large economic opportunities, where growth potential is greatest, because they require a greater initial income.

Based on this review, it can be concluded that on grounds of both principle and practice team entrepreneurship appears to be particularly associated with the establishment of higher than average growth potential ventures. From a public policy perspective, therefore, there would appear to be grounds for redirecting attention away from generic support for individual entrepreneurship or small and low-growth potential business start-ups and towards team-based entrepreneurship (Vyakarnam and Jacobs 1993). In the remainder of this chapter we summarise one regionally based attempt to do just that.

THE NOVATECH PROGRAMME

Awareness of the need to develop entrepreneurial teams with complementary skills rather than reliance on a single entrepreneurial individual is one of three major constraints on effective business development identified by the Novatech business and trade development programme established in 1991 in Northern Ireland. The other two constraints concerned identification of products with proven market potential and access to seed capital finance at the outset of a project. The Novatech project provides an innovative approach to stimulating the development of high-growth potential ventures in order to contribute to the economic development of a disadvantaged regional economy as it has been designed to support the creation of export based companies in a way which provides the lowest possible risk and highest growth potential.

The policy context for the development of the Novatech programme was established in two official regional policy reports in the late 1980s (DED 1987, 1990). Initially, this established an enterprise policy based on the identification of three major constraints on venture development in Northern Ireland: the lack of an enterprising tradition (although the extent to which this has been a problem relative to the UK has been questioned by Harrison and Hart (1992) and Blackburn et al. (1991)); the presence of few appropriate role models or mentors for would-be entrepreneurs; and the absence of positive triggers to business start-up for those most likely to be successful (in their 30s, educated, widely travelled and currently in employment). The enterprise policy to address those constraints later became subsumed within a wider-ranging regional economic development policy aimed at improving the competitiveness of the regional economy (Hitchens and Birnie 1989, 1992; Teague 1989; McEldowney and Sheehan 1993). Three issues in particular were identified (DED 1990): the high degree of concentration of most new and small firms in Northern Ireland on the local market; the consequent high level of job displacement associated with government assistance to small and new firms; and the continuing need for inward investment of high quality and lasting economic value to complement indigenous venture creation.

As Harvey and Harrison (1992) have noted, the Novatech process was specifically designed to address these issues. To achieve this, three key elements based on the identification of the three major hindrances to success have been built into the Novatech process. In attempting to address the problems Novatech has developed a business ideas bank, representing joint venture or licensing opportunities being offered by US companies with an interest in developing into the European market. A venture team-building development programme to develop a business around any of the opportunities identified has

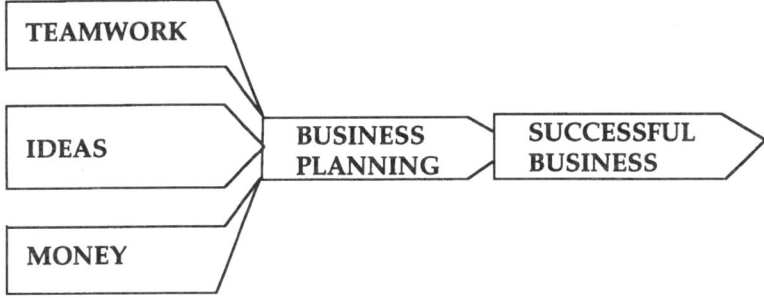

Figure 13.1 Novatech – the process

also been established, while a seed capital fund provides patient finance at the start-up stage (Figure 13.1).

Teamwork

Novatech companies are started by linking venture teams in Northern Ireland with American companies. The venture team manufactures the US products in Northern Ireland either on the basis of a joint venture or licensing agreement and exports the products into European markets. The programme is specifically premised on the argument that properly balanced venture teams have a better chance of success than those businesses established by a single entrepreneur. The ideal team would have core complementary skills such as marketing, finance and production. The Novatech process attempts to stimulate as high a rate of new venture creation as possible by introducing to each other 25 to 30 individuals with senior management experience, third-level education, and a range of key skills. Suitable managers identified from applicants to press advertisements are then individually screened before being accepted onto the Novatech programme. Novatech introduces selected managers into a business development programme which will be discussed later. However, as a number of authors have already highlighted, the formation of entrepreneurial teams has long been characterised as a random process (Silver 1983) which is very difficult to control (Silver 1983; Rick and Gumpert 1985), and although the Novatech system aims to stimulate the creation of a significant number of entrepreneurial teams there will be occasions when the process will be unsuccessful. This highlights one of the research issues identified by Kamm et al. (1990) that despite the importance of new venture teams relatively little is known about the process of assembling and maintaining an effective entrepreneurial team (see also Vyakarnam and Jacobs 1993).

Ideas

Most Novatech companies are started as joint ventures or on the basis of a licensing arrangement with existing successful companies in America. It was felt in the first instance that alliances should be established with American companies who are culturally similar to those in Northern Ireland, as opposed to those based for example in Japan or Korea even though Pacific Rim companies have already expressed an interest in the process. It is intended, however, to expand the business ideas bank network to include potential licensing agreements with companies located elsewhere. The targeted company in America is approached by Novatech personnel who are based in offices in Pittsburgh, Boston, Washington and New York to ascertain if an opportunity exists for exporting to Europe, and if so if use would be made of the Novatech programme. For the American company the attraction of working with Novatech lies in the business development opportunities and access to the European market it can facilitate. The companies and their products are assessed for suitability in three areas: technological advance, market opportunity and financial stability. The project provides innovative American businesses the chance to enter the European market with a local venture team developed and established around the parent company's specific product, thereby providing a market entry strategy which maximises response time and minimises risk.

Finance

Novatech originally had a seed fund of £900,000 which was used to take an equity stake in appropriate venture team companies. The seed fund was administered by an independent committee of five people from business and commercial backgrounds. Although the fund may provide a majority of the financing, it never takes a majority shareholding, as it feels that it is important that the venture team control their own company. At this stage of the process all of the seed fund has been invested and, therefore, it has been necessary to identify additional funds. In addition, the project has also attracted interest from private investors.

Business planning

When the project was initially established advertisements were placed in the business press in order to attract interested managers, who were subsequently screened, informed of the potential products and introduced to one another. However, as the programme has matured a number of refinements have been made. It was felt that the number of businesses being generated from the process was not adequate. Thus, in order to stimulate business start-ups press advertisements listing five or six available product ideas are released approximately every six weeks, and interested individuals apply to join the business development programme section of the Novatech process. This has been found to be more successful, as it encourages those actually interested in a particular product idea to apply to the project.

Managers interested in the various business ideas are enrolled onto a business development programme led by an experienced 'mentor' or programme leader who is generally an experienced businessman in his own right. He thus acts as a role model for the venture teams and, in addition – a point which cannot be stressed enough – has total credibility with managers who themselves are very experienced. The business development programmes are each run on a part-time basis, two evenings per week for approximately 12 weeks, and occur at eight-week intervals. Throughout the course and until the successful formation of a venture, managers remain in their existing employment. During the course of the programme managers are introduced to potential venture team partners, and are guided through the complete process of business formation. On formation of the venture team an introduction is made to the relevant American company, and the team begins the process of conducting a thorough market research survey for the US product.

The venture teams created during the business programme stage now embark on the process of identifying potential sources of capital investment. In addition to the seed funds made available to the project each venture team member is expected to invest between £15,000 to £20,000 in the business.

Achievements

Initial results of the Novatech process, as of December 1993, are summarised in Table 13.4. In Year 1 of the process 150 managers were involved in five business development programmes, resulting in

Table 13.4 Achievements of the Novatech process

	Year 1 (1991)	Years 1–3
Business development programmes	5	15
Managers	150	450
Venture teams	42	100
Members per team	3	4–5
New ventures established	7	15

the establishment of 42 venture teams. Within that first year seven ventures were established, representing a commitment of almost £1 million in invested capital. Although performance data are not available for all ventures at this point, at least one of these ventures has an annual turnover of almost £1.5 million within two years of start-up. Over the first three years of the programme, 15 ventures have been established, with a number of teams still actively engaged in product development or joint venture/licensing negotiations.

From Table 13.4 it is clear that over time there has been an increase in the average size of venture teams being established, from 3 to 4.5 members; this reflects initial experience in terms of the range of expertise needed to develop a business concept, particularly when the founders remain in full-time employment elsewhere during the development process. Despite this, it appears that only about one in six venture teams established are resulting in the establishment of a venture. In part, this reflects 'external' problems, either in a team's difficulty in identifying a suitable and viable quality idea in the product data-bank, or in achieving agreement in negotiations for joint venture or licensing deals with the potential partner company. However, it also reflects 'internal' problems in building successful and integrated venture teams: as Muller-Boling (1993) has recently noted in a slightly different context, German research suggests that most of the partners in a venture team meet each other at work, and teams arranged by agencies play no important role. As Kamm et al. (1990) argue, the process of successful team formation is relatively unexplored in the venture creation context. It does appear, however, that an emphasis on technical skills (finance, marketing, production) in the process, while important, is of secondary importance to a substantial personal development process which emphasises personal motivation and the ability to build and manage relationships (Jacobs and Pons 1993; Vyakarnam and Jacobs 1993). The initial evidence from the Novatech programme is that it can and does lead to the establishment of high-growth potential ventures. The key issues for further research are to explore in greater detail the dynamics of the team formation and development process, to increase the effectiveness of the process and thereby increase the number of new ventures started, and to track longitudinally the development and growth path of the ventures established through this process.

CONCLUSION

In this chapter we have sought to establish two major conclusions, drawn from the extensive research on small firms and economic development and on entrepreneurship and business development. First, in terms of making a significant and sustained impact on local and regional economic development, particularly as reflected in employment, new firms are more significant than small firms *per se*, and growth firms, which may only be a very small percentage of new firm start-ups, are more significant still. From an efficiency point of view, therefore, there are grounds for arguing, on an *a priori* basis at least, that public policy should be selectively targeted at those firms most likely to grow. However, against this, and reinforcing both the minimalist *laissez-faire*, 'do nothing and wait for the survivors' approach and the universalist, 'maximise the number of start-ups to maximise the chances of supporting a growth firm' approach, it is difficult if not impossible in practice to identify these growth potential ventures. Second, evidence from the entrepreneurship literature, increasingly supported by regional and small business economics studies, suggests that, *ceteris paribus*, team entrepreneurship, that is the involvement of multiple entrepreneurs at the pre-start-up and start-up stages of venture development, is associated with the establishment of growth ventures. While not on its own a panacea for regional employment creation through business development, this does suggest that the deliberate stimulation of team, or collective, entrepreneurship rather than individual self-employment and lifestyle business creation will make a greater long-term contribution to local and regional economic development. As a brief case study of one such programme in Northern Ireland suggests, team-based entrepreneurship can be successfully stimulated through policy intervention. However, if this type of selectively applied policy is to be developed and, in particular, if it is to benefit from a significant reallocation of resources away from the largely social-ameliorative policy of general start-up assistance, there is a need for a much greater understanding of the dynamics of entrepreneurial team formation in programme (rather than personal network) contexts. Kamm et al. (1990) refer to the random and difficult process of team assembly: the challenge for both researchers and policy makers alike is to develop an understanding of how to reduce that randomness and difficulty.

BIBLIOGRAPHY

Aldrich, H. E. (1992) 'Methods in our madness? Trends in entrepreneurship research', in D. L. Sexton and J. D. Kasarda (eds) *The State of the Art of Entrepreneurship*, Boston: PWS-Kent, 191–213.

Barkham, R. J. (1994) 'Entrepreneurial characteristics and the size of the new firm: a model and econometric test', *Small Business Economics*, 6: 117–25.

Barkham, R. J., Hanvey, E. and Hart, M. (1993) 'The determinants of growth in small manufacturing firms in the UK', paper to 23rd European Small Business Seminar, Belfast, September.

Birch, D. L. (1979) 'The job generation process', *Working Paper*, Cambridge, MA: MIT.

Birley, S. (1987) 'New ventures and employment growth', *Journal of Business Venturing*, 2: 155–65.

Birley, S. (1989) 'The start-up', in P. Burns and J. Dewhurst (eds) *Small Business and Entrepreneurship*, London: Macmillan.

Birley, S. and Westhead, P. (1993) 'A comparison of new businesses established by "novice" and "habitual" founders in Great Britain', *International Small Business Journal*, 12: 38–60.

Blackburn, R., Curran, J., Harrison, R. T., Hart, M. and O'Donoghue, J. (1991) 'Sixth formers and the enterprise culture', *Business Studies*, 4, 3: 36–9.

Bruno, A. V. and Tyebjee, T. T. (1982) 'The environment for entrepreneurship', in C. A. Kent, D. L. Sexton and K. H. Vesper (eds) *Encyclopaedia of Entrepreneurship*, Englewood Cliffs, NJ: Prentice-Hall.

Carsrud, A. and Johnson, R. W. (1989) 'Entrepreneurship: a social psychological perspective', *Entrepreneurship and Regional Development*, 1: 21–31.

Chell, E. (1985) 'The entrepreneurial personality: a few ghosts laid to rest?', *International Small Business Journal*, 3, 3: 43–54.

Chell, E., Haworth, J. M. and Brearley, S. (1991) *The Entrepreneurial Personality: Concepts, Cases and Categories*, London: Routledge.

Churchill, N. C. and Lewis, V. L. (1983) 'The five stages of small business growth', *Harvard Business Review*, May–June: 30–50.

Cooper, A. C. (1973) 'Technical entrepreneurship: what do we know?', *R and D Management*, 8: 50–65.

Cooper, A. C. (1981) 'Strategic management: new ventures and small business', *Long Range Planning*, 14, 5: 39–45.

Cooper, A. C. and Bruno, A. V. (1977) 'Success among high-tech firms', *Business Horizons*, 20: 16–22.

Davidsson, P., Lindmark, L. and Olofsson, C. (1994) 'Entrepreneurship and economic development: the role of small firm formation and expansion for regional economic well-being', *Journal of Enterprising Culture*, 1: 347–65.

Davidsson, P., Lindmark, L. and Olofsson, C. (1995) 'New firm formation and regional development in Sweden', *Regional Studies*, 28, 4: 395–410.

DeCarol, J. F. and Lyon, P. R. (1979) 'A comparison of selected personal characteristics of minority and non-minority female entrepreneurs', *Journal of Small Business Management*, 17, 4: 22–9.

Department of Economic Development (1987) *Building a Stronger Economy: The Pathfinder Process*, Belfast: Department of Economic Development for Northern Ireland.

Department of Economic Development (1990) *Northern Ireland: Competing in the 1990s – The Key to Growth*, Belfast: Department of Economic Development for Northern Ireland.

Foley, P. and Green, H. (1989) *Small Business Success*, London: Paul Chapman.

Fritsch, M. (1992) 'Regional differences in new firm formation: evidence from West Germany', *Regional Studies*, 26: 233–41.

Garofoli, G. (1992) 'New firm formation and local development: the Italian experience', *Entrepreneurship and Regional Development*, 4: 101–25.

Gartner, W. B. (1985) 'A conceptual framework for describing the phenomenon of new venture creation', *Academy of Management Review*, 10, 4: 696–706.

Gibb, A. A. (1993) 'Key factors in the design of policy support for the small and medium enterprise (SME) development process: an overview', *Entrepreneurship and Regional Development*, 5: 1–24.

Gibb, A. A. and Davies, L. (1990) 'In pursuit of frameworks for the development of growth models of the small business', *International Small Business Journal*, 9, 1: 15–31.

Greiner, L. (1972) 'Evolution and revolution as organisations grow', *Harvard Business Review*, July–August: 37–46.

Gudgin, G., Hart, M., Fagg, J. and D'Arcy, E. (1989) *Job Generation in Manufacturing Industry 1973–86*, Belfast: NIERC.

Hakim, C. (1989) 'Identifying fast growth small firms', *Employment Gazette*, January: 29–41.

Hanks, S. H. and Chandler, G. N. (1993) 'What shall we say about growth: a search for a common theory', in R. D. Russell (ed) *Preparing the Entrepreneur for 2000 and Beyond*, Baltimore: USASBE.

Hanks, S. H. and Chandler, G. N. (1994) 'The impact of new venture growth research on entrepreneurship education', paper to Babson College/Kauffman Foundation Entrepreneurship Research Conference, Babson College, June.

Harrison, R. T. and Hart, M. (1992) 'Encouraging enterprise in Northern Ireland: constraints and opportunities', *IBAR – Journal of Irish Business and Administrative Research*, 13: 104–16.

Harrison, R. T. and Leitch, C. M. (1993) 'From Cinderella to ditty bag: entrepreneurial education and development for the twenty-first century', paper to Third Global Conference on Entrepreneurship Research, Groupe ESC, Lyon, March.

Harrison, R. T. and Leitch, C. M. (1994) 'Entrepreneurship and leadership:

244   *Richard T. Harrison and Claire M. Leitch*

the implications for education and development', *Entrepreneurship and Regional Development*, 6: 111–25.

Harrison, R. T., Leitch, C. M. and McGuigan, M. (1994) 'Regional business creation as a response to unemployment push', paper to Fourth Global Entrepreneurship Research Conference, INSEAD, March.

Harrison, R. T. and Mason, C. M. (1991) 'Change and continuity in small firms policy since Bolton', in J. Stanworth and C. Gray (eds) *Bolton 20 Years On: The Small Firm in the 1990s*, London: Paul Chapman.

Hart, M. and Hanvey, E. (1994) 'New firm formation and the job generation debate: some evidence from the late 1980s', paper to ESRC Urban and Regional Economics Seminar Group Conference on New Firm Formation and Regional Economic Development, University of Paisley, January.

Hart, M., Harrison, R. T. and Gallagher, C. (1993) 'Enterprise creation, job generation and regional policy in the UK', in R. T. Harrison and M. Hart (eds) *Spatial Policy in a Divided Nation*, London: Jessica Kingsley.

Hart, M., Scott, R., Keegan, R. and Gudgin, G. (1993) *Job Creation in Small Firms: An Economic Evaluation of Job Creation in Small Firms Assisted by the Local Enterprise Development Unit*, Belfast: NIERC.

Harvey, S. and Harrison, R. T. (1992) 'Stimulating entrepreneurship: mechanisms for new venture creation', paper to Eleventh Babson Entrepreneurship Research Conference, INSEAD, June.

Hitchens, D. and Birnie, E. (1989) 'Economic development in Northern Ireland: has *Pathfinder* lost its way? A reply', *Regional Studies*, 23: 477–82.

Hitchens, D. and Birnie, E. (1992) 'Competitiveness and regional development: the case of Northern Ireland', *Regional Studies*, 26: 106–14.

Hoad, W. M. and Roskoe, P. (1964) *Management Factors Contributing to the Success or Failure of New Small Manufacturers*, Ann Arbor, MI: University of Michigan.

Hofer, C. W. and Sandberg, W. R. (1986) 'Improving new venture performance: some guidelines for success', *American Journal of Small Business*, Summer: 11–25.

Horne, K., Lloyd, P., Pacy, J. and Roe, J. (1992) 'Understanding the competitive process: a guide to effective intervention in the small firm sector', *European Journal of Operational Research*, 56: 54–66.

Illeris, S. (1986) 'New firm creation in Denmark: the importance of the cultural background', in D. E. Keeble and E. Wever (eds) *New Firms and Regional Development in Europe*, Beckenham: Croom Helm.

Inside the Inc. 500 (1983) *Inc.*, December: 66–76.

Jacobs, R. C. and Pons, T. (1993) 'Developing a new model of individual and team competence in small business', paper to 16th National Small Firms Policy and Research Conference, Nottingham, November.

James, B. G. (1973) 'The theory of the corporate life-cycle', *Long Range Planning*, 6: 66–74.

Jennings, P. L. and Beaver, G. (1993) 'Picking winners: the art of identifying successful entrepreneurs', paper to 16th National Small Firms Policy and Research Conference, Nottingham, November.

Johannisson, B. (1990) 'Community entrepreneurship: cases and conceptualisation', *Entrepreneurship and Regional Development*, 2: 71–88.

Kamm, J. B. and Aaron, N. J. (1993) 'The stages of team venture formation:

a decision-making model', *Entrepreneurship: Theory and Practice*, 17, 2: 17–27.

Kamm, J. B., Shuman, J. C., Seegar, J. A. and Wurick, A. J. (1990) 'Entrepreneurial teams in new venture creation: a research agenda', *Entrepreneurship Theory and Practice*, 14: 7–17.

Katz, J. A. (1990) 'Longitudinal analysis of self-employment follow-through', *Entrepreneurship and Regional Development*, 2: 15–25.

Keeble, D. and Wever, E. (1986) (eds) *New Firms and Regional Development in Europe*, Beckenham: Croom Helm.

Keeble, D., Potter, J. and Storey, D. (1990) 'Cross-national comparisons of the role of SMEs in regional economic growth in the European Community', *Working Paper*, SME Centre, University of Warwick.

Keeble, D., Walker, S. and Robson, M. (1993) *New Firm Formation and Small Business Growth in the United Kingdom: Spatial and Temporal Variations and Determinants*, Sheffield: Employment Department Research Series No. 15.

Kenny, M. and Florida, R. (1993) *Beyond Mass Production: The Japanese System and the Transfer to the US*, New York: Oxford University Press.

Kidd, J. and Gallagher, C. (1994) 'The role of new firms and their contribution to regional economic development', paper to ESRC Urban and Regional Economics Seminar Group Conference on New Firm Formation and Regional Economic Development, University of Paisley, January.

Kolvereid, L. and Bullvag, E. (1992) 'Novices versus habitual entrepreneurs: an exploratory investigation', in S. Birley, I. MacMillan and S. Subrammony (eds) *Entrepreneurship Research: Global Perspectives*, Amsterdam: Elsevier.

Levie, J. (1993) 'Can Governments nurture young growing firms? Quantitative evidence from a three nation study', paper to 12th Babson Entrepreneurship Research Conference, University of Houston, March.

Loveman, G. and Sengenberger, W. (1991) 'The re-emergence of small-scale production', *Small Business Economics*, 3: 1–37.

McEldowney, J. J. and Sheehan, M. (1993) 'A preliminary assessment of recent changes in industrial development policy in Northern Ireland', *Regional Studies*, 27: 490–5.

McGuire, J. W. (1976) 'The small enterprise in economics and organisation theory', *Journal of Contemporary Business*, Spring: 115–38.

MacMillan, I. C. and Katz, J. A. (1992) 'Idiosyncratic milieus of entrepreneurial research: the need for comprehensive theories', *Journal of Business Venturing*, 7: 1–8.

MacMillan, I. C. and Low, M. B. (1986) 'Techniques of the habitual entrepreneur: team building', Snider Entrepreneurial Center, Wharton School, University of Pennsylvania, *Working Paper*, Series No. 1.

McMullan, I. C., Kulow, D. M. and Khoylian, R. (1988) 'Venture capitalists', involvement in their investments: extent and performance', in B. A. Kirchoff, W. A. Long, W. E. McMullan, K. M. Vesper and W. E. Wetzel Jr (eds) *Frontiers of Entrepreneurship Research*, Wellesley, MA: Babson College: 303–23.

Mason, C. M. and Harrison, R. T. (1990) 'Small firms: phoenix from the ashes?', in D. A. Pinder (ed) *Challenge and Change in Western Europe*, London: Bellhaven Press.

Mueller, D. C. (1972) 'A life-cycle theory of the firm', *Journal of Industrial Economics*, 20: 199–219.

Muller-Boling, D. (1993) 'Venture team start-ups: an undiscovered field of research', in H. Klandt (ed) *Entrepreneurship and Business Development*, Aldershot: Avebury.

Mussati, G., Fumagalli, A. and Vivarelli, M. (1994) (eds) 'Special issue on birth and start-up of new ventures', *Small Business Economics*, 6: 79–163.

North, D. and Smallbone, D. (1993) 'Employment generation and small business growth in different geographical environments', paper to 16th National Small Firms Policy and Research Conference, Nottingham, November.

Northern Ireland Economic Council (1986) *The Duration of LEDU Assisted Employment*, Belfast: NEDO.

Obermayer, J. M. (1980) *Case Studies Examining the Role of Government R&D Contract Funding in the Early History of High Technology Companies*, Cambridge, MA: Research and Planning Institute.

O'Farrell, P. N. and Hitchens, D. M. W. N. (1986) 'Alternative theories of small firm growth', *Environment and Planning A*, 20: 1365–83.

Reich, R. B. (1987) 'Entrepreneurship reconsidered: the team hero', *Harvard Business Review*, 3, May–June: 77–83.

Reynolds, P. D. and Maki, W. R. (1990) *Business Volatility and Economic Growth*, final project report submitted to the US Small Business Administration.

Rick, S. R. and Gumpert, D. (1985) *Business Plans that Win $$$*, New York: Harper and Row.

Robson, G. and Gallagher, C. (1993) 'The job creation effects of small and large firm interaction', *International Small Business Journal*, 12: 23–37.

Sapienza, H. J., Herron, L. and Menendez, J. (1991) 'The founder and the firm: a qualitative analysis of the entrepreneurial process', in N. C. Churchill, W. D. Bygrave, J. G. Corin, D. L. Sexton, D. P. Slevin, K. M. Vesper and W. E. Wetzel (Jr) (eds) *Frontiers of Entrepreneurship Research*, Wellesley, MA: Babson College.

Scottish Enterprise (1993) *Scotland's Business Birth Rate*, Glasgow: Scottish Enterprise.

Silver, A. D. (1983) *The Entrepreneurial Life*, New York: Wiley.

Stanworth, J. and Curran, J. (1976) 'Growth and the small firm – an alternative view', *Journal of Management Studies*, 13: 95–110.

Stanworth, J. and Gray, C. (1991) (eds) *Bolton 20 Years On: The Small Firm in the 1990s*, London: Paul Chapman.

Steinmetz, L. L. (1969) 'Critical stages of small business growth', *Business Horizons*, 12: 29–34.

Stewart, A. (1989) *Team Entrepreneurship*, Newbury Park, CA: Sage.

Storey, D. (1982) *Enterpreneurship and the New Firm*, London: Croom Helm.

Storey, D. (1988) 'The role of SMEs in European job creation: key issues for policy and research', in M. Giaoutzi, M. Nijkamp and D. Storey (eds) *Small and Medium Sized Enterprises and Regional Development*, London: Routledge.

Storey, D. (1991) 'The birth of new firms: does unemployment matter? A review of the evidence', *Small Business Economics*, 3: 167–78.

Storey, D. (1994) *Understanding the Small Business Sector*, London: Routledge.

Storey, D. and Johnson, S. (1987) *Job Generation and Labour Market Change*, London: Macmillan.

Storey, D., Keasey, K., Watson, R. and Wynarczyk, P. (1987) *The Performance of Small Firms*, London: Croom Helm.

Storey, D., Watson, R. and Wynarczyk, P. (1989) *Fast Growth Small Businesses: Case Studies of 40 Small Firms in North East England*, London: Department of Employment Research Paper no. 67.

Teague, P. (1989) 'Economic development in Northern Ireland: has *Pathfinder* lost its way?', *Regional Studies*, 23: 63-69.

Teach, R. D., Tarplay, F. A. (Jr) and Schwartz, R. G. (1986) 'Software venture teams', in R. Ronstadt, J. Hornaday, R. Peterson and K. Vesper (eds) *Frontiers of Enterpreneurship Research*, Wellesley, MA: Babson College.

The IPO Fast Track (1989) *Venture*, 11, 4: 25–39.

Timmons, J. A. (1979) 'Careful self-analysis and team assessment can aid entrepreneurs', *Harvard Business Review*, November–December: 198–206.

Timmons, J. A., Smollen, L. E. and Dingee, A. L. M. (1977) *New Venture Creation: A Guide to Small Business Development*, Illinois: Irwin.

Tuck, P. and Hamilton, R. T. (1993) 'Intra-industry size differences in founder-controlled firms', *International Small Business Journal*, 12: 12–22.

Vesper, K. (1980) *New Venture Strategies*, Englewood Cliffs, NJ: Prentice Hall.

Vivarelli, M. (1991) 'The birth of new enterprises', *Small Business Economics*, 3: 215–23.

Vyakarnam, S. and Jacobs, R. (1993) 'Teamstart – overcoming the blockages to small business growth', paper to 16th National Small Firms Policy and Research Conference, Nottingham, November.

Walker, D. A. (1989) 'Financing the small firm', *Small Business Economics*, 1: 285–96.

Westhead, P. and Moyes, A. (1991) 'Reflections on Thatcher's Britain: evidence from new firm registrations 1980–88', paper to RENT V Conference, Vaxjo University, Sweden, November.

White, S. B. (1994) 'What can the public sector do to increase new business starts?', paper to 13th Babson Entrepreneurship Research Conference, Babson College, June.

Index